Small Business Employment Law For Dummies®

Cheat Sheet

The Employment Rights Checklist

Your employees have the right to:

- Be paid at least the Nation
- Work no longer than the ma
- Equal pay
- At least four weeks' paid ho
- Protection from discriminati
- A safe working environment
- Notice that their employment is ending (after one month)
- Written Statement of Particulars of Employment (within the first eight weeks)
- Statutory sick pay and statutory maternity, paternity, and adoption pay
- Maternity, paternity, and adoption leave
- Parental leave and time off for family emergencies
- Request flexible working arrangements.
- Protection from unfair dismissal (after one year)
- Redundancy pay (after two years)

What's Most Likely to Land You in Court

- Sacking an employee unfairly
- Refusing employees their legal rights
- Discriminating against people who work for you, want to work for you, or have worked for you
- Failing to provide a safe and healthy work environment
- Not paying the minimum wage
- Not paying all the other money owed for sickness, maternity, or redundancy
- Not paying men and women equal wages for the same work
- Not allowing employees to take their holidays or breaks
- Asking employees to work too many hours
- Not following disciplinary procedures

For Dummies: Bestselling Book Series for Beginners

Small Business Employment Law For Dummies®

Your Best Sources of Help and Advice

- **Business Link** is the government's small business service with offices in most big towns and cities and advisers with the whole range of business expertise. Visit www.businesslink.gov.uk or call 0845-600-9006. In Scotland: www.gateway.com 0845-609-6611. In the Highlands and Islands: www.hie.co.uk 01463-234-171. In Wales: www.businesseye.org.uk 08457-969798. In Northern Ireland: www.investni.com 028-9023-9090

- **The Federation of Small Businesses** offers various services including a legal helpline. Call 01253-336-000 or visit www.fsb.org.uk.

- **The Advisory, Conciliation and Arbitration Service** (ACAS) is an invaluable source of help to business. Call 0845-747-4747 or visit www.acas.org.uk.

- **Job Centre Plus** offices are helpful on recruitment and employing people with disabilities. Visit www.jobcentreplus.gov.uk or your local office.

- **The Disability Rights Commission Helpline,** call 08457-622-633.

- **The Women and Equality Unit** Web site at www.womenandequality.gov.uk can help on equal pay.

- **The Equal Opportunities Commission** is at www.eoc.org.uk.

- **The Commission for Racial Equality** is at www.cre.gov.uk.

- **Health and Safety Executive** is at www.hse.gov.uk or call the infoline on 08453-450-055.

- **Her Majesty's Revenue and Customs** is at www.hmrc.gov.uk or call your local office.

- **The Information Commissioner** gives help on the Data Protection Act. Visit www.informationcommissioner.gov.uk or call 01625-545-745 (England), 0131-225-6341 (Scotland), 02920-894-929 (Wales), or 02890-511-270 (Northern Ireland).

For Dummies: Bestselling Book Series for Beginners

Small Business Employment Law

FOR DUMMIES®

by Liz Barclay

JOHN WILEY & SONS, LTD

Small Business Employment Law For Dummies®

Published by
John Wiley & Sons, Ltd
The Atrium
Southern Gate
Chichester
West Sussex
PO19 8SQ
England

E-mail (for orders and customer service enquires): cs-books@wiley.co.uk

Visit our Home Page on www.wileyeurope.com

Copyright © 2005 John Wiley & Sons, Ltd, Chichester, West Sussex, England

Published by John Wiley & Sons, Ltd, Chichester, West Sussex

Wiley also publishes its books in a variety of electronic formats. Some content that appears in print may not be available in electronic books.

British Library Cataloguing in Publication Data: A catalogue record for this book is available from the British Library.

ISBN-13: 978-0-7645-7052-0

ISBN-10: 0-7645-7052-8

Printed and bound in Great Britain by TJ International, Padstow, Cornwall

10 9 8 7 6 5 4 3 2 1

WILEY

About the Author

Liz Barclay is presenter of BBC Radio 4's daily consumer and social affairs programme *You and Yours*. Before joining the BBC she worked for Citizens Advice specialising in Employment and Family Law and Money Advice. She writes on business issues for *BBC Online* and has written on business and personal finance for various national newspapers, magazines, and Web sites over the past 10 years. Liz has also produced and presented 60 small business and 10 occupational health and safety programmes for BBC2 and written several booklets on work and personal finance to accompany BBC television and radio programmes. She chairs and speaks at conferences and seminars on work and business, is a trained counsellor, and lives in London.

Author's Acknowledgements

Thanks to Stephen Alambritis, Head of Policy at the Federation of Small Businesses for all his encouragement, support, advice, and practical suggestions. The book wouldn't have happened without that.

Also thanks to Murray Fairclough, Director of Legal Services at Abbey Protection Group Limited, legal advisers to the Federation of Small Businesses, for access to reams of useful information; Claire Birkinshaw at Abbey Protection Group Limited for all her practical help; and last but definitely not least, employment lawyer David Jones for running a beady legal eye over what I've written and patiently answering all my daft questions.

Publisher's Acknowledgements

We're proud of this book; please send us your comments through our Dummies online registration form located at www.dummies.com/register/.

Some of the people who helped bring this book to market include the following:

Acquisitions, Editorial, and Media Development

Project Editor: Daniel Mersey

Content Editor: Simon Bell

Copy Editor: Sally Lansdell

Proofreader: Martin Key

Technical Editor: Mark Leach LL.B, LL.M, Barrister www.netlawman.co.uk

Executive Editor: Jason Dunne

Executive Project Editor: Amie Jackowski Tibble

Cover Photo: © Steve Hamblin / Alamy

Cartoons: Ed McLachlan

Composition Services

Project Coordinator: Maridee Ennis

Layout and Graphics: Andrea Dahl, Joyce Haughey, Stephanie D. Jumper, Heather Ryan

Proofreader: Susan Moritz, Brian H. Walls

Indexer: TECHBOOKS Production Services

Publishing and Editorial for Consumer Dummies

   Diane Graves Steele, Vice President and Publisher, Consumer Dummies

   Joyce Pepple, Acquisitions Director, Consumer Dummies

   Kristin A. Cocks, Product Development Director, Consumer Dummies

   Michael Spring, Vice President and Publisher, Travel

   Kelly Regan, Editorial Director, Travel

Publishing for Technology Dummies

   Andy Cummings, Vice President and Publisher, Dummies Technology/General User

Composition Services

   Gerry Fahey, Vice President of Production Services

   Debbie Stailey, Director of Composition Services

Contents at a Glance

Table of Contents

Chapter 4: Disciplining and Dismissing Staff 59

Chapter 5: Trimming Down to Size – Redundancies 75

Part II: Working Hours and Taking Time Off 89

Chapter 6: Working All Hours...........................91

Chapter 7: Holidays and Time Off........................105

Introduction

. . . .

*W*elcome to *Small Business Employment Law For Dummies*. If you're running your own business and already have some employees or you're just starting out and are planning to employ some staff, you need to know where you stand legally and what your obligations and responsibilities are. That's where this book comes in, explaining the areas of law you need to be aware of and as many of the intricacies of that law as can be fitted between its yellow and black covers.

About This Book

This book will give you a good basic knowledge of how you need to apply the law to your employees, but if any disputes arise between you and your employees don't hesitate. Get advice from some of the organisations mentioned in this book, because ultimately the outcome of any claim made against you by an employee will be down to the very fine detail of that individual case and the way it has been handled.

Running a business, even when you do have employees around the place, can be a lonely experience. If you're a really small operation there may be just you to worry about getting the deliveries out on time, paying the invoices, and managing the cash-flow. Employment law might not be your immediate priority. This book is meant to be a useful and caring companion, on hand to give a bit of advice when you need it, rather than nagging for constant attention. Sometimes the best place for a book like this is in the loo, where you can pick it up when you're having a necessary break from the day-to-day oper-ation of the business!

Finally, remember that court and tribunal cases go on all the time and their outcomes have an impact on the law. The law is changing all the time and some aspects may be out-of-date almost as soon as this book reaches the shelves. New laws on age discrimination, for example, will be introduced in October 2006, although there are no details yet. The government mentions the law on maternity and paternity leave, parental rights, and flexible working almost every month, so there will be changes there that we won't know the details of by the time this goes to print. There will be changes to the Disability Discrimination Act too in December 2005, which will extend protection of the Act to some people with cancer and HIV as well as mental illnesses that aren't covered at the moment.

Conventions Used in This Book

To help you navigate this book, I've set up a few conventions:

- *Italic* is used for emphasis and to highlight new words or terms that are defined for the first time; this includes a lot of the 'legalese' you'll come across.

- `Monofont` is used for Web addresses.

- Sidebars (the shaded grey boxes) contain information that, although helpful, might not apply to all readers – check out these sidebars by all means, but don't worry if the information within them doesn't seem applicable right now (it may in the future).

Foolish Assumptions

They say you should never assume as it makes an ass out of 'u' and an ass out of 'me', but I've had to make a few assumptions, such as:

- You're reading this book in the first place, so you'll agree that in these days of skills shortages it's difficult to find staff you need, therefore making sure you look after your employees has to be a priority. Look after your staff and they'll look after your customers.

- You're running a business of some sort and, while you know that any employees you take on have rights, you aren't fully aware of all of those rights or what your obligations are to deliver them.

- You take your employees and their welfare seriously. You want to keep them, so you'd like to stay on the right side of the law.

- Ultimately you'd like not just to do the bare minimum for your staff but, if you're in a position to, be a bit more generous than the law expects and would like to aspire to what people see as best practice.

- You'll appreciate my warnings as to the dire consequences of getting it all terribly wrong, but you'll also see from what I've written that it's easier to get it right if getting it right is part of your business culture. It can simply become second nature. It needn't be nearly as hard for employers to get it right as stories in the press sometimes suggest.

How This Book Is Organised

Small Business Employment Law For Dummies is organised into six parts. The chapters in each part cover specific topics in as much detail as possible given the limitations of space and given that I've tried not to get overly technical.

Part 1: Hiring and Firing

The first five chapters cover all you need to know to employ someone and get rid of them again. You can work out who has employment rights, what those rights are, and what other rules you may want to lay down about your workplace that will help you comply with the laws. You can read about recruiting staff; what to put in the employment contract; and what forms part of the contract even if you don't write it down. At some point you may want to dismiss someone. The law has given employees more protection in recent years. The most recent and most important changes came into force in October 2004. There are now dismissal and disciplinary procedures that you must follow if you're firing someone. Employers who take the 'fire first and ask questions later' approach can get themselves into serious trouble, but if you follow all the right procedures and are fair about your reasons you do have the right to get rid of employees. This part also covers what happens if the business isn't doing so well and you have to make staff redundant.

Part II: Working Hours and Taking Time Off

The law has changed with the introduction of the European Working Time Directive. There are now rules about the maximum number of hours that people should work on average and about the breaks they have to be allowed. Employees also have the right to paid holidays. This part goes into the details of working hours, breaks, holidays, and all the other reasons for taking time off such as having a baby, becoming a father or an adoptive parent, or being off sick. There's also information on time off for jury service, union duties, pension fund trustees, and magistrates.

Part III: Keeping the Workers Healthy and Safe

The three chapters in this part explain all you ever wanted to know and more about identifying hazards and making risk assessments. It's your job to make sure the working environment is safe, so you've got to look out for the things that can cause the problems. Remove those hazards or, if you can't, reduce the risks. If risks still exist, set about protecting people with goggles, ear plugs, non-slip shoes, machine guards, and such like. The law covers hazardous substances, dust, noise, temperature, lighting, uneven floors, fork-lift trucks – you name it! You also have a duty to make sure that work doesn't cause illness or injury, and stress is one of the biggest problems here.

Part IV: Respecting and Consulting Staff

Respecting employees means keeping their personal information confidential and secure; not being intrusive if you are monitoring calls or e-mails; not discriminating against people because of sex, religion, race, disability, or sexual orientation (or age, from October 2006); making sure they aren't victimised, harassed, or bullied. It also means consulting them if there are problems and changes around the workplace. Your employees are a wonderful source of good ideas and information that can make the whole operation run more efficiently and smoothly. Consulting and involving them will have positive business benefits and should help avoid disputes. You have to have a disciplinary policy in place that sets out how disputes will be dealt with so that everyone knows where they stand and what they might do that can lead to them getting the sack. You also have to have a grievance procedure that employees can follow if they have complaints to make. This part deals with all of those issues.

Part V: Paying Up – Everything to Do with Money

This part does what it says on the label – it deals with everything to do with employees and money, from their wages and holiday pay to sick pay, maternity pay, pay in lieu of notice, final payments when they leave, and pension plans. It deals with the amounts you pay people and the regular amounts you have to deduct for things like income tax and National Insurance. It also explains the circumstances in which you can deduct other amounts like overpayments or sums of money missing from the till.

Part VI: The Part of Tens

Two chapters with 10 sections each – the first covers how best to avoid conflict between you and your staff at work and stay out of the Employment Tribunals or courts; the second is a collection of 10 documents that I think you should find useful when it comes to dealing with your employees.

Icons Used in This Book

If you flick quickly through the book you'll notice some little icons in the margins. These are there to highlight suggestions and cautions when it comes to dealing with employees.

This icon is a target to aim for – an insight into best practice that can help you to get the best from an employee or a situation.

Make a note when you see this icon – it highlights an important piece of information that you'll do well to take in.

Stop and read this information to steer clear of mistakes and pitfalls that are common in employment law – following my tips and remembering the important pieces of information will help you to avoid these problems.

The icon that speaks for itself! It highlights points of law that you'll want to become familiar with.

If you like as much in-depth information on a subject as possible, make a point of reading this material.

Where to Go from Here

The law is always a very serious matter and it can be quite daunting so I've tried to make this book as easy to read as possible. While it really does help you to avoid the pitfalls if you've got the law under your belt before you take on employees, you don't need to read this book all at once. If you're planning to recruit start with Part I; if you already have employees and some are having babies, Chapter 8 is the place to start. If you're worried about how to set up a disciplinary procedure turn to Chapter 15. You can read the bits you need and then dip in and out of the rest as and when you've got the time. Don't forget though that there's only room for the very basic information in a book this size so follow up the leads I've given you for more information and advice. There are Web site and helpline numbers throughout.

Part I
Hiring and Firing

"Come now, Mr Scrimfold, aren't you a little too old to ask your parents to help you with your contract of employment?"

In this part . . .

1 explain who has rights under employment law. I take you through the process of recruiting, from advertising or using an agency, to interviewing and checking references and convictions. The contract between you and your employees may be in writing, or some may be written down while the rest is implied. Written down or not, a contract exists from the moment you make a job offer and the candidate accepts it; so if you're about to employ your first member of staff or replace someone who has left, this is the place to start.

I then look at why you might want to get rid of employees by making them redundant, because you don't have any work for them, or firing them because they're incompetent or have been guilty of some unpardonable behaviour.

The idea is to stay on the right side of the law at all times so that you don't end up in front of a tribunal panel accused of unfair dismissal, discrimination, or having selected the wrong person to be made redundant. Be forewarned!

Chapter 1

Staying on the Right Side of the Law

*A*s a small business employer or in the management level of a small company, you may feel that staying on top of the law is just too much hassle. As long as you don't do anything blatantly illegal, everyone should be content. After all, you've got a business to run and you have to make a living. While that's true, if you get on the wrong side of the law the results can be devastating. You can end up seriously out of pocket because a tribunal or court finds in favour of a disgruntled, or even worse a seriously injured, employee and awards large amounts of compensation against you. Tribunals can award anything from a very basic amount up to a maximum of £56,800 in unfair dismissal cases (see Chapter 4). But if they decide that you've discriminated against someone (see Chapter 13) when you've dismissed them or made them redundant there's no cap on the amount of compensation they can award. If they find that you didn't follow, to the letter, all the new dismissal and disciplinary procedures that came into force in October 2004 (see Chapter 15) they can increase the compensation they order you to pay and there's no upper limit in the case of a workplace accident or illness claim (covered in Chapters 10, 11 and 12). Many small businesses can't recover from that kind of a blow.

But it isn't only the financial penalties that can be seriously damaging. When a dispute or an accident occurs in the workplace it affects everyone, not merely the employee directly involved. People lose trust in an employer if they see that things aren't run properly and safely, or if the employer has no real respect for workers' rights.

Employers frequently struggle to find suitable employees or have to train applicants from scratch. You can't afford to lose employees because they have no confidence in the way your business is run. It costs a lot of money to recruit staff and train them. The more often people leave, the more time you spend fire-fighting instead of improving performance and increasing productivity.

Small business owners are always worried about the amount of legislation that applies to them. There are a lot of laws, regulations, and codes of best practice out there, and staying on the right side of the law can be a tough job. Knowing what the law says before setting up a business or before employing your first member of staff is important, and if you start out with all the information you need, it's not as difficult or expensive to apply the law as you go along – and take it into consideration each time you make a business decision. Changing your habits later on can be much trickier.

Good employment practices encourage good employee–boss relationships. In turn that breeds loyalty and staff stay. People who are loyal work better. They have the interests of your business at heart because you have their interests at heart. Everyone's a winner.

Cutting Through the Red Tape

'Red tape' is a term that conjures up images of bad regulations, strangling your business and making your life more difficult. Commentators sometimes blame the employment laws in the United Kingdom for putting too heavy a burden on business owners, but they're really intended to protect employees from bad employers, not from good ones. These laws also help employers protect themselves.

 The law isn't a burden to good employers who want to do right by their employees; it's a source of clear guidance that helps you to keep employees instead of losing them to better employers. When hard workers with the skills you need seem hard to find, your business's success depends on your reputation as a desirable employer; rather than seeing the law as just so much red tape, think of it as a guide to becoming that kind of desirable employer.

Business people most often cite the National Minimum Wage and family friendly legislation about maternity, paternity and parental leave as causing them difficulties. Yet motivated employees who feel fairly paid and who know they can take the time needed to take care of family matters can increase your company's productivity so it's well worth your investment in sound policies. You can read more about making sure your business complies with the National Minimum Wage in Chapter 16 and maternity, paternity, and parental leave in Chapters 9 and 18.

Perhaps the biggest problem is that the legislation relating to small businesses is scattered around so many acts and regulations that keeping a grip on them can be difficult. Some acts, like the Data Protection Act or the Regulation of Investigatory Powers Act 2000 (detailed in Chapter 14), have such a wide scope that it's easy to forget that they can apply to small businesses and their employees. The headache isn't always so much the red tape as pulling it all together and knowing exactly what it means for your business.

Working Out What the Law Expects from You

Working out what the law expects from you can sometimes be quite demanding. Most employers wait until something has gone wrong or an employee has taken legal advice and made a claim against them before checking out where they stand legally. But forewarned is forearmed when it comes to small businesses and the law. If you're setting up a business or about to take on your first employee, this is the time to get advice on your legal position. If you already employ people and you haven't put a lot of thought into the legalities of your situation, take the time now to find out what your obligations and responsibilities are as an employer. It makes good business sense and will stop you making costly mistakes in the future.

Employees, whether full-time or part-time – apart from those who are exempt and as long as they've been employed by you for the relevant qualifying period – have employment rights including the following:

- ✔ National Minimum Wage
- ✔ Maximum weekly working hours (with breaks)
- ✔ Equal pay for equal work
- ✔ Four weeks' paid holiday (at least)
- ✔ Protection from discrimination
- ✔ A safe working environment
- ✔ Notice that their employment is ending (after one month)
- ✔ Written Statement of Employment Particulars (within the first eight weeks)

- Statutory sick pay and statutory maternity, paternity, and adoption pay

- Maternity, paternity, and adoption leave

- Parental leave and time off for family emergencies

- To request flexible working arrangements

- Protection from unfair dismissal (after one year)

- Redundancy pay (after two years)

Phew, that's quite a list – but this book covers all these aspects.

If employees are unfairly treated and denied their employment rights, they can take a claim against you at an Employment Tribunal or in some cases in the civil courts (detailed in Chapter 15). If you break the law, you can face prosecution in the criminal courts by an enforcing body such as the Health and Safety Executive (a body you can find out more about in Chapters 10, 11 and 12).

In most cases the legislation is reasonably clear, but some areas of employment law are governed by common law. *Common law* is the body of law that builds up as cases are heard in court and in tribunals and judges make their decisions, as opposed to *statutory law* which is passed by parliament.

Going the Extra Distance

Whatever the law says is just the start. You can go further and offer your workers better terms and conditions than the law demands. Following various codes of practice helps you to act as a tribunal would expect a reasonable employer to act, rather than merely complying with the law. For example, the code on monitoring employees at work will not only help you comply with the Data Protection Act but following it will also help you to gain your employees' trust. ACAS – the Advisory, Conciliation and Arbitration Service – produces useful codes of practice on issues such as the new dismissal and disciplinary procedures which came into force in October 2004. You absolutely must comply with these if you are disciplining, dismissing or making someone redundant. Contact ACAS on 08457 474747 or through the Web site – acas.org.uk. Business Links will also point you in the right direction – their Web site www.business link.gov.uk has links to other organisations and departments which produce useful codes of practice.

Putting company policies in place dealing with workplace issues that don't come under the scope of legislation is a good idea. For example, you may decide to add a policy on the use of e-mail and the Internet (see Chapter 14). That's not a legal requirement but that way everyone knows up front whether employees can use company facilities for personal reasons.

None of this preparation costs much in terms of cash outlay, but planning, writing, and distributing policies does take time. However once you've brought yourself up to date with the law, implemented the codes of practice and drawn up your policies, all employees know where they stand, and staying on the right side of the law becomes second nature to your company's culture.

Deciding Who Has Rights

The people who work for you may not all have the same employment rights. Employees have different rights to people who work for you on a self-employed basis. Some rights are acquired by working for you for a particular length of time. Some are automatic no matter how long a person has worked for you and if you try to deny her those rights you will automatically be in the wrong. Some people who do particular types of work are excluded from rights that other people working in different jobs automatically have. Other rights apply to everyone who works in your workplace regardless of their status. Even people who don't work for you yet but have applied for jobs have some rights (see Chapter 2 on recruiting employees).

Potentially confusing? This section provides some definitions to help you navigate your way as your read through this book.

Employees

Employees work for you under a contract of employment. They include apprentices. It's all fairly clear-cut where a written document exists labelled 'contract of employment' or Written Statement of Employment Particulars (see Chapter 3). Problems arise when nothing is in writing and the worker argues that she's an employee and the employer argues that she's self-employed.

Employees start off from day one of your employment with some employment rights. Some of those rights are set out by law (known as *statutory rights*) and others are rights you give your employees through their contract terms and conditions (known as *contractual rights*). A contract exists as soon as you make an offer of employment and the employee accepts it, so anything in that contract stands and can't be changed without her agreement or you may be in breach of contract (detailed in Chapter 3).

An employee has statutory rights from day one, such as the right to be paid at least the National Minimum Wage, the right not to be discriminated against, and the right to a healthy and safe environment to work in. The right to paid holidays starts to build up from day one and the regulations on working hours and breaks apply. Employees have to be given a Written Statement of Employment Particulars by the time they've been with you for eight weeks (see Chapter 3 for more on this). If you try to deny an employee her statutory rights and sack her for asking for them, you have dismissed her unfairly in the eyes of the law (see Chapter 4).

You also give your employees rights through their contracts. You can give people better terms and conditions than the law allows – longer holidays, better rights to sickness pay, better redundancy payments – but you can't give them less than the law says. If you do offer better terms in the contract, you have to deliver or you're in breach of contact and the employee can take a claim against you.

If a contract is for a particular length of time – for example for three months – the employee has all the same rights as any other employee for those three months, but doesn't acquire the other rights that build up over time (such as maternity or paternity leave or redundancy payments).

Be careful if you go on extending someone's employment on short-term contracts: continuous employment for a year, or for two years, may allow an employee to argue at a tribunal that she has acquired rights, such as those to claim unfair dismissal (one year) and redundancy pay (two years) over that period of time.

Full-time

A *full-time employee* is someone who works the normal working hours for your business. Chapter 6 details the rules about the maximum number of hours someone can be expected to work in a week and the breaks you must give her, but all your full-time employees are entitled to all the statutory employment rights unless you work in certain employment sectors (See the section 'Exemptions', see later in this chapter).

Part-time

Anyone who works fewer than the normal number of full-time hours in your business is a *part-time employee*. Part-time employees have all the same statutory rights as full-timers and they can't be treated less favourably just because they don't work the same number of hours. Some employers try to give part-time employees less favourable conditions through their contracts – perhaps a lower hourly rate of pay – but you have to be careful not to discriminate.

You must pay part-time workers on a pro-rata basis. *Pro-rata pay* means that if they work half the hours of a full-time person you should pay them the same amount per hour for half the hours. You need to give them equal rates of pay, overtime pay, holiday pay, and the same rights in their contracts to training, career breaks, sick pay, maternity pay, and paternity pay. Similarly, if you offer full-time employees the right to join a company pension scheme and refuse your part time employees this scheme, you can be judged to be discriminating.

Self-employed

Someone who works for you on a self-employed basis isn't an employee and doesn't enjoy the same rights as an employee. However, not everyone who works for you on what you might consider to be a self-employed basis is in reality self-employed. Some employers hire people on a self-employed basis in order to avoid giving them employment rights, but if a dispute arises and the worker takes a case to a tribunal, the tribunal may find that she has been an employee all along.

Someone who is genuinely self-employed works under a contract for service rather than a contract of employment. You are contracting that person to provide services. She is genuinely self-employed if some or all of the following apply; if she:

- ✔ Can send someone else along in her place to do the work
- ✔ Can work for more than one business at the same time
- ✔ Can work as and when she's required
- ✔ Provides her own tools or equipment to do the job
- ✔ Pays her own support staff if she needs any
- ✔ Is responsible for her own profits and loss

Employers sometimes see proof of self-employed status in the fact that workers pays their own tax, National Insurance, and VAT, don't get sickness pay, paid holiday, or regular wages, and don't come under the firm's disciplinary procedures. Those factors do count, but if those are the only factors that can be used to prove self-employment, a tribunal might decide that the relationship is really one of employer and employee and that you're just trying to avoid employment legislation.

People who are brought in as genuinely self-employed to do some work for you may not qualify for the same employment rights as your employees, but if they are working on your premises they have the right to a healthy and safe working environment (see Part III for more on this) and they have the right to have information about them treated properly and fairly under the Data Protection Act (see Chapter 14).

Consultants

Consultants working in your workplace are usually either self-employed or employees of other companies. If you take them on under a contract of employment on a temporary basis, they become employees. If their firms send them to deliver consultancy services under a contract for services, their employers should take steps to ensure that yours is a healthy and safe environment for them to work in, but you have the same obligations as for other self-employed workers.

Agency workers

Companies often employ temporary workers through agencies. This saves you having to go through lengthy recruitment procedures to employ someone for a short time. These workers have a contract with the agency and the agency has a contract with you. In this case, the agency pays the worker direct and you pay the agency for delivering the service. The contract you have with the agency isn't an employment contract, so the worker isn't your employee.

However, it's not quite that straightforward. Over a period of time it's possible for a relationship to develop where something like a contract of employment exists between you and the agency temp, even if only in implied terms (see Chapter 3). If you insist that the agency can't send someone else along instead, if the person can't work for anyone else, if you supply all the tools and equipment, include the temp at your staff meetings, more or less treat her like one of your employees, and most importantly have control of the worker on the day-to-day supervision of her work a tribunal can decide that she is in reality an employee. A recent Court of Appeal case decided that once an agency worker has more than one year's service with a single 'end-user' employer they are almost bound to be the employer of the worker and other cases have followed suit. If you need to keep her on for longer than originally anticipated, offering her a job as an employee is a good idea.

A whole range of EU regulations giving workers protection have effectively given agency workers rights to paid holidays, rest breaks, minimum wages, maximum working hours, and protection from being treated less favourably if they are part time. The Secretary of State can extend individual employment rights to groups of people who aren't covered by current employment law, so it's likely that all workers, other than the ones who are genuinely self-employed, will eventually have the same protection as employees.

Home workers

If people work in their own homes they will be employees unless they are genuinely self-employed. If you have an obligation to provide them with work, they can't pass that work on to someone else, you supply the tools and equipment, and they can't work under more than one contract for different employers at the same time, they are likely to be considered employees.

Exemptions

There are exceptions to every rule and some employees aren't entitled to all employment rights. Police, share fishermen, and merchant seamen employed wholly outside the UK and who are not ordinarily resident in the UK have no right to claim unfair dismissal or statutory redundancy pay. People who work for government departments can't claim statutory redundancy pay or minimum periods of notice. Members of the armed forces have no statutory employment rights other than the right not to be discriminated against. Temporary and casual workers won't usually be able to claim unfair dismissal or redundancy pay because they won't work for an employer long enough to acquire those rights.

The law does not protect people working under illegal contracts. If someone is, for example, paid cash in hand to avoid paying income tax and National Insurance, she has no employment rights. Anyone who is employed to do something illegal won't be protected either. The principle is that a wrong-doer mustn't benefit from her wrong-doing.

New age discrimination laws come into effect October 2006, so the best advice is to be very careful about treating your older workers less favourably than your younger ones. Of course you won't be able to discriminate against younger workers either. See Chapter 13 for more details about the code of practice on ageing workers recently drawn up by the Dept. of Works and Pensions.

Young people

From the age of 18, workers are entitled to the National Minimum Wage of £4.10 an hour (£4.25 from October 2005), which goes up to £4.85 an hour (£5.05 from October 2005) when they're 22. And you have to pay 16- and 17-year-olds a National Minimum Wage of £3 per hour, although apprentices under 19 are exempt. Anyone aged 16 and 17 may be entitled to time off with pay to study and you may be expected to help with those costs. You can take on someone under the age of 24 on an apprenticeship scheme. The Learning and Skills Council Web site has the details – www.lsc.gov.uk.

You can't employ a child under 13. The only exception is for child actors. Strict rules govern the hours that 13- to 16-year-olds are allowed to work: they can't work, paid or unpaid, before 7 a.m. and after 7 p.m. They can't work more than two hours on a school day or a Sunday and they can't work more than 12 hours a week during term time. In the school holidays 13- and 14-year-olds can work up to 25 hours a week and over-15s can do 35 hours. Rules also exist about breaks and time off (see Chapter 6). Some local authorities have other rules about school-age children working, so you should check with them before you take any young people onto your books.

After they are over school leaving age and up to the age of 18, the Children and Young Persons Act still protects young people and they can't work more than 8 hours a day or 40 hours a week. Their breaks are clearly set out too (see Chapter 6).

Deciding What to Put in the Contract

Employees have statutory rights and you can't do anything that takes away those rights. When it comes to the contract you can offer more generous terms and conditions of employment, but you can't write in clauses that take away the statutory rights.

Employees are entitled to a *Written Statement of Employment Particulars* within eight weeks of starting work. That should include all the main terms and conditions of their employment or refer employees to other relevant written documents. Chapter 3 goes into all the details of what has to be in that statement and explains all the other terms that make up a contract even if they aren't in writing.

Drawing Up Other Employment Policies

Your policies on pay, working hours, holidays, sickness absence, maternity, paternity and adoption leave should all be covered in the Written Statement of Employment Particulars. Apart from those and the terms that form part of the contract whether in writing or not, there are also policies for running your business that the law says you have to have and there may be others that would help everyone be clear about where they stand.

Some working parents have the legal right to request flexible working patterns and you might want to extend these to your whole work force (see chapters 6 and 9).

You must have written policies on disciplinary procedures, grievance procedures (see Chapter 15), health and safety (see Chapters 10, 11 and 12), discrimination including dealing with bullying, harassment and victimization (see Chapter 13).

You might also want to consider drawing up policies on the use of alcohol and drugs, telephone, e-mail and the internet, smoking, even dress codes.

Your policies should all be in writing and you should make sure all your employees are aware of them and can have access to them at any time. They set the standards for everyone to aspire to and everyone knows exactly where they are from the start.

Managing without an HR Department

Big firms usually have special departments employing human resources specialists to ensure they stay on the right side of the law, respond to all the government's latest demands on flexibility, and draw up policies that make everyone aware of how the workplace should operate. Most small businesses don't, but that doesn't prevent good small business bosses getting it right. Many of the small businesses that do get it right are no bigger than yours and have no more facilities, no bigger turnover, and no more profit. They have the systems in place right from the start to help them make sure they are complying with the law and good practice has become part of the culture. Each time a change in the law comes along that can pile on the pressure, little change is required because they're most of the way there already.

You don't need an HR or personnel department if everyone in the workplace knows exactly where they stand and everyone knows who is in charge of what. The person who pays the staff knows the legislation on pay and making deductions from pay and deals with sick and maternity or paternity pay. Someone else looks after the workplace, making sure that you don't break the health and safety regulations. It gets harder when it's just you who has to know everything about everything and make sure you don't break the law. However, it's still a question of putting the systems in place right from the start and building the business around them, instead of grafting on the means of complying with each piece of legislation as you find out about it.

Getting Help and Advice

You need good sources of information and some way of keeping up-to-date with changes as they come along the pipeline.

Most big banks provide very useful information on all aspects of running a business. Your solicitor and accountant, if you have them, will be helpful, but don't take petty problems to them as you have to pay for their time and there may be more cost-effective ways of getting help and support. Make sure any solicitor and accountant you use are experienced in dealing with small businesses. Big businesses are quite different animals and experience of working with big firms doesn't qualify people to work with small ones.

The government runs Business Links around the country, with offices in most big towns and cities and advisers with a whole range of business expertise. The service is free and can give you advice, guidance and support on everything to do with setting up and running a business, including how to deal with all aspects of employees' rights. Business Link also has a very comprehensive Web site where you can get most of the information you need (www.businesslink.gov.uk). Nevertheless, Web sites can't always give you the necessary support. You can get details of the nearest office to you on the Web site or in the local telephone directory or call 0845-6009006.

The Department of Trade and Industry (DTI) Web site also has lots of useful information for employers: www.dti.gov.uk

ACAS (the Advisory, Conciliation and Arbitration Service) is an invaluable source of help to business. Its helpline number is 0845-7474747 and the Web site is www.acas.org.uk.

The Federation of Small Businesses is a group you may want to join. It has 185,000 members with 1.25 million employees between them. For an annual subscription of between £100 and £750 depending on how many employees you have, you get various services, including access to the legal helpline where you can talk to an adviser about any legal problems you have, including all aspects of employment law. The organisation lobbies government on issues of concern to small businesses, so as well as helping you stay on the right side of the law the Federation can give you a voice. Call 01253-336000 or check out the Web site at www.fsb.org.uk.

Chapter 2

Finding Person Friday – Advertising and Interviewing

*A*s a small business manager, situations arise requiring you to find new members of staff. Whether you're looking to take on your first ever assistant, hoping to replace a worker who's left the business, or are expanding and need an extra pair of hands, you need to get the recruitment process correct. Good recruitment practice should bring in good candidates, and ultimately benefits your business.

But first things first! Do you really need to take on a new member of staff? It costs time and money to employ someone new, so take a careful look at how you staff your business at the moment. Be sure that you really need another person or to replace someone who's left before you start advertising. Also make sure that the person you advertise for is really the employee you need – if you're replacing someone who has left, think about why he left and the skills he had that you need to replace (you can read more about exit interviews in 'Tying up the Loose Ends' in Chapter 4).

Before heading down an external advertising route, consider promoting current employees, or find out if any of your part-time workers would like full-time jobs, or if anyone would appreciate the chance to do some overtime. Something as simple as changing working hours – allowing some people to start earlier and others to finish later – may be enough to get the work done without recruiting. It has the added benefit of giving your existing employees flexible working patterns (see Chapter 6).

Filling the Gap

Work out the skills that your new recruit should have and what his job will really involve. Think about whether you need someone permanent or someone to see you through a temporary period of increased workload. Maybe you don't really need another full-time person. Can a part-timer do the job? For many small businesses, part-timers are the answer when it comes to filling the gaps. They have all the same rights as full-time employees, but being part time allows many people to work and still fulfil their family or caring obligations when working full-time isn't an option. That gives you a wider pool of experienced and skilled people to recruit from.

If the job you have to offer is full-time, think about job sharing. As the name suggests, job sharing means that two (or more) people in effect share one job. They may split the week, work alternate weeks or alternate days, or some of their hours might overlap, but they do one job between them and share the pay and benefits of a full-time job. It can cost you a bit more in terms of training and admin, but job sharing can benefit you in a number of ways. Job sharing:

- Enables you to keep on experienced people who can't continue working full-time but who still want to be employed

- Gives you more flexibility if you have peaks and troughs in demand

- Means one job sharer is around when the other is on holiday or off sick, and because they have more control over their hours, job sharers usually have less time off sick and suffer less from stress

You need to choose people to job share who get on well together, which is never an exact science! They should have complementary skills and experience. Make sure that they divide the work fairly, that they have a way of communicating if they rarely see each other, and that each doesn't end up doing less or more than the hours you're paying them for.

Other methods of employment can be useful to know about. You can consider having people who work for you in term time and don't work during the school holidays. Or you can employ people on contracts where they're available as and when you need them and you pay them for the work they do (called *zero-hours contracts* because you don't specify any particular number of hours). Or you can recruit people temporarily as and when you need them to see you over periods of increased production.

You also have to think carefully about how much you can afford to pay any new employees. Pay has a bearing on whether or not you can afford to look for someone better qualified than a person who has left, or whether you can afford to entice someone from outside the area (which can be expensive in terms of relocation expenses).

Don't forget the obvious factors like space and desks. If you're replacing someone and can use his old workspace that's fine, but adding an extra employee to the workforce means you'll need somewhere for him to work without leaving everyone else squashed and being in danger of breaching health and safety regulations (see Chapters 10, 11, and 12 for more on these).

Getting It Right from the Start

Getting your recruitment procedure right is crucial for the success of any business. If you hire the wrong person – someone with the wrong skills, someone who can't do the job, or someone who isn't competent and puts your other employees under stress or at risk – your whole operation is in danger of falling apart. At best working relationships become strained and at worst you start losing good employees or good customers or both. Don't waste time and money taking on the wrong person. And don't forget that certain aspects of employment law such as the laws on discrimination (Chapter 13) apply to people during the recruitment process, before they ever work for you.

Coming up with the job description

Having put a lot of thought into the kind of job or person you need, write a job description. No law says you have to have one, but it's a valuable exercise that helps you to define very clearly the job you want done. When you send the job description to potential applicants they can see exactly what they are applying for. A *job description* should:

  ✔ Give the job title

  ✔ Explain where the job fits into the overall structure – who the applicant will report to and who he will be responsible for

  ✔ Say where he will be expected to work

  ✔ Give all the duties he will be expected to carry out and the objectives of the job

As well as putting the details of the job on paper you can draw up a *person specification* of the kind of applicant you're looking for. You need to be careful when you're doing this: it's against the law even at this stage to discriminate against certain people (see Chapter 13 for more details about discrimination). If specific skills, qualifications, and experience are required in order to do the job, you can list those. You might then list the qualities that you'd like the applicant to have that aren't essential for the job, but make it clear what's essential and what isn't.

When writing a person specification, don't put down things that exclude a whole set of people from applying if that quality isn't essential. For example, if you don't need someone with 10 years' experience, by putting it in the specification you rule out all those who can do the job but have less experience. Don't discriminate, but equally don't reduce the pool of people you receive applications from or you may not get the best candidates.

Advertising – what you can and can't say

Writing a job description and a person specification makes writing an ad easier. You can say anything in your ad as long as it isn't discriminatory. If you say in a job ad that you want a man for the job, but in reality it's not absolutely essential, you're discriminating against women. But if you really do need a man (or woman) because it is a 'genuine occupational requirement', you're not discriminating. If, for instance, you run a shop selling women's clothes and you need someone who can help women in the changing-room, being female will be a requirement of the job.

Don't use words like waitress or manageress. Even if you will take on a man or a woman, it looks as if you intend to take just women and therefore discriminate against men. Use words that apply to both sexes or make it clear in the ad that the job is open to both sexes.

You can't discriminate against anyone on the grounds of race, sex, religion or other beliefs, sexual orientation, or disability. Age will be added to that list in 2006, although the Government already has a code of practice on age discrimination. You can find out more about the code in Chapter 13 or at www.agepositive.gov.uk. You also can't refuse to appoint someone because they belong to a union or won't join a union.

In certain instances, you can advertise for someone solely from a particular sex or race. If in the last year, for example, few men or black people have been working in your particular field and you want to get a better representation in your workforce, you can encourage them to apply through your ads. But because the discrimination laws are a minefield, it's advisable to take advice from an organisation like the Equal Opportunities Commission at www.eoc.org.uk or 0845-6015901 or the Commission for Racial Equality at www.cre.gov.uk or 0207-9300000.

Placing your ads

Your ad needs to be to the point, but give enough information to allow people to decide whether or not to apply. Good job ads list:

- ✔ Essential skills required
- ✔ Relevant experience desired
- ✔ Necessary qualifications
- ✔ Application processes – where to send a CV or who to contact for an application form
- ✔ The job title and an outline of the tasks involved
- ✔ The closing date for applications

Where you decide to advertise depends on the audience you want to reach. If you're just looking for someone who lives locally, try the local papers (including any free ones that get put through letterboxes), local radio, schools or universities, and your local newsagent's notice-board. If you know that you're likely to have to go further afield to get the skills you need, think about the national papers.

Don't forget the trade press and magazines that people who work in your industry read. More employers are now using the Internet to reach a wider audience quickly. If you go into a search engine and type in 'job vacancies' you will see that there are many Web sites that carry job ads: www.jobsearch.co.uk; www.jobsin.co.uk or www.fish4jobs.co.uk to name just three. Some Web sites like www.reed.co.uk will carry job ads for free. If you want to attract people with disabilities, Jobcentre Plus offices are useful, but other options such as the Talking Newspaper Association are also available. You can contact them on 01435-866102 or at www.tnauk.org.uk. Think about making job descriptions available in large print or on tape for people with visual impairments or in different languages for applicants whose first language isn't English.

The wider you advertise the more applications, CVs, phone calls, and e-mails you're likely to get. Make sure that someone's available to deal with enquiries, send out forms, and collate all the applications.

Using an agency

Employment agencies can advertise on your behalf and can provide lists of possible candidates for you to look at. You have to pay a fee for an agency's services, so find out what they charge before you decide which agency to use.

Many agencies specialise in particular areas of work. These types of agencies can save you a lot of time, but they can also be very expensive.

You can recruit people through an agency on a temporary basis, meaning that the agency employs them rather than you – so the agency looks after their pay, tax, and National Insurance. This system enables you to try people out on a temporary basis before deciding whether to employ them yourself permanently. Using an agency also means that your business name doesn't have to be included in the advertising if you'd rather it didn't. Of course, if the agency can't find you anyone suitable you're back to square one and have lost valuable time, but you don't usually have to pay a fee in these circumstances. Just be aware that if you take on agency workers for more than a year, an Employment Tribunal may decide you have become their employer even if they're described as being self-employed by the agency or by themselves. For more on agency workers see Chapter 1.

Alternatively you can employ a firm of recruitment consultants to take you through the whole recruitment process from deciding on your person specification, to interviewing, to making a final choice. A recruitment consultancy differs from an employment agency in that the agency offer you the pick of people registered on its books and a recruitment consultancy charges a fee to do the job of recruiting for you.. If the job is a very important one within your organisation you can use a firm of *headhunters* who actively look for the very best person on your behalf. They tend to be very specialised and because they know a lot about their industry they know where to look for people already working at the level you require.

Using the Jobcentre

You get a similar from Jobcentre Plus as from an employment agency (see the previous section 'Using an agency') but it doesn't cost you anything. You can advertise your job and get help from one of the vacancy managers. Advertising in the Jobcentre Plus can be a quick way to find new employees and you can arrange to take someone on, on a trial basis, before you offer them a permanent job. The people who use the Jobcentre are actively looking for work and often ready to start work straight away. If you employ someone through Jobcentre Plus you employ them and pay their salary direct to them, whereas if you recruit through an agency the person you take on may not be your employee, but paid by the agency (see the section 'Agency Workers' in Chapter 1).

Another advantage of using Jobcentre Plus is the advice the centre offers not only on recruitment but on just about every other aspect of employment, including help with employing people with disabilities.

The centres also run the *New Deal* scheme. Through New Deal you can get financial help if you take on a new employee and train them. Employers have been put off in the past because they felt that it was only people who were unemployed and therefore unemployable who went to Jobcentres to look for work, but as unemployment rates have fallen the people who use them are more often already employed and looking for better opportunities. You can find information on the New Deal and details of your local office at www. jobcentreplus.gov.uk or in the telephone directory.

Following up recommendations – and remembering to be fair!

Finding someone suitable to fill your vacancy can be as simple as asking around! Talk to your existing employees and colleagues, other people working in the area or industry, friends, family, or local business people and organisations. How successful this method is usually depends on the level of expertise you're looking for. You may find someone if you're looking for a receptionist, but you may not if you're looking for a highly experienced financial director. It's certainly well worth thinking about as part of your recruitment plan, but you may be seen as trying to poach other people's employees. Also, if you rely on word of mouth alone you're limiting the pool of potential applicants to people who know people you know.

Considering Diversity

More and more businesses are realising the advantages of having members of staff of different racial and cultural backgrounds, ages, genders, sexual orientation, religious beliefs, and those with disabilities. Customers and suppliers appreciate being able to do business with a diverse workforce that reflects the community around it and it may improve your reputation. If you spread your net more widely when recruiting you're likely to have more applicants to choose from, with different experiences, knowledge, and skills, and your employees from varied backgrounds can help you understand your customers better. Some customers, for example, may prefer to deal with older people because they feel that older staff are more experienced and understand their needs better. If you only have young people on your staff those customers may well take their custom elsewhere.

Think carefully about having an equal opportunities policy. If you do face a claim for discrimination an Employment Tribunal will ask to see that policy. See Chapter 13 for more details. Use these guidelines to help prevent discrimination:

- Make sure that you don't exclude any one group when you write your job ad and job descriptions.

- Think about where you advertise. You may have to advertise in a wider range of publications than you have done in the past in order to get to all the people you'd like to reach.

- Make sure that people with disabilities who apply for jobs with you are able to get to interviews, and have access to your premises – otherwise you risk falling foul of the Disability Discrimination Act (see Chapter 13).

Grants (often up to 100 per cent of the costs) may be available to help you make reasonable adjustments around your workplace for disabled workers and to comply with the Disability Discrimination Act (see Chapter 13). Talk to your local Jobcentre Plus office for help and advice.

Sorting the Wheat from the Chaff – CVs and Application Forms

You need to decide how to extract the information from your candidates' applications in order to decide which ones to interview. Application forms and CVs both have their advantages and disadvantages, outlined in Table 2-1 for application forms and Table 2-2 for CVs.

Table 2-1   The Pros and Cons of Application Forms

Pros	Cons
You can decide exactly what you want to find out from your applicants, and can design the form yourself or buy ones from stationery suppliers.	You need to put a lot of thought into how the forms are designed and they need to be easy to fill in, or some people will be put off applying.
Every applicant fills in the same form so it's easy to compare skills, experience, and qualifications.	You have all the effort and cost of producing them and sending them out.
Some people feel happier about filling in a form as it gives them a guide as to what information is needed.	You have to be careful not to ask discriminatory questions.

Table 2-2	The Pros and Cons of CVs
Pros	**Cons**
The way a CV and covering letter are laid out will tell you something about the applicant's abilities.	You have no control over the information that's included on an individual's CV.
You don't have any of the costs of production, design, or sending them out.	All CVs have different information and layouts, so they're harder to compare.
People are more likely to apply if they don't have to fill in a form.	Applicants can easily hide work gaps.

Some employers prefer to use application forms that allow them to remove the personal information. This takes away the temptation not to see anyone over a certain age or who is of a particular sex or ethnic background. They then use just the parts of the forms that refer to skills, experience, and qualification when deciding who to interview, preventing bias or discrimination against a candidate when drawing up their short list. That's harder to do with CVs.

Whichever you decide to use, you're likely to get a better response in terms of the information people give you if you send them a copy of the job description and the person specification. Doing so gives applicants a much clearer idea than an ad can of what the job entails and of whether they've got a chance of getting it.

If people lie on CVs or application forms about their qualifications or experience and you offer them a job, you can later withdraw the offer or dismiss them if you rumble them. Make it clear that you will check all their claims.

Under the Data Protection Act the personal information you collect about individuals has to be used for the recruitment process only. Only those people involved in the recruitment process should have access to it: You can't pass it on to anyone else without the applicant's consent and it should be kept confidential and in a secure place so it doesn't fall into the wrong hands.

Drawing up your short list

After you've got all the applications in you need to decide who to interview. Decide how many people you have time to interview (allowing 45 minutes to an hour is about right), and come up with a short list of that number. Five or six candidates is usually enough.

Whittle the applications down to the number on your short list by using this process:

1. **List all the candidates and work out how well they fit your person specification and the job description.** Some applicants probably won't have the qualifications you need so you'll be able to reject them straight away.

2. **Give the rest a tick or a number of points for how well they meet each of the essential requirements to do the job.** If you do use a points system, make sure that you apply it equally fairly to all the applicants.

3. **From that you may have your short list.** If you still have too many people in the running look at how well each one of those who have the essentials match the other qualities you'd like your new employee to have.

If you take personal information into consideration, be very careful. Having more than one person involved in the short-listing process is a smart move because it helps avoid any personal bias on your part. For example, many employers still fall into the trap of thinking that men who have children won't want to ask for time off to look after them but that women will and make biased decisions on that basis. One employer was sued after a candidate submitted the same CV twice – once using an Indian name, the other time using an English name. The application with the English name was short-listed for interview and the one with the Indian name wasn't. Be fair.

Dealing with the ones that don't make the short list

Write to the applicants you don't want to interview so that they aren't kept hanging on, hoping. Thank them for their interest. If any of them do contact you to ask why they didn't get an interview, simply explain that other applicants were better suited to the job because they had more relevant qualifications, skills, or experience. Don't go down the route of saying that people were too old or too young or that they didn't have skills that you didn't specifically ask for in the job description or person specification.

Handling the Practicalities of Interviews

After deciding who's on your short list, invite them for an interview. However you contact the short-listed candidates, it's wise to confirm the details in writing.

Include the following information with your invite:

- ✔ Where the interview takes place
- ✔ When the interview takes place
- ✔ How long the interview will be
- ✔ Whether any tests or presentations are required and whether the person will complete them at the time of the interview or during a separate appointment
- ✔ Anything the candidates need to bring with them
- ✔ Details of who will be on the interview panel
- ✔ Who to ask for when they arrive
- ✔ How to get to the interview (with a map)
- ✔ Details of travel expenses

Also give the candidates a person to contact with any questions before the interview if they have problems getting there at the time you've given them or if they have any information they'd like you to know in advance (such as needing a car parking space close to the building because of a disability).

Making flexible appointments

The fun starts when everyone on your short list phones up to ask for a different date or time to the one you've allotted. Remember that you do need to hire someone suitable – these few candidates are your best chance so try to be as flexible as possible. Think before you allocate the times: If you're interviewing in Glasgow and someone is coming from Glossop, either allow time for him to get there and back in a day for an interview at a reasonable hour, or offer to put him up overnight in Glasgow. Similarly, there may be people on the list who have caring responsibilities first thing in the morning. In fact, some people may have applied and not told their current employer that they have an interview, so be prepared to start or finish later or earlier, to fit them in before or after work. Don't let a request for a later start immediately set alarm bells ringing about bad timekeeping. Keep an open mind.

Making sure everyone can get into the building

When you invite people for interview, ask them to let you know if they have any special needs. Someone may be a wheelchair-user, for example. You aren't expected to take out walls or build ramps, but you should be prepared to make reasonable adjustments so that the interview can take place without the candidate being in any way embarrassed or discriminated against. That can be something as simple as making sure someone gives up their car parking space for a few hours so that the candidate can park close to the main entrance. It may mean moving the interview from a room on the first floor to one on the ground floor, or making arrangements to use a room somewhere away from your work premises.

If you do have to move the venue for one interviewee, move the venue for them all in order to avoid any embarrassment or confusion.

Paying for expenses

You don't have to pay for travel expenses. If your applicants are all from your local area, the issue probably won't arise. If they're coming from further afield and you don't cover expenses, you run the risk that your best applicants may not be able to afford the journey. After you've selected your short list, look at where people are in the country. If you decide that you probably do need to cover some people's costs, it's better to offer to pay everyone's expenses.

Planning the Interviews

Employers often give little thought to either the process building up to the interview or how to conduct the interview itself. You're spending time and money to recruit someone, so preparing for the interview is well worth doing so that you can be sure to get the best out of it.

You'll be making first impressions of the people you interview, but they'll also be making first impressions of you. If you don't seem very well organised they may decide there and then that they don't want to work for you.

Work out who, apart from yourself, should be on the interviewing panel. As a small business owner or manager you may decide to do the interviewing yourself, but it usually helps to have at least one other person's opinion. Two heads are normally better than one. Consider involving some of the following people on your interview panel:

> ✔ If you have business partners or management colleagues, see if one of them is available to help.

> ✔ If the new employee will report directly to someone other than you, consider involving that manager.

> ✔ If you have a human resources or personnel department, enlist their help.

> ✔ If you've used a recruitment agency to help find candidates, try to involve the agency in the interviews.

> ✔ If the job requires a particular skill, invite a relevant member of staff onto the panel, to assess the level of that skill for each candidate.

It really helps if everyone involved in the interview knows the candidates' application forms or CVs reasonably well and has them available at the interview. You can use this information to come up with the list of questions you want to ask. If there are any unexplained mysteries about gaps in employment, you may want to ask the candidate about those.

 Decide how long you realistically need for each interview and leave some time afterwards to discuss each candidate with the other people on your interview panel. The length of the interview is important for the candidates as well as for you. You need time to extract the information you want and the interviewees need to feel they've had time to get their points across. So 45 minutes to an hour is usually enough, although you may want to set aside extra time for specific tests.

Working out what to ask

 The essential skills, qualifications, and expertise to do the job are the most important issues to address at an interview. So those are the areas you should concentrate on! Asking good questions should get you good answers in return. Prepare the kinds of questions that don't invite a 'yes' or 'no' answer. Other questions will arise as the interview goes on, depending on what the candidate has to say.

Start by introducing everyone on the panel, explaining a little bit about your business and its structure and where the job fits into that. Outline how the interview will be conducted. That allows time for the interviewees to get settled. Give each interviewee a chance to ask you any questions they have at the end and explain what happens next.

Be very wary of asking personal questions. You can't ask women about their childcare arrangements and not ask men the same questions – unless you want to end up being sued for discrimination. Only ask questions that are relevant to the job: asking about whether someone is married or not or has children may be used against you later. Questions about disability have to be carefully worded too. You have to discuss how you can help someone with a disability to do the job you're offering rather than talk about why it would stop them doing the job. You can't use a disability as a reason not to employ someone unless it's justified. A person who is seriously visually impaired may not be able to drive your forklift truck, but if the job you are trying to fill is an office job his visual impairment may not rule him out. If he can do the job as long as you make reasonable adjustments around your workplace then you have to ignore the disability (see Chapter 13 for more details on adjusting your workplace to help disabled employees).

Don't make any rash promises during an interview – if you offer an interviewee the job there and then with a package that includes all sorts of benefits (such as a company car) and he accepts your offer, you can't then change the offer later if you realise you can't afford it.

Setting tests

If a job requires a very particular skill you may want to conduct some kind of test of that skill as part of the interview process – for example a typing or shorthand test or a forklift driving test. *Psychometric tests* (measuring intelligence, decision-making and problem-solving skills, aptitude, and personality) are popular, especially when it's difficult to compare every candidate's skills and experience. If you do decide to include any tests, they must be relevant to the job and not discriminatory.

Tests can be done during, after, or before the interview, but you need to use them as part of the selection process rather than as the one and only method of choosing the best person for the job.

Taking notes

After each interview, write notes of key information, otherwise you may mix up important points. Only record what was said in the interview. Stick to the facts.

To make accurate notes as soon as possible, build into the interviewing time breaks where you can discuss the candidates and compare notes with fellow interviewers. Otherwise, by the end of a day remembering which candidate said what can become tricky!

After all the interviews are finished, you may want to add some notes that explain the criteria you used to select the eventual winner. The candidates have the right to see interview notes and may ask to see those notes if you don't offer them the job and they plan to bring a case against you at a tribunal for discrimination.

After the interviewing is over, only keep personal information if it's relevant to the selection process, and make sure that the notes and personal information are kept somewhere safe where they can't fall into other people's hands.

Checking Up on Your Chosen One

After going through the selection process and picking your best candidate, you can carry out a few checks before making the job offer, or you can make the job offer conditional on all your checks being satisfactory. Some checks are essential, others are your choice, as explained in this section.

When making your checks on the candidate:

- ✔ Only do checks that are necessary and for specific purposes
- ✔ Do checks only for the candidates you want to appoint
- ✔ Let people know you're going to do checks beforehand and whom you're checking with
- ✔ Don't use information that doesn't come from reliable sources
- ✔ If the checks throw up something negative, give the person the chance to explain
- ✔ Make sure that the information you get is kept confidential and secure

Following up references

You can take up references at any point during the recruitment process, but don't forget that most candidates will probably prefer you not to contact their current employers unless you are making them a firm job offer. You can't contact referees without a candidate's agreement, and previous employers don't have to give references unless they work in the financial services sector.

Despite the fact that many employers complain that they've had good references for employees who later turned out to be a disaster, most bosses do still use referees to check out a candidate's details.

You can insist on referees' details being given and make a job offer conditional on getting satisfactory references but an outside chance remains that if the references aren't satisfactory, or someone refuses to give one, and you do withdraw the job offer, you can still be sued for breach of contract.

When asking for references, you're using personal information supplied to you on application forms and CVs. Under the Data Protection Act you have to keep that information confidential. Get the applicant's permission before you follow up references. You can have a section on the application form that you ask applicants to sign to give their consent and that makes it clear you will be using the information they've given you.

Employers have to tell it as it is. If they do agree to give a reference it has to be truthful. If you later find that someone exaggerated an applicant's skills and you lose out because of that, you can sue the referee. Similarly, employees can take claims against employers who give them references that they feel unfairly damage their careers. The upshot is that many big organisations will now only give references confirming the very basic facts such as length of employment and job title. If you don't get the references you want, think about offering the job on a trial basis.

Proving that potential staff are entitled to work in the UK

All your employees have to be entitled to work in the UK and you have to check that they are. It's a criminal offence to employ anyone 16 or over who doesn't have permission to work in the UK or to do the type of work you're employing them for. You can be fined up to $5,000.

The rules are very complicated, so check up with the Home Office Employers Helpline on 0845-0106677 or its Web site www.homeoffice.gov.uk.

British citizens, Commonwealth citizens who have the right to live in the UK, and European Economic Area (EEA) nationals and their family members can work in the UK without restrictions on the length of time or the work they do. People who come into the UK under the Highly Skilled Migrant Programme or under the Working Holidaymaker Scheme – which allows Commonwealth citizens aged 17–30 to stay in the UK for 2 years – can work without work permits. Some students from outside the EEA over the age of 16 can work in the UK for up to 20 hours a week during term-time and full-time outside term-time.

Getting work permits

If your best candidate isn't automatically eligible to work in the UK, you may be able to get him a work permit from Work Permits (UK). Your employee will usually only get a work permit if the agency is convinced that no suitable and available person settled in the UK or EEA can take the job. You can get all the information and application forms you need from the The Work Permits (UK) Enquiry Line on 0870-5210224. The person may also need a visa to come into the UK.

Check and keep a record of the documents you used to confirm that someone is entitled to work before employing him. If you have made your checks and kept copies of the documents used, and done all you can to make sure that the person who showed you the documents was the person they rightfully belonged to, you will have a good defence if it later turns out that he wasn't telling the truth.

Checking convictions

If the job you're offering involves working with children or adults who are vulnerable – disabled or elderly – you must check convictions with the Criminal Records Bureau Disclosure Service (www.disclosure.gov.uk). Only make these checks if you've decided to offer someone the job, and make the offer conditional on getting a satisfactory result. Some legal and financial jobs require these checks too.

Two types of conviction checks may be made:

- ✔ **A standard disclosure.** This tells you whether the candidate has any cautions, warnings, or reprimands and any spent or unspent convictions.

- ✔ **An enhanced disclosure.** This tells you all the same information plus information from local police forces such as regarding acquittals.

If the job involves child care you can also ask on the Criminal Records Bureau application form whether someone is on the government's lists of people considered unsuitable for that kind of work.

Convictions are *spent* if someone was convicted of a crime and had no further convictions during his rehabilitation period. Treat someone with spent convictions as if those convictions had never happened. If the person was in prison for more than 30 months because of a conviction, it can never be spent.

Wait until you make a job offer before asking for a disclosure. It costs £300 to register with the Criminal Records Bureau.

Checking health

Some employers insist on a potential employee having a medical examination before starting the job. If that's the case, make it clear when you make the job offer that you want a satisfactory medical report to show that the candidate is fit to do the job and that if he refuses or the results aren't satisfactory the job offer won't stand. Other employers ask for a health questionnaire to be filled in, which, if it does throw up problems, can be followed up with a medical.

Only insist on health checks if you are sure that you want to take someone on. Don't insist that someone with a disability has a medical if you wouldn't insist on someone else having the same checks or you will be guilty of discriminating. Checks should really only be necessary if there's a legal requirement, such as an eye test for someone doing a driving job.

Some employers worry that candidates may be drug users and insist on health checks for that reason. If the employee may be at risk if his judgement is impaired due to drug use or he may put other employees at risk, tests can be justified. Make it clear when you make the job offer that drug use would rule the candidate out as being unfit to do the job and that relevant tests would be part of the medical.

Candidates have the right to refuse a health check; you have to have their written consent before you ask a doctor to do a medical report. If his own doctor does the examination a potential employee has a right to see the report and can refuse to let you see it even though you'll have to pay the doctor's fee. But of course, you have the ultimate sanction in that if you insist on a satisfactory medical report and don't get it, you can decide not to take the person on.

Checking qualifications

If a qualification is essential for the job, check it! You can make a job offer that's conditional on that check being positive. You can ask for certificates, or check with colleges, universities, or any other professional organisations or examining boards.

Experian offers a service for checking out degrees (www.uk.experian.com), the Qualifications and Curriculum Authority has a database of vocational qualifications (www.qca.org.uk), the Learning and Skills Council can help you check on National Vocational Qualifications (www.lsc.gov.uk), and the National

Academic Recognition Information Centre can check overseas qualifications (www.naric.org.uk).

Offering the Job to Your Dream Candidate

As soon as you make an offer – whether it's over the phone, by e-mail, or by letter – and the candidate has accepted it, a contract exists between you and your new employee. What that entails is spelled out in Chapter 3.

In theory you don't have to put anything in writing at this stage. The law says that an employee has to be given a Written Statement of Particulars of Employment (see Chapter 3 for more details) not later than eight weeks after he starts his employment with you.

If you don't really want to appoint any of the candidates or you don't feel any are right, don't appoint anyone. Get a temp in to tide you over and start looking again. Better this than giving the job to the wrong person.

Making an offer that can't be refused

After you find the right candidate, you have to discuss money. You may have mentioned ball-park figures during the interview, but now it's time to make an offer and negotiate a deal that suits both you and the employee.

Think about the whole package you are prepared to offer. You may have already thought this through when you were considering employing someone in the first place. You can attract good employees with contributions to an occupational pension scheme, use of a company car, or better holiday and sick pay than most employers.

Sometimes it's not just money that matters to employees. The other terms and conditions on offer can be what makes or breaks the negotiations. Your chosen candidate may be happy to settle for the money you're offering as long as he has a few extra days of holiday or flexible hours of work. Discuss and negotiate and come up with a package he can't refuse. Don't forget that if he's moving from a job outside your local area he may have the costs of selling a home and buying another, plus the costs of moving and getting his family settled.

After an agreement has been reached, put the whole deal in a follow-up letter with the main terms and conditions of employment. It makes things easier for everybody and allows no cause for dispute.

Setting the start date

You may want your new employee to start straight away, but unless he's already out of work that's not likely to be possible. Most people have to give their bosses at least a week's notice and many have contracts that stipulate much longer notice periods. He isn't likely to be willing to hand in his notice while there are conditions to the offer and he may well want an unconditional offer, with all the main terms and conditions, in writing, before he takes that final step. He may be able to negotiate that his current boss lets him go sooner than the contract allows, but think about how you'd feel if one of your employees wanted to go without working out his notice.

Withdrawing a job offer

After the job offer has been made and accepted, a contract exists. If you made it conditional on getting satisfactory checks and the results weren't what you'd hoped for, you can withdraw your offer. However, if you made the offer conditional on satisfactory references and you don't get them and withdraw the offer, you can be sued for breach of contract.

If you just change your mind after making an offer or you made promises of terms and conditions that you later find you can't deliver, the employee can sue you for breach of contract and damages. Someone who has been unemployed would find it difficult to claim damages, but someone who gives up a good job and starts to make arrangements to move homes can run up quite a lot of expenses and have quite a sizable claim.

You can offer the job on a trial basis for a particular period of time – long enough to find out if the chosen candidate is really up to the job. If you then decide to withdraw the job offer at the end of that time, you have to give the employee the correct period of notice (see Chapter 4), or extend the trial period and provide some training. If you withdraw the job offer after a trial period but you don't come up with the training you promised at the outset, the employee can sue for breach of contract.

Dealing with requests for feedback

At some stage, you are going to disappoint someone by your decision not to appoint him and he may want to talk to you about why. Tell him what it was that gave the winning candidate the edge and discuss anything the rejected candidate can do better next time. Stick to the facts, such as that the person you've appointed had more experience or better qualifications. Suggest training courses that may make the person you've turned down more suitable next time. And be impressed that he's keen, really wanted the job, and felt that feedback from you can help him progress in his career. He may be exactly the right person for the job next time!

Chapter 3

Spelling Out the Contract

· ·

· ·

*A*n employer offering a job usually does it something like this (and you've probably done this yourself): the employer makes a verbal offer of a job at the end of an interview or on the phone a couple of days later, the would-be employee accepts that job in the same conversation, pay is discussed briefly, and then the employer puts the whole thing in a follow-up letter with the main terms and conditions of employment.

For a *contract of employment* (the legal term for what you or I would call 'a contract') to exist between you and an employee you have to make an offer of a job, the employee has to accept that offer, and some payment must be involved for the work done. All of that can be done verbally or in writing, but it doesn't have to be written down for a contract to exist. What you do have to write down is the statement of employment particulars, as outlined in this chapter.

A contract exists as soon as the offer is made and accepted and it's like any other legal contract. A contract is governed by *common law* (the law that comes from judges making decisions in courts and tribunals) and by the various pieces of legislation that cover issues such as pay, holiday entitlement, hours of working, dismissal, redundancy, disciplinary and grievance procedures, health and safety in the workplace, discrimination, and many other factors that I cover elsewhere in this book.

The *terms* of the contract of employment don't have to be in writing at this point. But, as I explain below, you do have to give your employees a Written Statement of Employment Particulars within eight weeks of them starting work. The terms of a contract may consist of:

- ✔ Express terms
- ✔ Implied terms
- ✔ Incorporated terms

A contract of employment usually includes some of each of these terms and this chapter contains examples of all three types. Of course certain laws govern those terms so that no term in the contract – whether express, implied, or incorporated – can be less favourable to the employee than the law dictates. You can give your employees better deals than the law sets out, but you can't make them worse off.

Putting Terms in Writing

Having said that, the contract of employment and the terms of the contract don't have to be in writing but for your own, and your employees' sakes, I suggest you do put everything in writing. That way the contract's clear to everyone and you have proof of what's been agreed.

 A good written contract is worth its weight in gold because it means that everyone knows, or has no excuse for not knowing, exactly how things are to work around your workplace. Both employees and the employer need to know what to expect and what the consequences will be if those expectations aren't met. That goes for both employer and employee.

You don't have to write all of a contract in one document. You can have the Written Statement of Employment Particulars covering all the details it has to include (see the next section, 'The Written Statement of Employment Particulars' for more on this) and a company handbook to cover all the workplace rules that have been negotiated with employees and unions if they're relevant in your workplace or that have come about because of the custom and practice that's built up over time. The handbook can cover all the small details that are particular to your business (such as staff meetings or car parking spaces) that the law doesn't get involved in, but that are relevant to all employees and important to the smooth running of the place.

The Written Statement of Employment Particulars

Even though a contract needn't be made in writing, the law does say that every employee has to have a *Written Statement of Employment Particulars* (a document outlining an employee's basic employment terms) that must cover the following long list of issues:

- ✔ Your company's name and the employee's name.
- ✔ The date the employment began.
- ✔ The rate of pay and date of payments.
- ✔ The hours of work.
- ✔ Holiday entitlement policy.
- ✔ Details of sick leave and sick pay.
- ✔ Details of pension scheme.
- ✔ The length of notice that either of you has to give to end the contract.
- ✔ The job title and job description.
- ✔ Where the work is to be carried out, with addresses.
- ✔ How long the employment is for (if it's not a permanent job), and whether it involves a trial period.
- ✔ The disciplinary rules and procedures, and the dismissal procedure.
- ✔ Who the employee should talk to if she's not happy about the way disciplinary procedures are handled, or has a grievance she wants to raise.
- ✔ If the employee will have to work outside the UK for more than a month, you need to give details of how long she will be expected to be away, what additional pay and benefits she'll be entitled to, what currency she'll be paid in, and any terms and conditions that will apply to her return to the UK.
- ✔ If there are any collective bargaining agreements that have been reached with staff or unions that directly affect the terms and conditions of employment you have to give details of those too.

This is a fairly comprehensive document already, but that's the minimum the statement should cover. If there's nothing to say about an item on the list, include a line to say so.

A contract of employment is at least partly made up of *express terms* – terms specifically agreed between you and your employee. Express terms don't all have to be in writing, but I recommend that you do confirm them in writing to avoid disputes at a later date about who said what, especially as many need be covered in the Written Statement of Employment Particulars anyway.

The law says that express terms override all other terms in the contract that are implied, incorporated, or there by custom and practice. This is because the express terms have been expressed and agreed. So express yourself, preferably in writing, and everyone will know where they stand.

The following sections give the low-down on what you probably want to include as details in your written statement.

Describing the job

Set out exactly what you expect the employee to do and what her job title will be. You most likely drew up a job description before the interview and sent that to the applicants so that they knew exactly what they were applying for. Now that you have selected your number one candidate you may find that together you can work out an even clearer description of what you expect and she can deliver. If there is a possibility that you may want her to do different or additional jobs from time to time, discuss that at the outset. You can use phrases such as 'you may be expected to perform other duties within the range of your capabilities and skills if it's necessary for the good of the business.' It's better that she realises that and what those tasks may be from the beginning.

Working out hours

The number of hours an employee can be asked to work is regulated by the European Working Time Directive (see Chapter 6), so you have to make sure that you aren't asking her to work longer than the law allows. You also have to allow her breaks and these should be set out clearly, along with details of any overtime. If you want employees to work from a particular time to a particular time, say so. If you can be flexible, be clear about how flexible, and give the range of starting and finishing times (for example starting between 8.00 a.m. and 10.00 a.m. and finishing between 4.00 p.m. and 6.00 p.m.). Set out the rules for employees claiming back time if they do longer hours on days when there's more work to be done. If you expect employees to fill in time sheets, say so.

You should write into the terms and conditions your flexible working patterns (see Chapter 6). If you let people work from home when they can't get childcare or need to be with elderly relatives, make it part of their contract and include this in the written statement.

On the other hand, if you want to reserve the right to lay employees off in times when work is scarce or if you want the right to vary their hours, you need to have this agreed in the written statement also. Make it clear how much notice you will give of those kinds of changes. If you don't and you just go ahead later and make changes without prior agreement, you can be sued for breach of contract. Spend some time thinking about where disputes or misunderstandings may arise and express your intentions clearly so that you can avoid problems down the road.

Setting out details of pay

Pay is covered by the National Minimum Wage legislation which is detailed in Chapter 16. Some employers do just pay those minimum hourly rates and some ignore the law and pay less – risking prosecution. Of course, you can set your own rates higher than the minimum. To attract and retain the best employees, you generally need to pay at least the going rate in your industry or in your area. You will probably also want to take into consideration qualifications and experience when deciding what to pay.

Because pay is an important area for all employees (would anyone really go to work if they didn't need the wages?), you must cover the following areas in your written statement:

- ✔ What the rate of pay will be (agree on this with the employee beforehand).

- ✔ What bonuses apply (making it clear how she qualifies for any bonuses, overtime, or commission payments).

- ✔ Pay schedule and method of payment.

- ✔ Review process and schedule for potential increases (provided employee performs well).

- ✔ How and when you pay work-related expenses.

- ✔ Any other benefits she may be entitled to (such as contributions from you to the company pension, or the company car scheme).

Explain all the deductions that you will make from an employee's pay, such as income tax and National Insurance. Be clear too about any situations that can arise in which you may make other deductions from her pay, such as if she's been overpaid by mistake or the till is short while she's been in charge of it. To reduce a member of staff's pay by making additional deductions may be a breach of contract on your part unless you have got the agreement of the employee at the very beginning that deductions can be made in certain circumstances. All aspects of pay are covered in Chapters 16 and 17.

You must pay men and women equal wages for equal work (see the section 'Applying the Laws that Affect the Contract' later in this chapter) and you can't discriminate against someone by paying them less for doing the same job as everyone else because they are from a different race, sex, nationality, have a different religion or beliefs, or because of their sexual orientation (see Chapter 13 for more on equality for employees).

Providing holidays

The law sets down the amount of paid holiday employees must have – at least 20 days a year (Chapter 7 goes into more detail about this) – but this is just a minimum. You may offer new employees a certain number of days' holiday including or excluding bank holidays and increase that entitlement for employees who work for you for longer.

Be clear about the rules, including when the holiday year runs from and to, how holiday entitlement accrues, and how much notice an employee has to give before taking leave. If you expect employees to take holiday at particular times, such as Christmas because you close down the business, make that clear in the written statement. If you don't allow your employees to take leave at certain times of the year, say so. There's more on all this in Chapter 7.

Sometimes the amount of holiday an employer offers is as important to an employee as the wages, so again you probably won't be able to afford to offer less than the going rates for your industry or region. The offer of an extra day here and there may make the difference between being able to attract the best employee or seeing her choose to work for someone else.

Explaining sickness policy

If an employee is off sick, rules apply about how and when you must pay her under the Statutory Sick Pay scheme (see Chapters 8 and 18 for more details). You can offer better terms under the contract of employment or at your discretion depending on the case.

Whether you pay the basic minimum or an amount over and above that, make it clear how employees qualify and how long sick pay will last for.

Pinpointing the place of work

The place of work may be your premises, but if you want employees to work from home or from premises belonging to your clients, some or all of the time, or if they will be travelling between workplaces make that clear. If they are to work from home also give them details of any equipment that you'll provide for them.

Explaining disciplinary and grievance procedures

You have to set out the disciplinary, grievance, and dismissal procedures in the Written Statement of Particulars of Employment or the statement has to refer to some other document such as the handbook where the employee can find the details. You also have to give details of the person to whom an employee should complain if she has a grievance about any aspect of her work or the workplace. The procedures are dealt with in more detail in Chapters 4 and 15.

Giving notice

You have to put in the Written Statement of Employment Particulars details of the notice that you or your employee should give if either of you wants to end the contract. You have to give the employee a period of notice depending on how long she's been in the job (statutory minimum notice periods are laid down by law, as explained in Chapter 4). Of course, as an employer you may decide to be more generous to your employees.

If you have to give an employee notice of dismissal and you want her to leave immediately because you've no work for her, you do still have to pay her for the weeks she would have worked during the notice period. If the contract is more generous than the statutory notice period, the contract is what you have to pay.

If an employee wants to leave and she's been with your business for over a month, she has to give one week's notice. Unless her contract or written statement specifies differently, that doesn't increase with the length of time she's been with you. So if you want an employee to give more notice than that, make sure that you've got the longer notice period specified in the contract.

Explaining redundancy

If you don't mention redundancy terms in the contract the statutory rules will apply.

The amount of notice you must give an employee if you're making them redundant, and the redundancy pay they're entitled to, are also laid down in law, but again you can offer better terms in the contract. If you do offer better terms those are the ones you have to stick to. Redundancy is explained in Chapters 5 and 19.

Deciding on retirement age

If you have a company policy that every employee retires at a particular age – when they reach 60, for example – put this in the contract. If you don't mention this, the fact that people have historically retired at 60 – so that it has become custom and practice to retire at 60 – will be part of the contract even though you haven't specifically said so. But it's better to be clear from the beginning (see the section 'Taking account of custom and practice' for more on how custom and practice are applied).

If nothing is expressed or implied about retirement age in the contract or written statement, and there's no history of people retiring at a particular age through custom and practice, and you then make an employee retire before they reach 65, you can face a claim for unfair dismissal.

Given that age discrimination rules come into force in 2006, that the government is trying to encourage people to stay on at work later, and that a skills shortage is looming, it may be a good idea not to have a retirement age and instead to look at ways of helping people to work longer, such as giving them the option to reduce their working hours later in life.

Providing pensions

You have to offer your employees a pension scheme if you have more than five employees, although you don't have to make employer contributions. Give details of the scheme in the written statement, along with any contributions employees have to make from their wages, any contributions you will make, and whether or not the pension is contracted in or out of the state second pension. Chapter 20 explains pensions in more detail.

Drawing up the lines of management

Although you aren't required to outline this in the written statement, it helps if employees know how the management of the business works, who their immediate line manager is, and who the employee reports to about various aspects of her job. You won't really be able to name names in a contract because people may leave your business or get moved to other jobs but you can set out the reporting structure. If and when the management structure changes, you need to discuss your plans with employees and give them a new clear reporting line.

Meeting the deadline

You must give the Written Statement of Employment Particulars to the employee not later than two months after she's started the job. Two months is quite a long time, certainly long enough for all sorts of confusion to have arisen. As most of your contracts will be basically the same apart from names, dates, and possibly pay and holiday entitlement, it's a good idea to get that statement to the employee as soon as possible after the job offer has been accepted. If someone has worked with you for a month or more and leaves before you issue the written statement, you must still give them one.

Using a Company Handbook

You don't have to have a *company handbook*, but it can be your most valuable asset! You can use it to pull together all the rules and regulations under which your business operates and it can incorporate the Written Statement of Employment Particulars or complement that statement. It's simply a good way of making sure that everyone has everything they will ever need to know about working for you in one place and in a useful reference format, instead of having to ask questions all the time.

The handbook can cover anything you want, from the time any post has to be in that day's out-tray to the procedure for handling paper for recycling. It can reiterate all the express terms and conditions of employment that are included in the Written Statement of Employment Particulars and explain all the implied and incorporated terms detailed later in this chapter. A company handbook helps:

 ✔ New employees to settle into a workplace, because they have something to refer to and don't feel they're asking daft questions endlessly for the first few weeks.

✔ Existing staff to find forgotten information or details that aren't written down anywhere else.

✔ You! Writing a company handbook makes you think through how all the operations in the workplace function, and whether they're running efficiently.

A good company handbook is an important reference tool for all your employees (and for you as the employer!). It can save you all sorts of misunderstandings and disputes. For example, an employee may never remember how many weeks' notice she has to give when she wants to take holidays. The notice is set out in law but if it isn't in the written statement, every time she thinks about holidays she has to ask someone, or she forgets to ask and gives you notice when it's too late. Then she may get upset when you say you can't let her go away.

A company handbook can be a working document that you can add to as you deal with new and different problems. Ideally, if your company can afford it, everyone should have their own copy, but if that's out of the question your best bet is to have it in the form of a file with loose-leaf sheets that you can change and amend as necessary. Keep the handbook in a place where any employee can get hold of it and encourage your staff to use it. Alternatively, if your business is based in an office environment, keep an electronic copy on a shared server or intranet page. In the absence of a Human Resources Department, which many small businesses can't afford, it's a very useful management tool.

Remembering the Unwritten Rules

Apart from the Written Statement of Employment Particulars and the company handbook if you have one, other rules also exist – whether written or not.

Some things are just so obvious that you don't discuss them, but they still form part of the terms of employment. For example, even if you don't write it down or discuss it, it's obvious that if you offer someone a job and they accept you will pay them. It's implied in every contract of employment, and such conditions of employment are known as *implied terms*. The following sections detail these implied terms.

As with any other terms that make up the contract, if you don't comply with the implied terms you'll be in breach of contract and the employee can make a claim against you.

Providing work

If you have employees in your workplace, legally you have to pay their wages, whether or not you provide work. If you employ people to do work and you pay them by the amount of work they produce, such as the number of jumpers they knit or the number of envelopes they stuff, you have a duty to provide them with work so that they can earn money. It may not be said, but it's implied in the contract when you offer the job and they accept. If you don't provide work and don't go on paying the wages you'll be in breach of contract and the employee can bring a case against you.

Caring for employees

It is implied that you will look after the health, safety, and welfare of your employees (see Chapters 10, 11 and 12 for more on this subject and the possible penalties of failing to comply). You have a legal duty of care to provide a safe working environment and safe equipment for employees to use and you have to have insurance to cover their compensation if they get injured at work. Whether or not your statement or handbook spells it out, it's part of the contract. Some breaches of Health and Safety legislation can result in you being prosecuted for criminal offences.

Paying expenses

If an employee has to spend money on expenses while doing her job, it's implied that you will pay her back. Instead of leaving money matters implied, however, you may want to spell out somewhere in the company handbook how to submit receipts for compensation of expenses and how an employee gets reimbursed. If you don't pay up you're in breach of contract and can be taken to an Employment Tribunal.

Trusting each other

The relationship between you and your employees has to be one of trust and confidence in each other. You wouldn't normally say this in the contract, but if one of you does something to upset that relationship and trust and confidence fall apart as a result, the other one can regard the contract as being at an end. You can dismiss the employee or she can sue you for unfair constructive dismissal on the grounds that your actions left her with no choice but to leave. For example, if you fail to pay her on time several paydays in a row, her trust that you are ever going to pay up is likely to erode rather rapidly.

Obeying instructions

Employees have a duty to obey your instructions as long as they're reasonable and lawful. Instructions are reasonable as long as they're part of the employee's job description, she's capable of doing what you ask, it isn't demeaning, or she's done it before without complaining. This is an implied term with the potential for dispute! The employee might argue that the instructions weren't reasonable and you left her with no choice but to refuse. This can result in you dismissing her and her suing for unfair dismissal, or her leaving and claiming constructive dismissal, either of which can end up before an Employment Tribunal.

Doing a good job

Another implied term for the employee is that she will do her work to the required level of skill and competence and she'll be careful to do it safely and effectively. Sometimes it can be hard to judge how well someone is performing, and people do have off days. In certain jobs you can set targets, but you must agree these with the employee beforehand and make sure they're realistic. In other jobs that won't be possible and a good way of working out what to expect from an employee is to have regular meetings to discuss the work and to have an annual appraisal system. There's more on appraisals in Chapter 14.

Being faithful

An implication exists in the contract that employees work for you in good faith and do not work for somebody else or for themselves, in a capacity which conflicts with your business, competes with it, or damages it in any way. If you find an employee selling the same clothes for half the price you sell them in your shop, on the market on a Saturday, she is in breach of her contract but if she does a second job in the evenings in a different kind of business, she isn't.

Ensuring confidentiality

The employee has a duty not to go around telling everybody about confidential information that she's found out about your business. If, for example, she finds a list of your clients and the details of the work you do for them lying on the fax machine – which is a very dangerous source of information – and shows it to one of your competitors, this can damage your business and the employee's likely to be in breach of her contract. Any contract of employment has an implied term that the employee has a duty not to betray your confidence.

With 'trade secrets' it's obvious when confidentiality is broken, but employees pick up other information while they're employed that this implied term may or may not cover and sometimes it's far from clear. If the information is something a competitor can easily have got hold of elsewhere, it probably wouldn't come under the duty of confidentiality. Be on the safe side. If you want something kept within your own four walls, make sure that employees know it's to be kept confidential.

Taking account of custom and practice

Something can become an implied term in the contract of employment through custom and practice. For example, if you've always allowed your employees to leave at 4.00 p.m. on a Friday instead of the usual 5.00 p.m., even though you have never discussed this or written it down, then it has become an implied term of the contract. If at the end of the working day people who've been out of the office visiting clients go straight home without reporting back to the office, that will become an implied term through custom and practice if you let it carry on happening – usually over a period of months rather than merely weeks.

If you don't want employees making up their own rules through custom and practice, stop the practice. Something does not become custom and practice over a set length of time, but the more regularly you've allowed something to go on happening without taking action to stop it, the shorter the period over which employees can claim it had become custom and practice. Write into the written statement or company handbook anything that you don't want to happen or nip it in the bud the first time it does happen. It can be much harder to change contracts later.

Incorporated Terms

Incorporated terms are those terms of the contract that are agreed between a union and an employer. They apply to all members of staff regardless of union membership.

Incorporated terms won't apply in small business where no recognised union is present (see Chapter 7 for more on union activities). If you have more than 20 employees, a union can write to you asking for you to recognise it to be entitled to conduct collective bargaining on behalf of your workers. If a tenth of your employees are already union members and the majority of your staff would be in favour of union recognition, there may be a ballot and a declaration that you recognise the union. If that's the case, the union can then negotiate with you on behalf of the employees.

The terms agreed between a union and an employer become incorporated into each individual employee's contract of employment. Incorporated terms may be negotiated on:

✔ Terms and conditions of employment

✔ Physical conditions in the workplace

✔ Allocation of work

✔ Disciplinary procedures

✔ Membership of trade unions, and facilities for union officials

✔ Engagement, non-engagement, termination, or suspension of employment

Applying the Laws That Affect the Contract

On top of express, implied, and incorporated terms, a whole host of other Acts and Regulations affect the contract of employment. Just a few examples are:

✔ All the legislation covering health and safety at work (see Chapters 10, 11, and 12) setting out your legal obligations to care for your employees' health, safety, and welfare at work.

✔ The Equal Pay Act 1970, covering the right of a woman to have equal pay to that of a man where the work she does is like work to a man, is rated as equivalent to work done by a man, and is of equal value to that done by a man (see Chapter 16)

✔ The various Acts that make it unlawful for you to discriminate against an employee on the grounds of race, nationality, sex, sexual orientation, religious or other beliefs, or disability (and to include age after 2006) (see Chapter 13).

✔ The Patents Act 1977, which covers the issue of who owns the patent for something invented by an employee in the course of the job – the inventions will usually belong to the employer.

Many more Acts and Regulations are explained as you read through this book. Even if you haven't written anything specific in the contract and you haven't discussed it, the law still applies. There may be areas of the law that this book doesn't cover but which are relevant to your business. Business Link will be able to help – go to www.businesslink.gov.uk or join the Federation of Small Businesses by calling them on 01253-336000 or go to www.fsb.org.uk or talk to ACAS on 0845-7474747 or www.acas.org.uk.

Avoiding Unfair Clauses

Contracts of employment are also covered by the *Unfair Contract Terms Act 1977*. This says that you can't put into the contract of employment to protect yourself something that would be unfair to the employee. You can't, for example, put in a clause that says you will have no liability for injuries the employee suffers as a result of you failing to provide a safe working environment. If you did put a clause like that in the contract and the employee later took a case against you, a court would be highly likely to say that it was unfair and find in the employee's favour.

Some employers try to get employees to sign contracts in which they waive their rights to something that, in law, they're entitled to (such as redundancy payments). You can't force people to waive their rights to redundancy payments and any such agreements won't be enforceable unless the employee is on a fixed-term contract of two years or more (agreed before the Fixed Term (Prevention of Less Favourable Treatment) Regulations 2002 came into force on 1 October 2002). She must also have agreed in writing, before she started work, to waive her rights to redundancy payments at the end of the contract.

Breaching a Contract

Throughout this book you can find examples of things you might do that would be in breach of an employee's contract and can result in the employee taking a case against you at an Employment Tribunal. For example, if you reduced an employee's pay without her agreement; refused her full holiday entitlement; did not give her time off to carry out public duties; or failed to carry out your duty of care for her health and safety by providing a safe working environment you would be in breach of contract. If you do find yourself faced with a Tribunal get advice – Chapter 15 explains the tribunal process and where you can get help and advice.

You must adhere to any terms and conditions set out in the contract, either in the Written Statement of Employment Particulars or implied terms that exist without discussion. You can't change them without your employee's agreement.

Changing Terms and Conditions

If you do want to change terms and conditions in an employee's contract you can be entering a legal minefield. If the contract doesn't contain a clause allowing you to vary a particular term or condition that you want to change you should negotiate with her and get her agreement. If you want to change her working hours by having her come in earlier and leave earlier or come in later and leave later, for example, you have to realise that such hours will suit some people and make life difficult for others. Discuss the situation with your employee. If you have a good business case for doing it and can argue that the viability of the business depends on it, you should negotiate and if you can't come to an agreement you will have to give your employee a reasonable period of notice during which she can make necessary arrangements for the change.

You may be taken to an Employment Tribunal over changes to an employee's terms and conditions. You can even face a claim for sexual discrimination (see Chapter 13) if a change particularly adversely affected women workers for example. The Tribunal will want to know that you have a good business argument for making the changes. It will also expect you to have acted reasonably, looked at alternatives that would suit everyone such as flexible working patterns, and acted in the way a 'reasonable employer' would have acted.

Chapter 4

Disciplining and Dismissing Staff

In This Chapter

▶ Implementing a disciplinary procedure

▶ Getting rid of employees – the correct way

▶ Avoiding wrongful or constructive dismissal

▶ Understanding what happens if you do get dismissals wrong

Sacking people isn't a nice job, but sometimes you're left with no other choice. If the job an employee has been doing no longer needs to be done and you have no other job that's suitable, you can make that member of staff redundant (and that's dealt with in Chapter 5); but if you want to dismiss an employee for another reason and their job still exists, you have to be sure of your standing and tread very carefully through the legal minefield of dismissal.

New Dispute Resolution Regulations came into force in October 2004 which substantially changed the way employers have to deal with disputes and disciplinary and grievance procedures. An employer who dismisses someone and gets those procedures wrong can have a case brought against them at an Employment Tribunal. They'll be found to have unfairly dismissed the employee, and as a result they can be ordered to pay greatly increased compensation. The new rules are set out in detail in Chapter 15. Don't think you can ignore the new rules and procedures. More and more cases are being brought against employers who simply don't know the law has changed.

Most importantly, the reason for the dismissal has to be fair; the way you dismiss also has to be fair and you have to follow all the right procedures. This chapter helps you to work out what's fair and what's not, and begins by taking a look at your disciplinary options *before* deciding to sack a member of staff.

Resolving Disputes

Firing an employee really should be the very last option you consider. If a member of staff's performance is causing you or other employees concern, your first step is to follow your company's disciplinary procedure (see the section 'Following a disciplinary procedure'). New statutory dismissal and disciplinary procedures came into force in October 2004, and your company procedures must at least comply with those minimum standards.

Pretty much every story has two sides to it, so if you go into a meeting or begin an investigation with the idea of resolving the problem, rather than being determined to get rid of the thorn in your side, it's better all round. A disciplinary meeting is an opportunity to find a solution to a problem rather than just to mete out discipline and punishment.

Morale around the workplace can plummet when an employee is sacked. Unless the person has been a complete pain, colleagues may feel you've just been looking for an excuse and weren't listening to the employee's views. Resolving a dispute and making things work can have a very positive effect on the rest of the workers and ultimately your business will benefit.

Following a disciplinary procedure . . . right through to dismissal

All employers are legally required to have a disciplinary procedure. I just outline the procedure here – Chapter 15 deals with it in a lot more detail. Some bosses have separate procedures dealing with conduct and underperformance; some use the same procedure for both. When employees join your firm you have to let them know how the disciplinary procedure operates and the kind of behaviour that gets employees fired. If this information isn't spelled out in detail in the Written Statement of Employment Particulars it has to be in a company handbook or in some other written document that your employees have easy access to (see Chapter 3).

ACAS (the Advisory, Conciliation and Arbitration Service) produces a code of practice on disciplinary procedures with details on how to draw up and operate a disciplinary procedure. The code is used as the yardstick to judge how reasonable an employer has been if an employee brings a claim for unfair dismissal to an Employment Tribunal so get a copy and incorporate it into your own procedures. You can contact ACAS at 0845-7474747 or through the Web site at www.acas.org.uk.

The minimum the law says you have to implement in your disciplinary procedure is the following:

1. **Get all the facts straight, and decide whether or not any further action must be taken.** Investigate the situation fully by talking to the employee concerned and any other employees who might be able to throw some light on events. Gather any evidence you can find – e-mails, letters and so on. Interview any witnesses and take signed written statements from them.

2. **Start informal discussions, coaching, or counselling for the employee involved.** Make it clear to them that this isn't part of a formal disciplinary procedure – you're trying to help them and to avert more problems.

3. **If the problematic situation doesn't change let the employee know in writing what they're doing wrong.** Be sure to include any evidence you have, and explain to them why the situation cannot continue, what you expect them to do to remedy the situation and by when.

4. **Hold a disciplinary hearing to discuss the situation.** The employee can bring along a work companion or a union representative. Before the hearing you must set out in writing the concerns which have led you to hold the meeting and the employee must have a copy of that statement. At the hearing explain your complaint and your evidence and give the employee the chance to state their case, ask questions, give evidence, and call their own witnesses.

5. **Let the employee know what you've decided in light of the hearing.** If you decide on disciplinary action rather than the sack, give them a written warning spelling out what the misconduct is, what has to be done about it, and by when. And explain the consequences if things don't change – perhaps a final written warning and then the sack.

6. **Allow the employee the right to appeal.** If they do, hold an appeal meeting. If your business is big enough try to have a different manager hear the appeal to the one who made the decision to dismiss. Once the appeal is over you have to let the employee know your final decision.

The list shows the basic statutory requirements – your own disciplinary procedure may allow for more warnings and more meetings and other courses of action such as demotion or suspension.

If you don't follow this basic procedure and you have employed the member of staff for more than a year, they can claim automatic unfair dismissal and the resulting tribunal can increase the compensation it orders you to pay.

Calling in the arbitrators

If you can't resolve a disciplinary problem inside your organisation, think about calling in an outsider as an arbitrator. If your organisation recognises a union (see Chapter 7), that union may be able to send someone in to arbitrate. ACAS may also be able to help – the contact details are earlier in this chapter.

Dismissing Staff – the Right Way

Most things in life can be done in a right way and a wrong way, and dismissing staff is definitely one of those areas where you have to get it right. The law protects most employees from being unfairly dismissed or from being forced to quit because of their boss's unreasonable behaviour. And that means that if an employee thinks they have been unfairly dismissed, they can take a case against you at an Employment Tribunal (flick through to Chapter 15 for more on these tribunals).

If you need any incentive to stop and reflect before you wield the axe, just remember that a tribunal can order you pay compensation if it decides you've got it wrong. That can be to anything from a basic award worked out based on a weekly wage figure of £280 and the number of years the employee has worked for you, up to a maximum compensatory award of £56,800 (a maximum that is index-linked and increases annually). It wouldn't take too many payments like that to bring many small businesses to their knees. If the tribunal also decides that the dismissal was discriminatory (see Chapter 13) the compensation is uncapped!

Having fair grounds to sack an employee

For a dismissal to be fair you have to have an acceptable reason for getting rid of your employee.

It's fair to dismiss a member of staff when:

- ✔ Their job no longer exists. But remember it's the job that's redundant, never the person (see Chapter 5 for more on this).

- ✔ They turn out not to be capable of doing the job or are not qualified (including lying about qualifications in a job application).

✔ They're guilty of some misdemeanour (constantly being late, absent, careless, or having a bad attitude, for example).

✔ They do something so bad that it amounts to gross misconduct (such as stealing something, hitting someone, committing fraud, or sexually harassing other staff). See the later section 'Dismissing for gross misconduct'.

✔ You can't let the employee go on doing their job because to do so would be breaking the law (such as a job that involves driving when the employee has been banned from driving).

If none of those reasons apply to the employee you want to sack, one more category may give you a get-out clause. You may be able to fire someone for 'some other substantial reason'. Isn't the law wonderfully clear? Basically, this other reason has to be one that you can defend in a tribunal hearing. One of the most common reasons is that you have to restructure your business for financial reasons and that means jobs aren't redundant but are changing and so your contract with your employee has to change too. If an employee refuses to accept these contractual changes it can then be fair to dismiss him.

Although employees past retirement age haven't been protected against unfair dismissal in the past, some recent legal cases cast doubt on this. If you haven't set a normal retirement age for your workplace, employees over 65 generally count as being of an age to retire. Starting in 2006, new legislation regarding age discrimination will kick in that may well prevent your firing old timers (regardless of whether they're past retirement age). Although the details haven't been worked out yet the government may give older employees the same rights to claim unfair dismissal and compensation as their younger colleagues. There's more on age discrimination in Chapter 13.

Applying your decision

If you've got good grounds for dismissing an employee, the next step is to go about the dismissal fairly. That means first giving the employee a fair hearing by going through all the necessary disciplinary procedures explained in the section 'Following a disciplinary procedure . . . right through to dismissal' earlier in this chapter.

Even if you have no choice but to sack someone because it would be breaking the law for them to carry on in their job, you still have to be fair in how you go about it. You have to discuss, investigate, and consider the possibility of keeping the person on in another capacity if other jobs are available. If you end up having to explain yourself to a tribunal panel they will want to know that you gave the employee a fair hearing; that you investigated the whole situation fully; and that you were being reasonable when you decided that the reason was substantial enough to merit the sack. A dismissal has to be fair all round.

 Keep detailed records of all the procedures you go through – copies of letters, warnings, records of meetings, and the evidence you gather. If the case does come to a tribunal, you'll need to be able to prove that you did everything fairly and squarely.

Giving written reasons for dismissal

If you've investigated, warned, followed the procedure, and finally decided you have good reason to dismiss someone, you've got to let the employee know what your reasons are. If you've followed the correct disciplinary procedure outlined in the section 'Following a disciplinary procedure . . . right through to dismissal', this shouldn't come as a surprise to the employee and they should be fully aware of all the reasons already – but you still have to put the reasons for dismissal in writing.

Giving notice of dismissal

Except in cases of gross misconduct, you have to give the appropriate period of notice for any dismissal. Details of an employee's notice entitlement should be outlined in their contract.

 The law says that someone who has worked for at least a month but less than a year is entitled to one weeks notice. Someone who has worked for two full years is entitled to two weeks' notice; three full years means three weeks' notice, and so on up to a maximum of 12 weeks' notice. You may offer more generous terms in your employees' contracts (see Chapter 3 for more information on contracts). You can increase the amount of notice employees are entitled to depending on how long they've worked for you, and your more senior employees – such as managers – may have longer notice periods.

Don't forget that an employee who is retiring is in reality being dismissed (because of retirement) and so is entitled to be given notice of dismissal in the same way as anyone else or to be paid money in lieu of notice.

If you don't want the employee around the workplace after you've given them notice, you can let them go immediately but you have to pay them in place of the notice period anyway. So if they're entitled to six weeks' notice, you have to give them six weeks' pay. They also have to be paid for any other fringe benefits they may be entitled to under the contract such as the use of a company car.

Dismissing for gross misconduct

Examples of misconduct can be constantly being late or not turning up at all, making careless mistakes, or not really caring how their work goes! Misconduct is irritating in the extreme and possibly a reason to sack someone. While ordinary misconduct may be annoying, beyond that it becomes gross misconduct.

Gross misconduct is something so serious that it brings the contract between you and the guilty party to an end immediately. Examples of acts at work that may constitute gross misconduct include:

- Theft
- Dishonesty
- Fraud
- Violence
- Deliberately damaging company property
- Sexual harassment
- Bullying
- Downloading pornographic material from the Internet
- Inciting racial hatred
- Gross insubordination

If you sack someone for gross misconduct, without notice, you have to be able to justify that action. What you are actually saying is that the employee has done something that has damaged the relationship of trust and confidence between you, destroyed their working contract, and made it impossible to carry on as boss and employee. If you can't prove that, the employee may make a claim for wrongful dismissal at a tribunal.

In such cases, the tribunal will want to know:

- Whether any of your other staff ever acted in the same way and whether you took that case seriously enough to fire them without notice.
- If whatever has happened really has broken down the trust and confidence between you and your employee.

This means that you have to have fully investigated the incident and given the employee a fair hearing before you come to your decision. The principles of fairness apply just the same to cases of gross misconduct as they do to ordinary cases of misconduct or poor performance (read the section on 'Avoiding wrongful dismissal', later in this chapter). Employees should already know what kind of gross misconduct will get them fired on the spot – this should be in your staff handbook (outlined in Chapter 3).

Be very careful about summarily dismissing someone for what you see as gross misconduct. If they bring a case against you at an Employment Tribunal and the tribunal decides the conduct didn't amount to gross misconduct, you can end up having to pay greatly increased compensation. You must follow all the basic dismissal and disciplinary procedures outlined earlier in this chapter.

If employees are guilty of actions outside the workplace that would constitute gross misconduct at work you may be able to fairly dismiss them. If that happens take your solicitor's advice.

Plain old ordinary misconduct is handled differently. Ordinary misconduct doesn't bring the contract to an immediate end, and you must follow a fair disciplinary procedure with all the necessary warnings.

Dismissing for underperformance

We all have days when we go home without having done much (although my development editor insists he doesn't). But you can't sack an employee for the occasional lazy day unless it happens week in, week out.

If an employee is seriously underperforming – their work isn't up to scratch, they just aren't capable of doing the job, or they're always off, sick, or late so that the job isn't getting done properly, or they haven't got the qualifications they need – you can have a reason for firing them fairly on the grounds of lack of capability or qualifications.

The minimum procedures you have to go through are the same as for other disciplinary procedures (see the section 'Following a disciplinary procedure . . . right through to dismissal' earlier in this chapter) or follow your company's own disciplinary procedure.

Give people the chance to improve before dismissing them, and be reasonable about the timescale you set for seeing their work improve. You can allow any amount of time between a few weeks and several months. A tribunal considers how long the employee has been with you, how bad the performance was, what warnings you had given that things had to improve, the effect on your business, and the size of the workforce. If you have other people who can 'carry' underperforming employees while they are trying to improve, you can afford to give them a bit longer than if you are dependent on that one person.

Getting to the root of underperformance

An underperforming employee isn't necessarily being that way because they're not qualified for the job or they're just plain lazy. If their underperformance is the result of being off sick every so often and you can show that this has affected the operation of your business, you may have a fair reason to dismiss them. But you must still follow procedures and give a chance for things to change. You might discover that the reason for your employee having so much time off sick is that the job is making them ill – worry, stress, pressure of too much work – resulting in nothing getting done. The real problem can be that you are understaffed and the solution can be hiring someone extra.

Be objective about deciding whether or not an employee has made an improvement. Getting exasperated and being determined not to see any improvement isn't your best way forward. Taking a second opinion from another manager or a colleague is a good idea.

Annual appraisals are a good way of assessing how people are performing and they give you a legitimate reason to discuss any problems. It's good to talk.

Dismissing Staff – the Wrong Way

If you just snap and fire a member of staff without a full investigation, without giving her the chance to put her case across or to improve, and without going through all the correct procedures, your sacked employee will likely feel very aggrieved and seek legal advice. And a solicitor is likely to tell her that she has a case for unfair dismissal, if she has at least one years' service. The next thing you know, your former employee has filed a claim, and you have to prepare your case for the defence.

Avoiding wrongful dismissal

Wrongful dismissal is when you decide to end a member of staff's contract by dismissing them without notice or by giving them a period of notice less than what they're entitled to. Doing so means you're in breach of contract and the aggrieved party can file a claim against you at a tribunal within three months of the event or within 6 years in the courts.

You must give the notice period set out in the employee's contract unless you are firing them for gross misconduct (refer to the section 'Dismissing for gross misconduct' earlier in this chapter). If you haven't put a notice period into the employee's contract, the statutory minimum applies. See 'Giving Notice of Dismissal'.

You have to give notice or pay in lieu of notice. If the employee can show that they didn't get the right notice and that they have suffered financially as a result, they can claim at an Employment Tribunal or in the County Court for amounts up to £25,000. For sums over £25,000 the employee can apply to the High Court.

If you haven't made clear in the contract how much notice an employee gets and you fire them using the statutory minimum, in some cases they can also ask a court or tribunal to rule that the period of notice, although perfectly legal, was unreasonably short. The more skilled, well-paid, and senior an employee is, the more likely the tribunal is to agree.

Steering clear of constructive dismissal

If you behave in such a way that employees feel they have no choice but to quit, that's *constructive dismissal* (to use the full title, constructive unfair dismissal). Once the employee has gone, providing they have one years' service, they can take a claim against you for unfair dismissal and possibly wrongful dismissal too if you haven't got the notice period or pay right.

If as an employer you just keep forgetting to buy the teabags and coffee or are merely an irritable pain, no-one can quit and claim constructive dismissal. You have to have done something seriously wrong – such as changing the job they do without any discussion. The trust and confidence that exist in the employee's contract, whether in writing or not, have to be broken.

If you do something serious, such as reduce an employee's pay without his agreement, the longer he stays on after the event, the more he would be seen to have accepted the change and the less likely he would be to win a constructive dismissal claim. If, however, the employee works 'under protest', making it clear that she does not accept the changes, it's possible for her to resign some time after the breach of contract and successfully sue you. If she left because she had a better job offer, she would have a hard time proving that your behaviour was the catalyst pushing her into going.

Automatic unfair dismissal

You can't dismiss an employee for being pregnant or because she has dared to ask for something that she's entitled to by law (such as written terms and conditions of employment or parental leave). A situation where you sack an employee for asking for something she had the right to ask for is known as *automatic unfair dismissal*. In cases of automatic unfair dismissal, the tribunal will automatically come down on the side of the employee. The tribunal has no choice – because you have broken the law – and this is costly for the employer. For example, the minimum basic award where you dismiss someone because of their union membership or activities or for being a health and safety representative or occupational pension scheme trustee is £3,800.

As I've said earlier in this chapter if you dismiss someone without following all the right procedures that will also be automatic unfair dismissal and you can be penalised by being ordered to pay increased compensation.

Tying Up the Loose Ends

Even when all the procedures have been gone through and a leaving date is settled, that's not the end of the matter. You aren't under any obligation to offer an exit interview to an employee who is leaving, but it can be useful for you as well as the employee. They may have comments to make about the way your business operates that would be useful to consider – as well as letting them get it off their chest! It can help to clear the air.

Don't forget the paperwork. Just as you have to do when an employee hands in their notice and chooses to leave, there are loose ends that need to be tidied up (see Chapter 19 for more on this).

Handing over paperwork to a new employer

Paperwork is always involved when an employee leaves. Tax forms need to go to HMRC (HM Revenue and Customs – formerly the Inland Revenue) as well as to a new employer. Here's a summary of the paperwork that you need to sort out before your dismissed employee leaves:

> ✓ **A P45.** This form is the most important piece of paperwork, because it details where you're up to with deducting tax and

national insurance for the year so far. The P45 can be passed on directly to a new employer, but if the employee doesn't have a job to go to you should give it to them. They will need it to claim Job Seeker's allowance until they get back into work.

✔ **A P60.** If the redundancy happens near the end of the tax year, the employee should get a P60, detailing all of their tax deductions for the year.

✔ **A P11B.** This form shows all the benefits in kind that the employee has received so far during the year. The HMRC's Web site (www.hmrc.gov.uk) has details of all the forms you need and provides downloadable forms too.

Chapters 5 and 19 contain more detailed information on what to do if you are dismissing someone because of redundancy.

You must also give new employers details of all the entitlements employees have taken so far in the current year of employment – maternity leave, paternity leave, or parental leave, for example.

Give the dismissed employee a copy of all their tax and benefits details plus any certificates they may have gained while they've been employed by you (such as qualifications or safety certificates or courses related to their job).

Sorting out outstanding payments

Check that the dismissed employee has been paid everything they're owed. They may not have taken their full holiday entitlement up to and including their last day.

If this is the case they may be entitled to be paid for that accrued holiday under the terms of their contract or under the working time regulations (see 'Calculating holiday entitlements' in Chapter 7). You can agree that they take their remaining holiday during their notice period, but if you want them to do that, make sure that you give them enough notice to do so (depending on how much notice they have to work that may not be practicable – Chapter 7 explains more about this).

You also need to check that a dismissed employee has been fully paid for any overtime, extra hours they've put in, expenses they're due, or for anything else that they would normally expect to have been paid for while in your employment, such as bonuses and commissions.

If you decide to take a company car away from an employee during their notice period, you have to work out how much they should be paid to compensate for that loss.

You need to check if the employee is entitled to any tax rebates through the PAYE (Pay As You Earn) scheme. The member of staff who works out wages should be able to sort this out with the help of the Inland Revenue – now HM Revenue and Customs. Chapter 16 gives more details on paying wages.

Any overpayments are returned in the employee's final pay cheque. All the money due to them should be detailed in the final pay slip; there's more about final payments in Chapter 19.

Paying instead of allowing staff to work their notice

If you want your employee to go this minute and never darken your door again, you have to pay them money for the period they would otherwise have had to work – money in place of the notice that their contract or the law says they're entitled to. Not only that, but they have to be in the same financial position as they would have been in if you had let them work through the notice period. That might mean paying out more than just a few weeks' pay. For example, if the employee had the use of a company car, they can have expected to use that during the notice period so you will have to compensate them for the loss of that too.

The right to pay in lieu of notice is always an option open to an employer, whether or not it says so in the employee's contract, and the employee doesn't have the right to demand to work out their notice.

The other thing you might do is to send the employee on garden leave. *Gardening leave* means that your dismissed employee spends the period of their notice still employed by you but at home and with no work to do while still being paid. You might decide to do that if you're worried about what damage they can do to your business if they worked out their notice in the office – maybe by stealing all your best customers or contacts.

Dealing with pensions

When employees leave a job and start a new one, they have to decide what to do about the money they've paid into your company pension, if you provided one. The same goes for employees you dismiss.

Chapter 20 has much more about pensions.

Restricting what employees can do after leaving

In certain cases, the new business activities of a recently dismissed employee can harm your company. For example, if you are a hairdresser and a former employee sets up her own salon in close proximity and takes her customers away, you will lose out.

You have the option of taking steps to protect your business by putting into your employees' contracts terms that limit what they can do when they leave you. These are known as *restrictive covenants*. You can say that former employees are not to set up in competition with you for a period of three months after leaving your firm or restrict them to setting up their business outside a particular geographical area.

You have to be reasonable about any restrictive covenants you put in a contract if you're not likely to be able to enforce them if the employee ignores them. If you try to sue for breach of contract the courts can find your restrictive covenants too restrictive and you will lose – and be out of pocket for the legal fees. Take advice from a good lawyer before you draw up contracts with these kinds of restrictions.

Giving references

You don't have to give any employee a reference, whether they've resigned or been dismissed, but if you do agree to, the reference has to say what you believe to be accurate and fair and you have to give it without malice.

If you give an unfair, malicious, or negligent reference and the employee loses out as a result, they can sue you. On the other hand, you have to be truthful for the sake of any prospective employers as well. If they lose out as a result of a negligent reference, they can sue you too!

If you've dismissed an employee you may not be too bothered about how quickly they get back to work, but be objective about this. They may have been in the wrong job and may be rather good in a different company with a job that suits them better.

Be truthful in your reference, but don't be tempted to exaggerate an employee's negative points. Employees will have the right to see what you have written about them in references once they've started work with their new employer, so make sure that what's in the reference is what has already been discussed in the course of the fair dismissal procedure and can be proved to be true. Don't add little extras out of spite.

Make sure you don't give a discriminatory reference to someone because of their sex, race, disability, religion or religious beliefs, or sexual orientation, and be careful too about age! Even though the age discrimination legislation doesn't come in until October 2006, that's no excuse for discriminating beforehand. Chapter 13 has more on age discrimination.

Don't be tempted to try to smooth things over with an employee you're dismissing over a dispute by offering a glowing reference. This can backfire on you. The employee can use your reference to prove that they weren't guilty of misconduct or incompetence after all.

Facing Tribunals – Something to Be Avoided

Tabloid writers love a good story about an unfairly dismissed employee managing to win thousands of pounds from their employer. Some very high-profile cases take place, for example where employees of big financial firms win huge sums at Employment Tribunals for discrimination or in court for breaches of contract. They should act as a warning that you can't afford to be unfair.

If you do unfairly dismiss, wrongfully dismiss, or constructively unfairly dismiss an employee, they can take a claim against you at an Employment Tribunal (find out more about Employment Tribunals by heading on to Chapter 15).

Sometimes, even when you are in the right, vexed employees feel you've acted unfairly and want their day in court. If you really do have good reason to dismiss and scrupulously follow the correct dismissal procedures (explained in the earlier section 'Following a disciplinary procedure . . . right through to dismissal' and in more detail in Chapter 15) you'll be able to convince a tribunal should it come to that. But avoid this scenario if at all possible!

If an ex-employee brings a claim of unfair dismissal against you and wins, the tribunal can instruct you to:

- ✔ Pay compensation ranging from a basic award up to the top compensatory award of £56,800 depending on the details of the case (the maximum amount is index-linked and increases each year).
- ✔ Reinstate the employee in their former job.
- ✔ Re-engage the employee in a different job.

The employee is less likely to want reinstatement or re-engagement because it isn't likely that the two of you will be able to work together again comfortably. For a small business, even sums of far less than the maximum compensation figure can be crippling. So you really do want to make sure that you are on a very solid footing before you decide to sack someone. It pays to be fair.

Chapter 5

Trimming Down to Size – Redundancies

*R*edundancy isn't just another word for sacking people. *Redundancy* means that the reason members of staff are leaving is because jobs are going and therefore the people who do them have to go, rather than you sacking them for disciplinary reasons. Redundancy is fair grounds for dismissing employees, as long as a genuine reason exists and you aren't merely using it as an excuse to get rid of someone. But as with any dismissal, you have to be fair about how you choose whom to make redundant and you have to follow all the correct procedures otherwise your employees can claim unfair selection for redundancy and take a case against you at an Employment Tribunal. And unlike employees sacked in disciplinary circumstances (as covered in Chapter 4), most employees who are made redundant are entitled to an extra redundancy payment.

Understanding Redundancy

For a redundancy to be a redundancy and not a dismissal for some other reason, you must be able to prove that jobs really are redundant. Jobs have to disappear or there has to be less need for the work that your employees do or your place of business moves. You can't simply make a person redundant on Friday and take on someone new to do the same job on Monday. That is a dismissal for another reason, rather than a redundancy. Redundancy has to be non-discriminatory, fair and handled fairly (refer to Chapter 4) or you can end up being taken to an Employment Tribunal.

Forecasting your company's future

Sod's law dictates that just when your business is going really well the orders start to dry up, the customers stop spending, and some of the staff have next to nothing to do. This isn't so bad if you know that more orders are in the pipeline and you're simply in a lull. Perhaps you have enough cash in the bank to ride out the storm. Or you may be able to ride out a temporary crisis by laying off your employees or putting them on short-time working (see the section 'Laying Off Staff and Short-Time Working').

But if the lull goes on too long and you can no longer pay all the salaries at the end of the month, you may have to face facts and let some of the staff go.

It's a blow to the people who have to be 'let go', but it's a blow for their colleagues and for your business too. Why? Because you've spent a lot of time, effort, and hard cash recruiting and training your employees and they've got a lot of useful knowledge about how your firm works and how the market in general operates – so you'll be losing that knowledge and expertise. And of course when things do pick up, your former employees will probably have new jobs and you won't be able to get them back, so you'll have to start all over again.

No one wants to have to make good staff redundant, but sometimes you have no choice because economic factors have:

- ✔ Forced you to shut down your business or a part of it.
- ✔ Made you reorganise your business for efficiency.
- ✔ Created a downturn in business and your workforce no longer has enough work to do.
- ✔ New technology or processes mean you need fewer employees.

You can move someone else already working for you into a job from which you've made another employee redundant, but an overall reduction in the number of jobs at your workplace or a reduction in the need for a particular kind of work must occur.

When colleagues are made redundant the ones who are left behind often suffer from *survivors' syndrome*. They feel guilty about still having a job when their friends don't. The whole workforce can become very unsettled and work flow can be affected, so handle redundancy carefully and sensitively.

Laying Off Staff and Short-Time Working

Before you decide redundancies are the only way you can consider laying employees off or putting them on short-time working. The rules are explained in Chapter 6. If your employees have contracts which allow you to lay them off or put them on shorter hours, they may still leave and can be entitled to redundancy payments if the lay-off or short-time working lasts

> ✔ for 4 consecutive weeks or longer
>
> ✔ for a series of six weeks or more – of which not more than 3 were consecutive – within a 13 week period.

For redundancy purposes, short-time working is where an employee's pay in a week is less than half a normal week's pay.

Deciding Who's Going to Go

After you've decided that redundancies need to take place you have to decide who should be shown the door. Sometimes it will be immediately clear who that is. If you no longer need anyone with a particular skill, because you've had to stop a certain part of your business, then the person with that skill is the one to go. But if updated technology means that machines or computers can do more of the work and employees have less to do, or you simply have to implement job cuts across the board, it can be a lot more difficult to decide who should be given their P45 (that's the paper-work that shows how much Income Tax and National Insurance you've deducted from the employee's pay and passed on to HM Revenue and Customs – previously the Inland Revenue – at the date he stops working for you). What you can't do is use the need to make employees redundant as an excuse to get rid of all those workers you aren't happy with.

For an employee to be fairly made redundant your company must:

> ✔ Have stopped (or intend to stop) doing the business for which you employ them.
>
> ✔ Have stopped (or intend to stop) carrying out business in the place where they work.
>
> ✔ No longer need them to do that particular kind of work.

Here's an example. You have ten people working in the part of your business that bakes cakes and because demand has dropped off, you decide to shut down your cake-baking section. Those cake-baking jobs are redundant, so you can fairly make the ten people doing those jobs redundant. But if only one job has to go in the cake-baking section – because business has only dropped off by about ten per cent and you don't expect a cake recovery any time soon – it's less easy to decide who to fairly make redundant. The employee who does the icing may have all the same skills as the rest of the bakers and the icing skill is extra (you can say it's the icing on the cake). Then who goes? You can shuffle the jobs around, but one job has to go and so you have to choose one employee to be made redundant. But you can't just use this as an excuse to get rid of the one baker you like least. You have to be fair and non-discriminatory about whom you select. It would be unfair to select someone because of their disability or because they are pregnant for example.

Fair dismissal by reason of redundancy requires that the job is redundant and not the employee.

Last In, First Out – ways of choosing who loses their job

Some workplaces still use the principle that the last person to be taken on should be the first person to go if jobs have to be cut. This method has the advantage that everyone knows where they stand and no heart-rending choices need be made. But it's rather an out of date method to use in the modern workplace. From your point of view as the employer, the employee who has been with you for the shortest time may be the least experienced. On the other hand, using a policy like that can result in you losing your best workers. Despite having been with you for the shortest time they can have been very experienced when they joined you or they may simply have worked better and developed faster than those who've been there much longer.

Another alternative is to ask for volunteers to be made redundant, before forcing yourself to choose who goes. Maybe some of your employees are coming up to retirement age and would be glad to go early – especially if you offer them some money in a settlement. Others may feel that they've a good chance of getting a better job somewhere else or have ambitions to do something different and jump at the opportunity to leave with a few weeks' wages in their pockets to tide them over. But for most employees, losing their job is one of the worst things that can happen and they will want to stay on if at all possible – especially if you are a good employer.

If you have a redundancy procedure already agreed with a union or with your workforce, you have to stick to it. If you don't have such a procedure, go with *custom and practice* (previous procedures that have been traditionally used around your workplace). If you think custom and practice are due for a change, you have to get your employees to agree first.

You can take skills, knowledge, qualifications, and experience into account when deciding who's for the chop and that's fair as long as you can show how those skills, knowledge, qualifications, and experience are necessary for your business. You're entitled to try to keep a balanced workforce in terms of experience and skills. But whatever you decide, you have to be able to show that the workers to be made redundant were chosen fairly. ACAS can give you practical help on methods for redundancy selection. Contact ACAS on 0845-7474747 or have a look at the Web site `www.acas.org.uk`.

If you select for redundancy on the grounds of the quality of an employee's work or their attitude or ability to get along with colleagues and customers – which are all rather a matter of opinion – you can well run into trouble, facing a claim for unfair dismissal (refer to Chapter 4 for more on this).

It isn't fair to make a member of staff redundant because they

- ✔ Have demanded their statutory rights – such as the right to the minimum wage or paid holidays (or paternity leave for fathers).

- ✔ Are pregnant, on maternity leave, or have asked to be allowed to work flexibly so they can have time with their children.

- ✔ Are a member of a trade union.

- ✔ Have refused to do a job because it's a risk to their health and safety, because the job's against the law, because it means working on Sunday in a shop, or if the job's to do with betting, all of which they're legally entitled to refuse. See the section 'Working on Sundays' in Chapter 6.

- ✔ Act as an employees' representative in a consultation on redundancies, business transfer, or as a trustee of an occupational pension fund.

Avoiding discrimination

Be wary of discriminating against an employee when you're deciding who should go. If you choose to make someone redundant because of their sex, race, disability, religion or religious beliefs, or sexual orientation, that is discrimination. Similarly, you can't choose to make a member of staff redundant just because they're pregnant or off on maternity leave.

You can make an employee who is pregnant redundant, but this must be a fair choice, and not one made because of her pregnancy.

Be wary too about selecting part-time workers ahead of full-time workers as this can amount to indirect discrimination on the grounds of gender, if all your part-time employees are women, for example (see Chapter 13 for more on discrimination).

In the same way that it's discriminatory not to take someone on because of any of the above reasons, you have to be careful not to discriminate even after the redundancy, for example by giving them a less than accurate reference. The section 'Giving references' later in this chapter provides more information on supplying references.

Offering suitable alternative jobs

If you have to cut jobs in one part of your business but things are good in other parts of that business, you have to consider whether you can offer suitable alternative jobs to some or all of the members of staff whom you're intending to make redundant.

If a limited number of alternative jobs are available and an employee who is being made redundant is on maternity leave, you must offer her any suitable alternative vacancy, no matter how inconvenient that is for you. If you don't she can claim automatic unfair dismissal.

If an employee accepts an offer of an alternative job that involves different terms and conditions of employment or a different kind of work, you have to allow them to try it out for four weeks. You and they can agree that the trial period should be longer than four weeks if they are being retrained. Before the trial period begins you should put in writing the date on which the trial will end and the terms and conditions that will apply once it does end. If at the end of that time the employee carries on doing the job they will have accepted it. If during or at the end of the trial they turn down the job because it isn't suitable after all, you have to treat them as if they were made redundant on the day their old job ended (if they were entitled to a redundancy payment then they'll still be entitled to that same payment). Entitlement to redundancy payments is covered later in this chapter (in the section 'Paying Redundancy Money') and the amounts payable are dealt with in Chapter 19. If during or at the end of the trial the employee turns down the job and unreasonably refuses to accept it, you can treat them as having been dismissed when the original contract came to an end and you don't have to pay a redundancy payment.

Consulting with your staff and unions

Many small businesses don't have enough employees to fall into this category but if you are intending to make 20 or more people redundant over a three-month period you have to consult with your workforce as well as with the individual employees before you issue any notices. This means consulting the union if you recognise one (see Chapter 7). If you don't recognise a union, you have to get the workforce to elect a few employees to represent them or consult with the whole workforce if it isn't too big. If you're making fewer than 20 employees redundant you must still consult the individual employees, and it's good practice to consult their representative.

The aim of the consultation is to come up with ways of avoiding the redundancies or reducing the number of people who have to go. You might not come to any agreement, but you do have to go in with an open mind and make a genuine attempt to come up with a solution. You have to be open with the union or the workers about the reasons for the redundancies, the numbers and jobs affected, how you are selecting who is to go, and how any redundancy payments will be calculated.

If between 20 and 99 jobs are to go over 90 days or less, you should have at least 30 days in which to consult with unions and staff. And if more than 100 jobs have to go you need to have at least 90 days to consult. So if you are running a business of that size, you do have to start the consultation process well in advance of issuing redundancy notices and as soon as the thought of redundancies comes into your head!

If you don't meet all the consultation requirements the union can make a complaint to an Employment Tribunal, which can make a *protective award*. It can require the employer to pay employees covered by the award their normal week's pay for a specified period – known as the protected period – regardless of whether or not they are still working, and the maximum award is 90 days' pay for each employee. It pays to consult!

Some bosses do try it on and offer alternative jobs that they know will be unsuitable. They hope that when the employee eventually does turn the offer down that will be the end of the matter and they will avoid having to make a redundancy payment. You can only avoid paying a redundancy payment if the person unreasonably turns down a suitable alternative job.

Giving the Right Periods of Notice

As with any other situation in which you have to get rid of staff, they are usually entitled to *notice* that their employment will end on a particular date. The amount of notice to which an employee is entitled should be explained in their contract. The minimum notice you can legally give is one week's notice after an employee has been with you for a month and up to two years; two weeks' notice after two years; three weeks' notice after three years; and so on up to 12 weeks' notice after 12 years or more. If you have been more generous in the contract than the legal minimum, you have to stick to that. If you don't give the right notice periods or pay the equivalent in lieu, you can be sued for wrongful dismissal (see Chapter 4).

If an employee has been with you for a year or more they're entitled to have a written statement of the reasons they're being dismissed. If an employee asks you for a statement you have to let them have one within 14 days. If the employee is pregnant, on maternity leave or is sick at the time you make them redundant, you should automatically give them a written statement without them having to ask for it – no matter how long they've worked for you.

Time Off for Job Hunting

After you've given an employee notice that they're to be made redundant and of when their last day of work will be, you may have to allow them reasonable time off to look for another job or to make arrangements to have training.

Members of staff who've been with you for two years continuously have this right to time off and you have to pay them for it. It's back to the old question about what's reasonable. Discuss the situation with the employee and come to a sensible agreement. For most employees, it will be a case of time to go to interviews or to see recruitment agencies. Take into account, though, that if an employee is the main breadwinner in their household, they are more likely to be applying for more jobs and seeing more agencies than if they are considering having a rest between jobs.

Paying Redundancy Money

Once you've issued redundancy notices, you'll need to calculate how much each employee is owed.

Most people who've been employed by you for at least two years are entitled to a *statutory redundancy payment*. This payment is compensation for the loss of a job and is meant to tide your former employee over until they get back into work (and they're still entitled to this payment even if they've got a new job to go to immediately).

If any employee has been employed by you for less than two years, they're not entitled to a redundancy payment. They're only entitled to the correct period of notice or money in lieu of that notice period – unless you choose to give them some money as a severance payment.

Being entitled to redundancy pay

To qualify for a statutory redundancy payment an employee has to have been employed by you for two years continuously and has to have been dismissed because of redundancy.

If you issue a redundancy notice to an employee who then leaves you before her period of notice is up – to go to a new job – she will normally still be entitled to a redundancy payment. However, you may get away with refusing to pay if:

- ✔ You asked her, in writing, not to leave early.

- ✔ You warned her that she would lose her right to the redundancy payment if she did so.

- ✔ You had good business reasons for wanting her to work up until the last minute.

The employee can make a claim at an Employment Tribunal and it would be up to the tribunal to decide who was in the right. Most will be reluctant not to order a redundancy payment.

An employee isn't entitled to a redundancy payment if:

- ✔ Her fixed-term contract is immediately renewed.

- ✔ Her contract is renewed with a break of less than four weeks between leaving and returning.

- ✔ She accepts an alternative job offer from you.

- ✔ She resigns before her redundancy notice is issued.

- ✔ She unreasonably turns down an alternative job offer from you.

- ✔ She is dismissed for misconduct during the notice period.

Defining continuous employment

What constitutes continuous employment? You need to look carefully at each case. If an employee has been with you on and off for two years but had breaks where they've been employed by someone else, they won't have been continuously employed by you so won't be entitled to a statutory redundancy payment. On the other hand, if you took over your business from someone else a year ago and a member of staff was employed by the previous owner for more than a year, that will count as over two years' continuous employment.

If you make an employee redundant without notice and she has just less than two years' service, she can add one week to her termination date. If that extra week brings her up to two years' continuous service, she will be entitled to claim a redundancy payment. This 'Statutory Extension Rule' as it's called applies to notice payments too.

Redundancy close to retirement

If an employee is 65 (or the age at which people in your firm usually retire), she usually isn't entitled to a redundancy payment, because she would have left your employment at that point anyway – without a pay-off. But that may change when the Age Discrimination Laws come into force in 2006. Employees who are 64 when they are made redundant lose one twelfth of their redundancy payment for every month they are over 64. (See Chapter 19 for more on working out redundancy payments).

 Age discrimination laws coming into force in October 2006 may have an impact on redundancy at retirement age and people who previously weren't entitled to redundancy payments may become entitled to them. Several legal cases muddy the waters on this too – so take good legal advice before refusing to pay up.

Dismissal because of redundancy

As well as having been continuously employed by you for two years or more, an employee must be dismissed by you because of redundancy to be entitled to a redundancy payment. For an employee to be dismissed you have to end her contract. As with any dismissal you have to be very careful to follow all the right dismissal and disciplinary procedures: These are outlined in Chapter 4 and explained in more detail in Chapter 15. These new procedures came into force in October 2004. You must set out the reasons why you have made the employee redundant, invite her to a meeting before you take any action, and advise her that she has a right to appeal. Many employers are unaware of these new rules and are leaving themselves open to claims at Employment Tribunals. Take legal advice from an employment lawyer or talk to ACAS if you're having to make people redundant.

Remember to give an employee notice that her contract will come to an end – see the section 'Giving the Right Periods of Notice'. An employee who is dismissed because of redundancy will usually be entitled to a redundancy payment as long as she also qualifies on the grounds of the length of her employment.

Paying the legal minimum

What *statutory redundancy payment* (the minimum you can legally pay) an employee is entitled to depends on how long they've worked for you, how old they are, and how much they earned before being made redundant. Chapter 19 gives more details.

Being more generous

The statutory redundancy payment is what the law says an employee is entitled to, but you can be more generous and give members of staff better redundancy payments. The same applies to notice periods: just because the law says a week's notice for every year of service over two years up to a maximum of 12 weeks, this doesn't mean that you can't offer better terms.

Offering better terms in your employees' contracts means that you must pay on those terms rather than the statutory minimum.

Companies that do have to make people redundant are often on the brink of going under. If you're in that position and you can't pay people's redundancy money or pay in lieu of notice or holidays owed, you should advise your employees to contact the HM Revenue and Customs National Insurance Fund, which may be able to help them.

Paying in lieu of notice or holidays due

If an employee has been employed by your company for five years, for example, you should give them at least five weeks' notice of redundancy (see the section 'Giving the Right Periods of Notice' for more on this). However, you may want to close down your premises sooner, or may not have work to give the employee for the next five weeks. In this case, you can pay them money in lieu of working until the termination date. You're effectively ending their contract without notice and paying them compensation for the lack of notice. Paying in lieu of notice can suit everyone, because the employee leaving has a few weeks' wages to keep them going and can look for work full time, and you benefit by being free to close redundant premises.

If an employee hasn't taken all their holiday entitlement by the time they're scheduled to stop work, you may have to pay them in lieu for that. You have to work out how much holiday they would be entitled to – under the Working Time Regulations or in their contract if those terms are more generous – up until their last day whether they stay on at work or not, and either give them those days off with holiday pay or give them the money instead. If on the other hand they have already taken more holidays than they would be entitled to up to the last day of employment, you may be able to take that holiday pay back if there's a term in the employee's contract that allows you to. But that would be a bit mean, wouldn't it?

If you are considering redundancies you may decide that the best way forward is to sell your business or transfer it to a new owner. The sale or transfer of a business is covered by the Transfer or Undertakings Regulations. These are very complicated, both as they affect your responsibilities as an employer, and as they protect your employees' rights. Not only that but there will be changes to those regulations from October 2005. You must take advice on your employees' rights before you make any decisions or you can leave yourself open to claims against you. ACAS will be able to help. Their details are in the section 'Last in, First Out' earlier in this chapter.

Tying Up the Loose Ends

As well as making sure that redundant workers are paid all their outstanding holiday pay, overtime pay, notice pay, and any other money they may be entitled to, a few other bits of paperwork may also need to be dealt with. Employees may want to be sure they can come back to you for references, and various forms and pension details can be needed too.

Giving references

If you're making an employee redundant you don't have to give them a reference. But you'll probably be keen to help them get back into work as quickly as possible and so you probably will give references. Just don't be tempted to be overly glowing and exaggerate their positive attributes because you're feeling guilty about making them redundant.

Any reference you provide has to be the truth, the whole truth, and nothing but the truth, so don't gild the lily. If you lead a prospective employer to believe that they are hiring someone better than the employee really is, the new employer can sue you. You can only say what you believe to be accurate and fair.

Handing over paperwork to a new employer

Paperwork's always involved when an employee leaves their job. And the same applies when an employee's been made redundant as when an employee's been dismissed or resigned. See Chapter 4 for the forms that have to be filled in and the information you should let a new employer and your former employee have.

Dealing with pensions

If employees who've been made redundant have company pensions they will have to decide whether to leave them with the existing scheme, or to transfer to any scheme run by a future employer. If possible arrange for them to talk to an independent financial adviser about their options. Chapter 20 has details about occupational pensions.

Taking Staff Back When Business Picks Up Again

With any luck the downturn that's caused redundancies is only a blip and you'll be thinking of taking staff on again soon. If you have to refill the same vacancies you made redundant, and less than three months have passed since the redundancies happened, offer the jobs to the people who originally held them before you go out and recruit new employees. The chances are your former employees are now working elsewhere and won't come back to you so you'll have to start all over again (meaning recruitment and training costs), but if you do fill posts with new staff less than three months after making someone redundant, the former employee may take a case against you for unfair dismissal on the grounds that the job didn't really cease to exist.

Part II
Working Hours and Taking Time Off

"Look, Filligrew, this company has always insisted its employees leave their private lives at home."

In this part . . .

*T*he rules on working hours, breaks, and when you have to allow employees time off for public duties are explained. Flexible work patterns are high on the government's agenda and there's a good business case for introducing flexibility into your workplace if you can.

All employees now have the right to some paid holidays. And if they're off sick or having babies, there are rules about the leave they can take and when they have to be paid. Fathers can take leave when their babies are born, as can people who are adopting children. Parental leave is a possibility for employees with children under five, and they have the right to request flexible working. This part deals with all the details of when people should be in work and when they can be away from the workplace.

Chapter 6

Working All Hours

Many surveys claim that Britons are the hardest workers in Europe. And doesn't it just feel like that? Our counterparts in France work a 35-hour week, which is just part-time by our standards. The average working week in Britain is around 43 hours, and about 4 million of us work more than 48 hours each and every week. We don't take siestas (sometimes not even lunch-breaks), and our long-hours culture means that our jackets are always hanging from the backs of our office chairs. We've too much work to get through, we want to get promoted, and we worry about losing our jobs.

Employers seem to think that long hours equal more productivity. But the opposite is more likely to be true. The more flexible employers are about how long people work, and when and where they work, the more likely they are to get the best from their staff. This chapter explains your employees' basic rights with regard to their working hours.

Working Out Working Hours

The *European Working Time Directive* protects employees from working over-long hours and improves the organisation of their working time. The member states of the EU started discussing the aims of such a directive in 1989 and signed it in 1993. The terms of the directive mean that, unless workers are exempt (see the section 'Exceptions to the directive'), they can't be made to work more than an average of 48 hours in a working week. There are also rules on the breaks that must be allowed. As ever, there are exceptions and different rules for children and under-18s, people working in family businesses, and those in certain jobs. Despite the directive, working hours are a complex area and well worth checking out to make sure you get them right.

Legal requirements in Britain state:

- ✔ Employees should work a maximum of 48 hours in an average working week.

- ✔ Employees working more than 6 hours a day have to be allowed a break.

- ✔ Employees have to have a daily rest period of 11 consecutive hours in every 24.

- ✔ Employees should have 24 continuous hours off in every 7 days.

- ✔ Employees working at night should work, on average, a maximum of 8 hours in every 24.

Rules about holidays come under the Working Time Directive too, and are outlined in Chapter 8.

The 48-hour working week

The 48-hour maximum is an average rather than a definite limit each week, and you can work out average hours in different ways for different types of jobs.

In most cases you can calculate average hours by counting up the employee's working hours for the last 17 weeks and dividing the result by 17. Those last 17 weeks are called the *reference period*. If staff have been on holiday or had time off sick during those 17 weeks, you start counting earlier. If they've had a week off, count their working time from the previous week. If they've had two weeks off, count from two weeks earlier, and so on.

Different methods of deciding how to calculate the 48-hour average is can also be used. You can agree to use successive 17-week blocks to work out the average working week rather than a rolling 17-week period, or you can agree to extend the reference period.

The 17-week reference period is not set in stone. Some employers use a 26-week reference period, and some workplaces have agreed to extend the reference period to a year. This allows workers to work longer hours at times when greater demand exists for their services, but gives them extra time off when things slow down again. A year-long reference period is known as an *annualised hours contract*.

The European Working Time Directive suggests using a 17-week reference period. But the directive also allows you the right to change the reference period to any length 'not less than four months'.

At the time of publication, individuals or groups of workers can opt out of the 48-hour maximum for a definite period or indefinitely and they can reverse that opt-out at any time, as long as they give you up to three months' notice (the exact period can be negotiated between you and the employee). But most of the other EU countries don't have this opt-out and the UK may be forced to drop it.

You can't push your employees to opt out of the 48-hour maximum if they don't want to. And you're committing an offence if you dismiss them or treat them less favourably than other employees because they won't opt out. If you do they can take a case against you at an Employment Tribunal (see Chapter 15 for more on tribunals).

Exceptions to the directive

All categories of workers – including freelance and agency workers – have the rights that the directive outlines. But to complicate matters, some people are exempt from all or some of the rules. For example, doctors are famous for working long hours while they're training. The government has changed their hours, but doctors won't come under the maximum 48-hour average working week rule until 2009.

You may not have to worry about junior doctors in your workplace, but anyone working for you who is genuinely self-employed – running their own business – is exempt. So are employees who decide their own working hours or whose working time isn't measured (such as managers).

Domestic workers in private houses are also exempt. People working in transportation who are mobile (like drivers and train guards) do come under the 48-hour rule, but they are only entitled to 'adequate' rest breaks rather than those listed above . . . and what's adequate isn't defined. So there's plenty of scope for confusion. If you need to clarify someone's working hours situation, The Advisory, Conciliation, and Arbitration Service (ACAS) can help – call it on 0845-7474747 or have a look at www.acas.org.uk.

What Counts as Working Hours?

Working time is the period (usually a set number of hours) when you need to be at your workplace carrying out your working duties under the direction of your employer. Table 6-1 gives some examples of what constitutes working time.

Table 6-1	Defining Working Time
Working Time Does Include:	*Working Time Doesn't Include:*
Overtime	Breaks during work
Training at your workplace by your employer	Training at college
Travelling to visit clients if part of your normal job	Travelling time to a meeting away from your normal workplace
A working lunch (see the sidebar 'When is a lunch a working lunch?')	Travelling time to and from work
Time when you're on call at your workplace	Being on call but not in the workplace

The examples in Table 6-1 are all reasonably clear. But arguments do exist about people who take work home with them. Are they doing so on a purely voluntary basis, in addition to the hours set out in their contracts, or are they taking work home because things will become more difficult for them if the work is allowed to pile up and isn't done? A thin line exists between the two and, as an employer, you don't want to end up with the courts being asked to decide whether you have to pay for that additional work or not. You should discuss working from home with your staff, so that everyone's clear what they can expect to be paid for.

If staff members are taking work home that needs doing but there isn't time to do it in a working day, you may have to manage a workload problem. Maybe managers aren't sharing out the work properly or you need an extra member of staff. You have a duty of care to your staff to look after their health and safety, and this includes making sure their workload isn't so heavy that they suffer from stress. See Chapter 12 for more on staff welfare.

It's up to you to make sure your employees don't exceed the 48-hour average. At any one time you should have records for all of your staff who haven't opted out, for the previous two years (refer to the section 'The 48-hour working week' for more on calculating these hours).

When is a lunch a working lunch?

A *working lunch* is a business lunch taken with a client, or with a colleague if you are carrying on working at the same time as having lunch – to put it another way, 'having a meeting while you're eating'. Employees who choose to stay at their desk for lunch and carry on working can also count this as a working lunch, so long as you agree that your employees can count that time as working time, and take time off at another part of the day – maybe to start late or leave early.

Taking breaks

In most reasonable workplaces staff are allowed an hour off for lunch. Having said that, Britain's long-hours culture means that workers are increasingly tied to their desk and the lunch hour has now shrunk to an average of 27 minutes. But the good news for workers is that, by law, it can't shrink much further.

If the working day is more than six hours long, staff must be allowed one break of 20 minutes away from their desks or other workstations. If for some reason they can't take that break, you have to give them time off at another time (maybe a longer break on another day, or starting late, or leaving early). Some staff may be entitled to more frequent breaks for health and safety reasons. People working on computers need breaks to prevent RSI – repetitive strain injury – resulting from repeating the same keyboard strokes for long periods, so they are legally allowed a break of 10 minutes in every hour of work at the computer screen. Those 10 minutes aren't meant to be a break from work, just a break away from the screen – always an opportunity to catch up on some filing! See Chapter 11 for more on health and safety.

In addition to one 20-minute break if working for more than six hours, the law sets down some other rules about time off. Employees must have:

- 11 hours to themselves in every 24-hour period.
- 24 continuous hours off in every 7 days (but the day off doesn't have to be on the same day each week).

Exceptions to the laws governing breaks during working time do exist. For example, different rules apply for jobs

- Requiring someone to be permanently present to protect people or property (such as security guards and caretakers).

> ✔ Involving long-distance journeys (such as lorry drivers).
>
> ✔ Requiring continuity of work (such as in hospitals, prisons, or the media).
>
> ✔ Involving work that can't be interrupted (such as utilities workers).
>
> ✔ Experiencing seasonal rushes (such as tourism, post deliveries, or agriculture).

You don't have to make sure that your staff take the breaks that they're entitled to – you just have to make sure that they aren't prevented from taking them. And you don't have to keep a record of the breaks they do take. But insisting that they do take them will show clearly that you're concerned about their health and welfare.

Starting and finishing times

No rules govern start and finish times in the workplace. You set them to suit the work you need doing and you should lay these hours out in your employment contracts (refer to Chapter 3 for more on contracts). Start and finish times are worth thinking carefully about: Does everyone need to start and finish at the same time? Can you afford to be flexible?

If you can be flexible, this makes things easier for employees who have external commitments (such as dropping their kids off at school, or helping elderly relatives before their home help turns up). It can also avoid arguments that you are acting in a discriminatory way (see Chapter 13).

What the contract says

When you employ someone and give them their Written Statement of Employment Particulars (explained in Chapter 3, if curiosity gets the better of you) the hours you expect them to work and the breaks they're entitled to should be included. You may expect them to work far fewer than the 48-hour maximum. You may employ people on the basis that they work a 40-hour week of 5 x 8-hour days with an hour off each day for lunch. The contract can give your workers better terms and conditions than the minimum rights they have by law, but you can't make them worse off through their contract. For more information on contracts, refer to Chapter 3.

Flexibility also makes an employee's life easier – it means they can arrange deliveries or make doctors' appointments without having to take time off, and they won't get in a panic about being late for work if they're stuck in a traffic jam.

Being flexible about hours makes work less stressful for employees, and can work better for you too. Having someone start at 8.00 a.m. instead of 9.00 a.m. or finish at 6.00 p.m. instead of 5.00 p.m., can mean that you can answer customer calls over a longer working day rather than diverting them to a machine. Change can be good for your business!

Special Working Hours Considerations

Just when you think you have all the possible working hours permutations covered, you'll find that a whole raft of other situations may need to be taken into account. For example, people with families, night workers, and those under 18 all have their own special considerations. So this section explains what's what.

Flexible working

Just because staff have always clocked on at 9.00 a.m. and left at 5.00 p.m. doesn't mean that's the only or the best way to manage your workplace. Good employers have recognised that being flexible can pay dividends, and have adopted flexible working. Flexible working is just that – flexible – so it's hard to define. *Flexible working* can include employees:

✔ Working from home some of the time

✔ Sharing a job with someone else

✔ Working in school term-time but not in school holidays

✔ Working longer hours, fewer days of the week

✔ Starting and finishing at different times on different days

✔ Working an agreed number of hours over a year (rather than an agreed number each week)

✔ Working at times to suit themselves

Flexible working may be written into staff contracts or Written Statement of Employment Particulars or the staff handbook (refer to Chapter 3). Parents are legally allowed to request flexible working, but you can choose to open the offer out to everybody.

If you recognise a union then you may already have an arrangement with that union about flexible working. If so, or if flexible working conditions are written into a contract, you're legally bound to honour those terms and conditions. If you don't recognise a union but have more than 20 employees, a union can write to you asking for you to recognise it to conduct collective bargaining on behalf of your workers. You have 10 days in which to reply. You can refuse, but ultimately, if a tenth of your workers are union members and the majority of your staff are in favour of recognition, they may hold a ballot to decide if the union is recognised.

Not all small businesses can afford to have all their employees work in a complete free-for-all, but if your business can allow it, being as flexible as possible will make for a happier, less stressed, and more productive workforce. Talk to your employees to see if you can come to an agreement that gives everyone a bit of flexibility.

Flexible working and families

If people are working on average 48 hours a week – and about 4 million Britons do – they have less time to spend with partners and children. This puts a strain on relationships and can cause problems when it comes to finding childcare.

Parents have the legal right to request flexible working – maybe they'd like different working hours to the rest of the staff, such as different start and finish times, or to be able to work from home a couple of days a week.

Employees have the right to apply for flexible working arrangements if they fulfil three criteria:

- ✔ They have worked for you for at least 26 weeks continuously and are not agency workers.

- ✔ They haven't made a previous application to you for flexible working in the past 12 months.

- ✔ They have *responsibility for a child* under 6 or a disabled child under 18 (meaning that the employee is the parent, lives with the child's parent, or that the child lives with the employee).

You must give the employees your answer within 28 days of their application or arrange a meeting with them within that time and then tell them 'Yes' or 'No', in writing, within another 14 days.

If you turn down a flexible working request from a parent, you have to set out a clear business reason for saying 'No'. If you don't hold a meeting or tell your employees about your decision, they can complain to an Employment Tribunal (for more on tribunals, see Chapter 15).

You can only refuse a flexible working request from a parent on one or more of these grounds:

✔ It will mean extra costs for your business.

✔ You won't be able to meet customer demand.

✔ You can't reorganise the work among existing staff.

✔ You can't recruit additional staff to help out.

✔ Quality or performance will suffer.

✔ The employee won't have enough to do during the preferred working times.

✔ You have structural workforce changes in the pipeline that may change the employee's role.

If you reject the request the applicant can appeal. If you reject the appeal the employee can take a case to an Employment Tribunal on the grounds that you didn't follow all the correct procedures, that you rejected the request for reasons other than those listed above, or that you didn't know all the facts. You also have to be careful that a refusal doesn't amount to discrimination – for example it might indirectly sexually discriminate against working mums (see Chapter 13 on indirect discrimination). A tribunal can order you to reconsider or pay compensation if it agrees with your employee.

An employee has the right to be accompanied by a colleague or union representative at meetings or appeals regarding flexible working.

If parents are always the employees who are seen to get the breaks in the workplace, this can breed resentment among other employees. Make sure that all employees are treated fairly.

New mums and dads also have rights to paid maternity and paternity leave and to parental leave during the first five years of each child's life. Some employees who are adopting a child are entitled to leave too. These issues are covered in Chapter 9.

Working nights

About 1 million people are hard at work at 11.00 p.m. when the rest of us are drifting off to sleep. And as we increasingly embrace the joys of the 24-hour society – with shops, call centres, and night buses all busy in the wee small hours – night workers will become more commonplace.

Night workers are people who have to work more than three hours at night as part of their normal job. In this context, *at night* means between 11.00 p.m. and 6.00 a.m. If some of your staff regularly work nights, they shouldn't be working more than an average of 8 hours in every 24. You must provide night workers with regular free medical checks and if the medical advice says they should switch to other shifts you should do your best to accommodate that.

If night working is making someone ill and you refuse to transfer them to other shifts on request, you're committing a criminal offence and can be prosecuted and fined by the Health and Safety Executive or the local authority.

If staff members only occasionally work nights, they don't have these rights. If they work nights, say, one week out of three or one week out of four, it's not legally clear-cut whether they will qualify as night workers. The courts may have to settle any disputes. But if in doubt, always give your staff the most favourable employment terms possible.

Working nights . . . with special hazards

If your staff are night workers and their job involves working with special hazards – perhaps dangerous machinery or chemicals – or the work is very physically or mentally demanding, they must not work more than 8 hours in any 24. As soon as they've worked 8 hours they must stop and they can't opt out of this protection. You must carry out a risk assessment (see Chapter 11) to decide whether any of your staff come into this category.

The 8-hour limit doesn't apply to people who are treated differently as far as days off are concerned – see the section 'Exceptions to the directive' earlier in this chapter for more details.

Working on Sundays

Sundays are no longer a day of rest in Britain. The laws changed in 1994; before this date many shops couldn't trade, and racetracks and betting offices weren't allowed to operate.

People who already worked in those businesses before the law allowed Sunday opening are now protected when it comes to working on Sundays. They can refuse to work if they don't want to, unless they have accepted jobs on the basis that they will work on Sundays.

If members of your staff are protected in this way, you can't fire them for refusing Sunday working. You can't get rid of them by choosing to make them redundant because of their refusal and you can't punish them in any other way for refusing.

Even if workers have agreed to work Sundays, they're entitled to change their minds. They should give you three months' notice that they will no longer work on Sundays, and can take up a legal case against you if you won't accept their change of heart.

If your company isn't a retail or betting business, Sunday is just another day and you can expect your staff to work if necessary.

 Consider the sensibilities of your workers who are religious and talk to them about days they might prefer not to work – for example Saturdays for Jewish people. This helps you to avoid discriminating against them on the grounds of religion.

Zero-hours contracts

Zero-hours contracts mean that you don't guarantee work for staff but you expect them to be available if work comes in. As they aren't on call in the workplace their on-call hours don't count as working hours (refer to 'What Counts as Working Hours?' earlier in this chapter). Employees on zero-hours contracts get paid for hours actually worked, and while they are working the rules about maximum hours and breaks apply.

However the whole issue of 'on call' working is extremely complicated. If nursing or care home workers are on call or required to sleep over are they working whilst on-call or asleep? The law on this is still developing, through cases coming before tribunals. You should take legal advice on your employees' rights if you employ people on this basis.

Laying off staff

Occasionally you may not have enough work to keep everyone busy and may decide lay off some employees or put them on short-time working. This is also something you might consider instead of making people redundant (see Chapter 5) if there's a fall-off in orders. Be careful, however. If there's nothing in your employees' contracts that allows you to lay them off or put them on short time you'll be in breach of contract and if you cut their wages they can claim for unauthorised deductions from wages.

If employees' contracts do allow you to lay them off or put them on short time those employees who have worked for you continuously for at least one month will be entitled to a guaranteed payment for up to five days in the three-month period following the first day they were sent home because no work was available. If the staff contract, Written Statement of Employment Particulars, or the staff handbook says that employees will be paid their usual pay if they're laid off, then you must pay them that amount. But if not, then you must pay them the legal minimum.

Employees who have been laid off or put on short time may leave and may be entitled to claim redundancy payments (see Chapter 5).

Rules for children

Children of 13 or older must not work during school hours, before 7.00 a.m., or after 7.00 p.m., but they can work for two hours on school days and Sundays. Children under 13 cannot legally work. Local authorities supervise children's employment and other by-laws may exist in your area affecting the hours you can employ children for or the type of work they're allowed to do. Check with your local authority.

Young people over 16 but under 18 are covered by the Young Workers' Directive. They can't work more than 8 hours a day or more than 40 hours a week. They must have a continuous break of 12 hours every day and of 48 hours every week – although these can be split in some cases – and the timing of the two-day break can vary from week to week. For example, they can work for 10 days in a row with a two-day break at the beginning and again at the end.

Of course, exceptions exist to almost every rule, and children's working hours are no different! You can ask them to work longer hours if necessary to keep production going or if no adult is available to do the work. But you still have to give them breaks to make up for those longer hours and ensure that you supervise children properly.

Young people can't work nights (11.00 p.m. to 6.00 a.m.) unless working in

- ✔ Hospital jobs
- ✔ Sports-related jobs
- ✔ Cultural or artistic jobs
- ✔ Advertising jobs

And young people can work from 10.00 p.m. or 11.00 p.m. until midnight, or from 4.00 a.m. until 6.00 a.m. or 7.00 a.m. if in farming, shops, hotels, catering, restaurants, bars, bakeries, or postal and newspaper deliveries.

In emergencies, if you don't have any adult workers around to help, you can suspend the breaks defined by the Young Workers' Directive, but you have to catch up with the required breaks within three weeks.

Rules for close family

No rules govern close family members working in your business. They can work as little or as much as you and they agree, often working long hours for little money because they want to see the family business succeed. But don't take advantage just because you can or you might find they take their skills elsewhere!

Working Full- or Part-Time

Part-time workers have the same working hours rights as full-time workers – so all the same rules apply. You must not treat them less favourably than comparable full-timers working for you doing similar work. That means that part-timers should have pro-rata terms and conditions.

Chapter 7

Holidays and Time Off

. . . .

In This Chapter

▶ Understanding and calculating what holidays people are entitled to

▶ Allowing and refusing holiday requests

▶ Deciding on the holiday year and where bank and public holidays fit in

▶ Knowing other occasions that demand paid and unpaid leave

. . . .

*N*ot only are people legally entitled to breaks in their working day and working week (refer to Chapter 6 for more on this), the law also has a say in how much holiday your staff are entitled to. Gone are the days when they had no legal entitlement at all; now almost everyone's entitled to a minimum number of days (causing sighs of relief all around the office). This chapter helps you to understand when and for how long your employees can lie on a beach, and other circumstances when your staff can take leave.

Setting Annual Holidays

Holidays are very important. People need time off to recharge their batteries and they work better when they come back. Just about everyone enjoys a well-earned break from their daily toil. Paid leave – better known as *annual holiday* or *annual leave* – allows employees to take time off to use in whatever way they wish, be it a dream holiday to Disneyland, an afternoon of football fun in Peterborough, or even a job interview in Carlisle.

 Most people are entitled to a minimum of four weeks' paid leave each year. So if employees work five days a week they get 20 days off. If employees work part-time, they get four times their average weekly working time. So if employees work three days a week, for example, they get 12 days' holiday (4×3 days).

Bank holidays and public holidays (such as Christmas Day) can count towards that total minimum entitlement as long as you normally pay people for those days. If you want to find out more about working out holiday pay, head on to Chapter 18.

Exceptions to the rule can be found, of course. People who work in inland waterways and lake transport, sea fishermen, members of the armed forces, police, and civil protection services aren't entitled to paid holidays by law – although they may get paid holidays through their contracts.

If you can afford to, you can be more generous than the legal minimum when setting annual leave! But you can't give less than the law says. Spell out holiday entitlement in the contract so that your employees know where they stand.

You can offer four weeks' paid leave on top of all the bank and public holidays, or even five or six weeks off as well as bank holidays. You may give employees a certain holiday entitlement when they start with you and increase that entitlement at various intervals – four weeks of leave for the first four years, rising to five weeks of leave if they stay with you for five years. Or you can give people who are in more responsible jobs more time off than others.

Look at what other firms – particularly your competitors – are offering. You're competing for the same staff and you want to be seen as a good employer, so make sure you aren't offering less than everyone else.

Working out the holiday year

As your staff are entitled to a certain number of days off a year, you need to decide when your year runs from and to. Most bosses opt for a holiday year running from 1 January to 31 December or from 6 April to 5 April the following year – usually the same 12 months as they use for their accounts.

If you don't make the start of the holiday year clear, each employee's holiday year runs from the date they started on, unless they started before 1 October 1998 (23 November 1998 in Northern Ireland). In that case the holiday year starts on 1 October (23 November in Northern Ireland). Imagine how much more difficult it is to keep tabs on who is entitled to what if you have 50 staff with all sorts of different holiday years!

Calculating holiday entitlements

Holiday entitlement starts to build up from the first day someone works for you; but that doesn't mean they can start work on Monday and take four weeks off from the following Monday.

If employees start working at a company after 25 October 2001 (14 April 2002 in Northern Ireland), their holiday entitlement builds up monthly at ½ of the annual allowance each month in advance for the first year of employment. If employees started work before that date, no set rules govern holiday allocation.

After the first year, employers simply need to keep records of the days employees have off, and make sure they don't exceed the total by the end of the year.

If an employee starts working for you on 1 January and only stays with you for six months, by the time they leave at the end of June they should either have taken half of their total year's holiday entitlement or be paid for the days they haven't taken. If they work from January through to the end of December, they should have taken their full year's entitlement and be starting again from January. If they have taken more time off than they were entitled to, you can ask them to pay back the holiday pay for those extra days if that's in their contract. If it's not in the contract and you take the money out of wages the employee can take you to an Employment Tribunal for an unauthorised deduction of wages.

On the other hand, if someone joins you on 1 September and your holiday year runs from January to December, then by December they will only have been entitled to a quarter of a total year's holiday.

If employees leave to go to a new job they can't take unused holiday with them. Their remaining holiday can be used in the period between them telling you they are leaving and their last day in the job (if the employees choose that), but you will have to pay them for any unused days.

Working out entitlement for part-timers

The rules are basically the same for part-timers as full-timers. If employees work a three-day week and you've given them a holiday entitlement of five weeks, they are entitled to 15 days off in the year (5×3 days).

If employees work different hours each week, they are entitled to five times the average number of hours they work.

Deciding when holidays can be taken

Your staff can tell you when they would like to take their leave – but if they all want to take the same few weeks you'll be in big trouble. So you can decide who goes on holiday when – no rules exist about how much holiday can be taken at any one time. This means that you can

- ✔ Set aside certain times of year when no one is to go on holiday – usually at particularly busy times.

- ✔ Say that holidays have to be taken at particular times provided you give the right notice – usually when you know you won't be busy.

- ✔ Refuse holiday requests.

 Even though you may refuse holiday requests, be as reasonable as you can. People may want to take holidays when other members of their families are off, such as during school holidays. And employees will co-operate more if you discuss their holiday requests with them rather than just say 'no' without giving your reasons.

 Staff should give you notice when they want to take leave; this notice period should be twice the amount of time the employee wishes to take as leave. If employees want two consecutive weeks off, they should give you four weeks' notice; if they want four days they should give you eight working days' notice. But even with the right notice you can refuse – as long as you also give the right notice. To refuse you must give notice equal in length to the duration of the requested holiday (two weeks in the first example shown here, four days in the second).

If you want employees to take holidays at a particular time – for example you want everyone to take the days between Christmas and New Year as holiday, because work will be at a standstill – you need to give them two weeks' notice of this. As with refusing leave, notice that holiday has to be taken at a particular time should be twice the length of the holiday period.

In the staff handbook (see Chapter 3), explain how decisions are made about when holidays are taken, so employees know when requests should be submitted by. Also explain the limit on the number of people who can be on leave at any one time, if you have a policy on this.

 If you simply refuse to let employees take any holiday at all or give them less than their legal entitlement, they can use the grievance procedure and then bring a claim against you at an Employment Tribunal (see Chapter 15).

Carrying holidays over to next year

If employees aren't able to use up their holiday entitlement, you don't have to allow them to carry forward any of their minimum legal entitlement of four weeks and the law doesn't say you have to pay them for the unused days. But it is your duty to try to ensure that employees do take their holidays.

If you have allowed your employees more holidays than the legal minimum, you should make it clear what happens to unused leave days. It's much easier all round if you have made your policy clear to all employees so that everyone knows what happens if they don't take all their holiday.

Your unused leave days policy can take one of three forms:

✔ You allow employees to carry over holiday into the next year (you may wish to specify the maximum number of days that may be carried over).

✔ You pay employees their daily rate for any unused leave (again, you may wish to specify a maximum).

✔ You don't allow employees to carry over holiday or pay them for unused days; any unused days are 'lost'.

If you don't have a policy on unused holiday, discuss the options with the employees concerned. If employees have requested time off and you haven't been able to say 'yes', they will probably feel less aggrieved if you talk to them about it.

If you often face the dilemma of unused annual leave, take a look at your staffing arrangements. Employees may not be able to take all their leave because they have too much work and worry about how much they'll have to catch up with when they get back. It may be that you are simply short staffed.

Taking bank and public holidays off

All sorts of myths and conjectures have sprung up about bank and public holidays. We have eight of them in England, Wales, and Scotland, and ten in Northern Ireland. You can count them as part of the four weeks' holiday you must allow employees to have every year provided that you pay for them. Or you can let employees have them off in addition to however much holiday you give them in their contracts.

What if things go wrong?

If members of staff are off sick, their holiday entitlement carries on accruing just as it would if they were at work. But if they are off for a whole holiday year, they lose the holiday and you don't have to allow them to carry any of the legal minimum over into the next holiday year, nor do you have to pay them for unused holiday. If your contract allows employees more than the legal minimum and says that you will allow unused days to be carried over or that you will pay for them, you have to stick to the terms of the contract.

If your business goes bust and you can't pay employees for holiday that they've built up but not taken, or the holiday pay for time they have taken off, they can claim up to six weeks' holiday pay from the National Insurance Fund, which is operated by the Inland Revenue – now HM Revenue and Customs – www.hrmc.gov.uk.

The rules aren't always as clear and straightforward as you may like them to be. Make sure you give everyone at least their minimum entitlement and avoid any conflicts over holiday rights by making sure it's all spelled out in the contract, Written Statement of Employment Particulars, or the staff handbook (you can read more about this in Chapter 3). That way everyone is clear what to expect.

But do employees *have* to have bank and public holidays off? That is the question – and 'no' is the answer. People who assume that they're entitled to have bank holidays off or to be paid twice – or even three times – the daily rate to work on those days are wrong. It's a myth.

If you give employees 20 days' holiday in total and 8 of these are bank holidays, your staff can request to have the bank holidays off as they would any of the rest of the 20 days. You can say 'yes' to those requests; or you may make the bank holidays days that people have to have off as part of their 20 days (as long as you give the right notice); or you can refuse requests for those days off as long as you give the right notice. If employees do work on bank holidays, they're entitled to a normal day's pay unless their contract states that you'll pay them extra if they work on those particular days. If people have 20 or more days' holiday plus the bank holidays the same rules apply.

Giving Time Off for Other Reasons

As well as the rules for taking holidays, certain other situations may arise that allow your employees to take time off work. This section deals with those circumstances where your staff are entitled to be absent on paid leave for reasons other than requested holidays.

The law says you have to give employees paid time off if they are:

✔ trade union officials carrying out certain trade union duties

✔ trade union health and safety representatives carrying out union duties

✔ company pension fund trustees

✔ facing redundancy and needing to look for work

✔ pregnant and have ante-natal appointments

✔ taking maternity, paternity, or adoption leave

✔ accompanying colleagues at certain disciplinary or grievance procedure hearings

On top of those rights to paid leave, all employees are entitled to reasonable time off – unpaid – to perform various public duties. You can of course make it part of a person's contract that you pay for time off for reasons other than those that the law says you must pay for.

You can allow more leave than the minimum, but you can't allow less than the law expects.

Magistrates, councillors, and others performing public duties

Where would the country be without all those people who give up their time to be local politicians, magistrates, or voluntary, charity, and community workers? But the snag for you is that while they do their bit they may be expecting you to help them in their altruistic endeavours by giving them time off work.

Some employers accept that time off should be allowed for public duties (like local councillors and magistrates) but draw the line there. Others allow people to take time out of their paid working week to go into local schools and mentor pupils from disadvantaged backgrounds, seeing it as their way of putting something back into the community.

All employees are entitled to reasonable time off to carry out public duties, although the law isn't clear about how much time off or which duties. It's down to what you (as an employer) think is reasonable and that depends on what the duties are, the amount of time entailed, and the effect the person's absence will have on your business. You don't have to pay them in these circumstances, but you can decide to be more generous.

If you refuse employees time off for public duties you can end up in an Employment Tribunal facing a claim for compensation. The tribunal members will weigh up all those factors. Discuss and agree with your workforce, unions, or individuals what's reasonable and what isn't.

Even if you say 'bah humbug' to the notion that all businesses should be socially responsible, the bottom line is that if local people see your staff getting involved for the good of the community, this rarely harms your business.

Jury duty

This is an interesting one! No legal right exists allowing people to take time off work for jury service, but if an employee asks and you refuse you will be in contempt of court. Not really worth the trouble, is it? Give in gracefully! Not only that but from the 6th of April 2005 it has been automatically unfair to dismiss employees who are required to attend court for jury service (see Chapter 4 for more on automatic unfair dismissal) regardless of how long they've worked for you or what age they are. Employees on jury service can claim travel and subsistence expenses, as well as some loss of earnings. The employer has to provide proof of the losses the employee has suffered.

Union activities

As a small employer you may not come across many union members. But if you have more than 20 employees, a union can write to you asking for you to recognise it to be entitled to conduct *collective bargaining* on behalf of your workers. Collective bargaining means the union and the employer coming to an agreement about procedures and policies that affect the employees' terms and conditions of employment – for example an agreement about pay or holiday entitlement. Chapter 6 explains more about recognising a union.

Most staff have the right to time off to take part in union activities such as meetings during working hours as agreed by you. Officials in recognised unions also have the right to take time off, with pay, to carry out their trade union duties – such as preparing for negotiations with employers and keeping members up to date on progress.

The right to take time off for union activities doesn't apply to members of the police or armed forces, or those working in parts of the security and intelligence service, or share fishermen.

Union learning representatives are people who are trained to advise union members on their training, education and developmental needs. They are allowed time off for analysing learning and training needs, providing advice, and arranging and consulting with you about training.

The Advisory Conciliation and Arbitration Service (ACAS) has a code of practice on time off for union activities and duties. You can obtain this by contacting ACAS on 0845-7474747 or at www.acas.org.uk.

You can't refuse to employ someone because they hold union membership or because they aren't a member of any or a particular union – that would be discrimination. And you can't get rid of employees because they join a union or get involved in union activities – that would be unfair dismissal.

Antenatal care

During pregnancy an employee is entitled to reasonable (that word again!) time off to attend antenatal appointments made on the advice of the doctor or midwife. Antenatal care may include medical examinations and relaxation or parent-craft classes. And she has to be paid at her normal hourly rate. Reasonable time off depends on the person and the pregnancy. If an employee were to complain to a tribunal that you didn't give her reasonable time off, the tribunal would look at whether or not you behaved as a reasonable employer would have done.

You can ask the employee to produce medical proof of her pregnancy and an appointment card showing the date and time off required – although you can't expect medical proof if your employee's taking time off for her first appointment to find out if she is pregnant! These rights exist from day one of employment and if you don't comply, an employee can complain to an Employment Tribunal within three months of the date of the appointment you refused her time off to attend. You will find more detail on rights to maternity, paternity, and parental leave and requests for flexible working in Chapter 9.

Compassionate leave

What happens if someone close to one of your employees dies? It really depends on how closely related the dead person was. If the deceased was a dependant, as described in the section 'Caring for Dependants', you can't refuse compassionate leave without risk of being taken to an Employment Tribunal. And the closer the person, the longer the time off that may be needed for the employee to make all the arrangements and recover sufficiently to be able to get back to work.

You don't legally have to pay for the time off, but you probably don't want to be seen to be a totally uncaring Scrooge. Again, take into careful consideration how close the person was to your employee.

Giving Career Breaks

Some companies are geared up to giving employees *career breaks* – longer periods of time off to be with their children full-time in their early years; to study; travel; or even to go off and work at something else for a while, safe in the knowledge that their real job will still be open for them (or that they will be offered a suitable alternative job with the company when they are ready to return). Career breaks are periods of unpaid leave agreed between the employer and employee. Some companies have a policy of allowing anyone who's worked over a certain length of time – for example 10 years – to take a certain amount of time off: For, example a week per year of service.

Most small employers would be hard pushed to entertain the idea, but if employees do make such a request, think about just how valuable they are to your company and how much you'd like to keep them. A refusal might offend and result in them resigning to pursue their dreams . . . and you'll have lost valuable assets.

You're under no obligation to agree to an employee's career break, and you don't have to pay for their time away. Discuss the options with your employee!

Caring for Dependants

Chapter 9 explains the rights to time off for parents. As well as those rights, employees have the right to take a reasonable amount of time off – unpaid unless you're feeling generous – to deal with unexpected or sudden emergencies that present themselves when the employee has relatives who are dependent on them for care.

Again, this right starts on day one of the employee's time with you. A *dependant* is usually a spouse, child, parent, or any other relative (or even someone who isn't a relative but lives in your employee's household as part of the family). But boarders, lodgers, the nanny, or friends staying on holiday don't count. In other cases, a dependant can be someone who depends on your employee for most of the care they need or as the only person who can help in an emergency.

The government has helpfully suggested some situations that may arise where you will be expected to give time off:

- ✔ To help or arrange help if the dependant becomes ill, is injured, assaulted, or gives birth.

- ✔ To deal with the dependant's death and funeral arrangements.

- ✔ To sort out an unexpected incident at school or during school hours.

- ✔ To sort out problems where care arrangements have failed.

No law sets a limit on the amount of time that an employee can take off for these circumstances. Usually, you can expect employees to be able to resolve these situations in a day or two, but you have to allow enough time for the employee to cope with the crisis because you never know what unusual circumstances may be involved (such as a parent dying in Australia). There's also no limit on the number of times the employee can take time off (sometimes family crises come in a string: a baby is born the week after grandmother dies). But she has to tell you as soon as possible that she will be off, why, and how long she expects to be away. If you say 'no' she can complain to an Employment Tribunal.

Taking Unpaid Leave

Sometimes the four weeks' annual holiday simply isn't enough time for employees to recharge their run-down batteries. If they have no paid leave left to take, they may ask you to agree to unpaid leave. Of course, what you decide depends on the effect their absence will have on your business.

Don't dismiss requests for unpaid leave out of hand. Good employees are worth keeping and a few weeks off might just be the thing to keep them from throwing in the towel and taking all their valuable knowledge with them.

Chapter 8

Being Unwell or Throwing a Sickie

*A*bsence because of sickness costs the UK economy an estimated £12 billion each year. This means that sickness is costing you money as an employer. The average number of days off sick is 8.7 per year according to research by the Chartered Institute of Personnel and Development. Have a look at your staff records and see how your average number of sick days compares. If your figure is higher than average, maybe something's wrong in your workplace. Coughs and colds, stress, and back problems all figure high up the list of reasons for absence, and you can't do much to stop people getting sick – or can you? Some of those 'sick' days may not be taken because the employee is genuinely unwell. People may be taking the odd sickie because they can't face coming in to work.

A well-motivated workforce, where every employee understands the added pressures that fall on his colleagues when they are off sick, tends to have lower absence levels than one where everyone is stressed, working long hours, and dealing with bullying bosses. When people are working in a happy, healthy environment, there's less temptation to take a day off for no reason other than not feeling like getting out of bed in the morning. Employees are also genuinely sick less often in a well-run, safe, secure working environment. It is becoming more and more evident that the culture in which people work has a bearing on absence levels.

Paying for Time Off Sick

Your employees' contracts need to clearly lay out your company's policy about sick pay, so that all employees know exactly where they stand. The law determines the minimum amount your employees are entitled to, known as *Statutory Sick Pay* or SSP (Chapter 18 has more information on this). In many cases employers pay well over the SSP amounts and sometimes even give full pay for at least the first few weeks of a period of illness; this is known as *contractual sick pay*.

An employee starts receiving SSP from the fourth day of his or her illness. Each employee can receive up to a maximum of 28 weeks of SSP per year at £68.20 per week. Chapter 18 explains how SSP is paid and administered through HM Revenue and Customs and you can get help from HMRC. The Web site www.hmrc.gov.uk has a section called 'What to do if your employee is sick'; you can pick up relevant leaflets from your local office or call the HMRC Employer's Helpline on 0845-7143143.

If you refuse to pay SSP you need to tell your employees why (see the section 'Relying on the law for sick pay' later in this chapter). If you think they aren't entitled to SSP and they think they are, they can ask HM Revenue and Customs (formerly the Inland Revenue) to decide whether or not you should be paying up. The HMRC's decision is legally binding, although you can appeal. If an employee is entitled to SSP and you still refuse to pay, they can take a claim against you for unlawful deduction of wages at an Employment Tribunal. You can refuse to pay if you have good reason to believe that the employee is not genuinely ill, but a tribunal will have to be convinced by your evidence if the employee brings a claim against you.

If an employee is disabled and you refuse to pay SSP for a reason connected to that disability you can be breaking the law – and again facing a claim by an employee at a tribunal.

Abiding by the contract for sick pay

If your employees' contracts state that they get better sick pay than the SSP rates, you have to stick to those contractual amounts or you're in breach of the contract. You need to make the details of any contractual sick pay clear in the contract and stick to them. You may also provide your employees with private medical treatment. Give your employees the details of such schemes, as most don't cover every type of illness and treatment.

Relying on the law for sick pay

In smaller firms most employees depend on SSP to tide them over an illness because employers running small businesses often don't pay contractual sick pay. A long list of people won't qualify (Chapter 18 fills you in on this list in more detail) but basically, to qualify for SSP an employee must:

  ✔ Have four or more consecutive days off sick on which he would normally work (qualifying days) including weekends, non-work days, and holidays.

  ✔ Notify you of their absence.

  ✔ Supply you with evidence that he is too sick to work – usually in the form of a self-certificate (see below) for the first seven days and a doctor's sick note for the eighth day onwards.

Unless you've allowed for it in their contract, your unwell employee won't be entitled to any pay at all for the first three days (the waiting days) that they're off sick. A lot of employers do pay people for odd days off sick without any questions and an employee may be tempted to stay in bed or have a day out shopping knowing that their pay won't be affected. On the other hand, a genuinely sick employee may force themselves to come into work when they really should be at home in bed, to make sure that they're being paid.

If an employee has already used up all their 28 weeks of SSP or doesn't qualify for it, you have to give them form SSP1 to tell them why. You can get SSP1 forms from the Department of Work and Pensions Web site www.dwp.gov.uk or the local Benefits Agency or Job Centre Plus (you can find your nearest branch in the phone book). The employee can then use that form to claim Incapacity Benefit or Sickness Benefit from the Benefits Agency or Job Centre Plus.

Assessing Illness

You must have rules setting out what your expect people to do if they're ill and you need to make sure they know what those rules are. They need to know who to contact and when, and what evidence you expect them to provide that they're sick.

What you can and can't demand from your employees in terms of notification and evidence when they're sick depends on whether you are paying them contractual sick pay or just paying them SSP.

Calling in sick

An employee who is sick and needs to let you know about it should be aware of who to call and should call them as soon as possible. A common procedure is to specify that sick employees should call their direct manager or the human resources department.

If you are paying contractual sick pay you do have more freedom to set down rules. But if you pay your employees the minimum SSP when they're off sick, then you cannot ask them to:

- ✔ Let you know before the first day that they would normally be at work that they're sick if for example they've already been sick over a weekend that they wouldn't normally have been working.

- ✔ Provide a medical certificate until the eighth day of their illness.

- ✔ Phone you by a certain time of the day to say they're off sick.

- ✔ Phone you more than once a week while they're off.

- ✔ Call you themselves rather than getting someone to do it for them.

If you do pay contractual sick pay and timing is crucial in your workplace, make sure that employees know that you expect them to call in by a particular time (which as you'll see above you can't do if you pay just SSP). This allows you to organise the day's work-load as efficiently as possible without putting any more pressure than necessary on other staff or calling in extra help.

If you pay contractual sick pay you can also ask unwell members of staff to speak to you themselves – although you have to be reasonable as this may not always be possible. (Again as you'll see above you can't do this if you pay just SSP.) Try to get an idea from absent employees of how long they expect to be off work so you can plan ahead. Most bosses are happy to accept an employee's word that they are sick for a few days, but you can ask for a medical certificate.

DIY certificates

Unless your contracts say that your employees will get paid as usual when they're unwell, they won't get paid for any periods of fewer than four days off. If an employee is still off on day 4 (qualifying for SSP), you'll need to see proof of their illness. A written note explaining what's wrong or a certificate that employees fill in themselves is adequate proof for the first week off. This is called a *self-certificate SC2* and can be downloaded from the HM Revenue and Customs (formerly Inland Revenue) Web site (www.hmrc.gov.uk) or you can provide your own version.

Getting a doctor's certificate

If a member of staff is still off on day 8 you can ask them to supply a medical certificate as proof so that they can qualify for SSP. If you're paying contractual sick pay you can ask for a medical certificate straight away, but in most cases absences only last one or two days and are caused by something uncomplicated like a cold, so there's really no point in insisting that someone goes to the doctor for such a short absence. A medical certificate needn't necessarily come from the employee's GP or hospital doctor. You should consider accepting certificates from other health professionals such as osteopaths or acupuncturists.

Dealing with Short-Term Absences

If an employee is off work frequently or for an unacceptable length of time in total, ask them for an explanation.

You might discover that the person has genuinely had a series of less serious illnesses and that their job is making them sick. They may be getting sick because of worry, stress, or pressure due to a high workload. The real problem can be that you are understaffed and the solution can be to hire someone extra.

We can't stress this enough

Stress is one of the biggest reasons for sick leave – even overtaking back problems (which can themselves be stress-related). Because there's so much debate about stress – what stress is, how much stress we can cope with, the causes of stress, and why some people are better at dealing with stress than others – it can be a difficult problem to deal with.

Remember: Different people show different symptoms too. You do have a duty of care to keep your employees healthy and that includes dealing with the causes of stress. You won't recognise the causes or symptoms unless you talk with and listen to your employees about their workloads and work–life balance.

You may discover that an employee is being harassed or bullied and it's actually someone else in the workplace who needs to be dealt with. Sometimes employees are simply too concerned about losing their jobs to say anything and you should view your investigation as an opportunity to talk to staff and make the workplace better.

And of course, you may occasionally find that an employee is just taking you for a ride, in which case you will probably want to consider disciplinary action. Chapter 15 goes into detail about resolving disputes.

Investigating recurring sick leave

If an employee is off sick for several short periods in a year, you can contact Medical Services through you local HM Revenue and Customs office (the Inland Revenue) and ask them to look into the reasons. Medical Services can ask the employee for permission to contact their doctor. If Medical Services reports back that your employee has been off for no good reason, you need to use your disciplinary procedure (see Chapter 15) to warn them about the level of absence. Tell your employee what level of improvement they must make and what the consequences will be if they don't.

If Medical Services reports back that the person has genuinely been off sick, you can ask it to decide if the employee is capable of doing the job. Alternatively, you can request the employee's agreement to see another – independent – doctor for a second opinion.

Sometimes short, frequent absences can point to a person having a problem with alcohol or drugs. You do need to be sure that this is not affecting employees' concentration at work. If they work with heavy machinery they can become a risk not only to themselves but to other employees. If that's the case you may be able to dismiss them for misconduct but be very careful to follow all the correct dismissal and dispute resolution procedures as outlined in Chapters 4 and 15). If you do suspect there's a problem of that sort talk to the employee. Beware of being intrusive but explain that you're concerned and want to offer help rather than consider dismissal.

You sometimes simply find that a member of staff has been throwing a sickie. Employees should be made aware through your firm's handbook or contract that you will use your disciplinary procedures to deal with such behaviour and that if it amounts to a serious breach of contract he can even be dismissed.

You do have the right to say that enough is enough regarding staff absence. Even if the employee's absences are genuinely because they are sick, you can dismiss them if this is having an adverse effect on your business on the ground of not being capable of doing their job. You must have evidence to back up your claims and follow all the right procedures – see Chapter 4 for more about the correct way to do this.

Getting the job done

If someone is just off for a day or two, it might be that the work they would otherwise have done can wait until they get back. But be careful about that. They can return to a whole pile of work and find it impossible to catch up . . . the result might be another few days off because of stress, and then you're both caught in an endless cycle.

Take the opportunity to look at how your workplace runs. Can someone else do unwell employees' work while they're away so that they come back to a clean slate? Is there someone in the workplace who would benefit from moving up into their shoes while they're off? Sometimes holidays and sick leave give you opportunities to see how other people would cope with a new role. You have to manage these options carefully though. You can't simply pass the work on to someone who is already fully employed or they may get stressed too! And you can't afford to have employees sick and feeling that they're surplus to requirements when they return. Redistributing work is a delicate situation that needs handling sensitively.

The further up the company hierarchy your unwell member of staff is, the more difficulty you'll have getting someone else to take over the work – partly because someone coming in from outside won't understand your business or because the work that person does is very specialised. Bringing in temporary help can be easier if you do move a few employees up the chain temporarily, and employ a temp at the bottom of the pile.

If you're worried about being able to afford temps, remember that you may be able to claim some of the SSP back through tax and National Insurance – see Chapter 18 for more details on this.

Dealing with Longer Absences

If a member of staff is off for the long-term and no one knows when their return is likely, you have to make some tactical decisions. If they have been paid SSP and the maximum SPP period of 28 weeks is up, they'll have to apply for *incapacity benefit* which is the state welfare benefit paid to people who can't work on a long-term basis. You need to give your employee form SSP1 explaining why his SSP has stopped.

If your employee is absent for long enough to qualify for incapacity benefit, you're not paying them anyway and so you can simply allow them to stay on your books and take them back to a suitable job when they are well enough to return. Or you can dismiss them on the grounds that their absence is having a detrimental effect on your business and you need to get someone in to do the job on a permanent basis.

If 'generosity' is your middle name, and you pay your employees contractual sick pay, you can operate a *discretionary sick pay scheme* so that in cases of serious illness you can extend the period for which you go on paying unwell members of staff before they must apply for incapacity benefit.

Is your employee ill or do they have a disability? The *Disability Discrimination Act 1995* applies to people with a physical or mental impairment or medical condition that has substantial and long-term effects (lasting 12 months or more) on their ability to carry out day-to-day duties. If they do have a condition that's classed as a disability under the Act (you can find out more about this by logging on to the Disability Rights Commission Web site at www.drc.org.uk or calling the helpline on 0845-7622633) they'll have certain rights and protection, and you need to be sure that you treat them fairly or they may have a case against you for discrimination – see Chapter 13 for more on this.

Talk to an employee who's on incapacity benefit about his abilities, inclinations and hopes for the future. If an unwell employee's condition won't allow him to come back to his current job, but he may be able to manage other jobs, you may be able to offer him a suitable alternative. Flexible working patterns may make it viable for him to return; adjustments can be made in the workplace that will allow them to work; or they may be able to do most of their work from home.

Don't forget any private health care policy you have to cover your staff. Check to see if long-term absentees are entitled to permanent health insurance, because not everyone will satisfy the rules of the scheme.

Holding the job open

If you value an employee who is currently absent on long-term sick leave, you may want to hold their job open for him. Whether or not you can do that very much depends on how your business operates. You may simply not be able to get someone to replace them on a short-term basis because it's a very specialised job for example but it could be a job that could be filled by a temp from an employment agency.

You can promote another employee on an acting basis, provided that they understand and agree that they will have to move back to their usual job when the post holder comes back. If you decide to pay extra money for added responsibility, then you need to agree with your temporary post-holder that this extra money is for that job only and that their wages will go down again when they return to their usual job. Another option is to discuss the situation with your member of staff who's off sick and agree with them that you'll promote someone permanently or recruit someone new to do their current job, but that when they're ready to come back you'll find them a suitable alternative job.

If you do decide to hold a job open, you should contact your employee regularly to see how they are. Don't be intrusive or make them feel pressurised into coming back before they're really well – reassure them that they shouldn't worry, that you do still want them back, and that you are genuinely interested in their welfare. They will probably like to be kept up-to-date with what's going on too so that they still feel a part of the organisation.

Retiring early on grounds of sickness

If you run an occupational pension scheme (Chapter 20 gives more details on these), you need to provide for employees who have serious long-term illnesses or disabilities to retire early with a lump sum and an annual pension. Talk to the people who operate your scheme to organise this.

Holidays and sickness

Under the Working Time Regulations 1998 just because an employee is off sick doesn't mean that their holiday entitlement stops building up. However in a recent case in the Court of Appeal the judge decided that the right to four weeks' statutory paid holiday (see Chapter 7 for more on holiday entitlement) does not continue to accrue while an employee is off on long-term sick leave. This case overturned other Employment Tribunal decisions. If an employee is off on a long-term illness you should take legal advice on whether or not they are still entitled to holiday pay. ACAS, the Advisory, Conciliation and Arbitration Service, should be able to help if you call the Employers' helpline on 0845-7474747.

Dismissing Employees Who Are Sick

If an employee's absence is adversely affecting the operation of your business and you have fully investigated and considered all the other options, you may have a fair reason to dismiss them. But you must still follow the correct dismissal and dispute resolution procedures (see chapter 15) and give a chance for things to change.

If an employee has been taking time off sick when they haven't been genuinely ill, this can amount to misconduct. You have to fully investigate and have evidence before you can act. See Chapters 4 and 15 for more detail about the ins and outs of misconduct and the correct procedures to follow.

If employees aren't happy about the way you handle their misconduct, they can take out a grievance against you. See Chapter 15 for more information on managing grievances.

If you dismiss an employee, they are entitled to the correct period of notice – depending on how long they have worked for you and what's in their contract (refer to Chapter 4). If they've returned to work and you subsequently fire them and want them to leave immediately, they're entitled to money in lieu of notice (see Chapter 4).

References are a big worry for employees who have been sacked for taking too much sick leave. Agree with an employee before they leave what you're going to say in any references you are asked for, but remember that you have to be absolutely honest in any references you do give. The kind of references you agree to provide will depend on whether the employee has been genuinely ill or not. You may agree to give only straightforward information about start and finish dates and the nature of the work they did. For more on supplying references, see Chapter 4.

Getting Back to the Grindstone

If an employee has been off for some time you need to manage their return carefully, to help them settle back into their working environment. The longer they've been away, the more important your role in assisting a returning employee becomes.

Talk to returning employees about their return date and whether or not they'd like to ease back into work – perhaps doing fewer hours for the first couple of weeks and building up to their usual working pattern, by working part-time or doing some of the work from home. Your employee may feel confident that they can simply turn up and pick up where they left off without realising the lasting effect that a period of illness may have had. In such circumstances, a returning employee may lose confidence if they feel they haven't immediately got back into the swing of things or if they find the pace of work tiring.

Think about all the things that have changed around the workplace since the employee went off sick. You may need to offer them another induction, taking them around to meet new people or to learn about new processes, machinery, or technology. You might need to offer some retraining or refresher courses.

Don't just put return-to-work measures in place and assume that they're working. Have regular chats with an employee who's been off sick for more than a few days, to see how they're coping now they're back at work. You need to monitor the situation making sure that the return to work has been successful and that over the longer term any factors that may have caused a problem in the first place aren't allowed to build up again.

If a returning employee has a disability that will change their way of working, you need to make reasonable adjustments to ensure that they have access to all necessary areas of the workplace and make it possible for them to do their job.(See chapter 13 for more information about reasonable adjustments.) This may take quite a lot of planning and help from an outside organisation such as the Disability Rights Commission (see previous section for details) or a local disability charity which offers advice. Such reorganisation is an opportunity for you to make sure that you are fully complying with your obligations under the Disability Discrimination Act. You may also need to pave the way for a disabled employee's return by making sure that everyone else in the workplace is fully aware of any issues that may arise from their disability, such as health and safety considerations.

Managing Absence

If employees phone in sick, they may have all sorts of other reasons why they've taken the time off. Many employers don't even realise the size of this problem, which can range from a parent throwing a sickie to take their children to the doctor or go to a sports day, to other employees taking time off to deal with the demands of elderly parents (see Chapter 7 for more information on when employees can take time off to look after dependents). Other absences may be related to alcohol or drug problems. Some not-really-sick absences can be down to the atmosphere at work if disputes or personality clashes are taking place. If you don't know what the problems are, you can't start to resolve them.

Monitoring the problem

You need to keep records of who is off when and why. Try providing a simple form that everyone has to fill in every time they take a day off. That way you can track who is taking agreed leave and who is off sick at a glance. One trend some employers notice when they do this is that there are more sick days taken on Fridays, Mondays, and on the days of big sporting events. From the records you may start to see patterns, and this may give you clues about why members of staff are absent. As with all the information you keep about your employees, make sure it is kept secure and that only people within your business who really need to see it have access to it. See chapter 14 for more on keeping information about your employees.

Looking for patterns – individually and corporately

If employees are often off sick during big sporting events such as the World Cup or the Olympic Games that can be a problem for your organisation. How about addressing this issue by letting people take the afternoon of an important match off and make up the hours another time? You can even allow radios or televisions in the workplace for the duration of the match.

If your workplace has above-average sickness levels, or Fridays and Mondays are particularly 'sick' days, you may have an internal morale problem to deal with. Take a look at the working environment. People may be working overly long hours and be completely exhausted by the end of the week. Or you can have a bullying problem that leaves employees unable to face Monday mornings.

Of course, plenty of other reasons can cause absence too. If your employees are always getting colds and flu, can the workplace itself be unhealthy and require better ventilation or heating? Maybe too many employees work in an open-plan space and they can't hear themselves think, adding to their stress. Maybe their workstations are poorly laid out, giving people back problems. Chapters 10, 11 and 12 have more on how to protect your employees from workplace illness and accidents. Maybe your employees aren't taking enough breaks from their computer screens, so are getting headaches. Unless you take a really good look at how things are run, you may go on experiencing high levels of absence, costing you money and adding to your own stress levels.

Possibly your own closed door is the problem – employees don't feel they can talk to you about their problems!

Flexible working patterns

Introducing flexible working patterns can give employees (especially those with family commitments) the freedom to take time when they need to and make this time up before or afterwards rather than just taking time off 'sick'. You can read more about flexible working in Chapter 6.

Duvet days

Some employers have tried to pre-empt members of staff taking sickies by writing into their contracts the right to take a couple of days a year off – with or without pay – at short notice, on top of holidays and genuine sick leave. These days, known as *duvet days*, are useful because employees can take them without planning ahead as they would have to if they wanted to take some of their holiday entitlement, when they really can't face going into work. They don't have to worry about being seen out shopping and accused of shirking and that day away from the office may be the one that averts the need for a longer time off sick.

To grant your members of staff duvet days, you must make sure they all know the rules that apply to them, such as whether or not they've got to let you know they won't be in that day and whether they'll get paid or not.

Return-to-work interviews

A quick chat with an employee who's had a few days off sick can be very useful. You have no right to know the precise nature of their illness if they want to keep it private. Don't interrogate them and make them feel you don't believe them or are prying, but this is an opportunity for them to tell you if they have any problems with the way the place operates and try to work out a solution between you. It's also somewhat of a deterrent against throwing sickies, as members of staff are less likely to lie to you face-to-face about the reason they were off. And of course, a boss who listens and acts is a very motivational person to have around the workplace.

Getting a second opinion

If all else fails and an employee is off sick repeatedly but you're unconvinced by their explanation, you can ask for doctors' notes and then refer the employee to an independent doctor of your choice. Employees should know what to expect, so write this option into their contracts.

Chapter 9

Having Babies and Bringing Up Kids

N*early three quarters of a million babies are born each year in the UK, so the chances are you'll come across a fair few mums-to-be at your workplace. Working mothers have a range of rights both before and after their babies are born. About two thirds of working mothers are back at work within nine months of the birth, and by treating such an employee fairly during and after pregnancy, you're protecting a valuable asset. You want her back at work with all her skills and knowledge. And you're also protecting the next generation of employees.

This area of employment law is particularly complicated. If you are faced with pregnant employees; requests for maternity, paternity, or parental leave; or flexible working patterns, make sure you dot all the *i*s and cross all the *t*s.

Mum's the Word

In the past many employers simply sacked an employee who got pregnant, or treated her unfairly because she was pregnant, or made her job mysteriously disappear while she was on maternity leave and refused to take her back.

The law now doesn't allow women to be unfairly treated or dismissed as a result of being pregnant or having a child. The law makes provision for:

✔ Paid time off for antenatal care

✔ Protection against unfair treatment or dismissal

✔ Maternity pay (read more about this in Chapter 18)

✔ Maternity leave (dependent on how long the employee has been with you)

✔ The right to return to work

You must take extra care to protect an employee's health and safety when she's pregnant or breastfeeding. If she works in the kind of environment that can put her or her child at risk, you should offer her a suitable alternative job if you have one. If not, she has the right to be suspended from work, on full pay, for as long as the risk exists. You can't dismiss her on the grounds of becoming or being a mum. The same goes for working nights – if a doctor says working nights will adversely affect her or her child, you can't make her work nights.

Dismissing an employee or selecting her for redundancy, in preference to somebody else who can equally well be made redundant, for any of the following reasons is legally unfair:

✔ Because she is pregnant

✔ Because she has had a baby

✔ Because she has taken maternity leave

✔ Because she has been suspended from work for health and safety reasons

As women have babies and men don't, any unfair treatment because of pregnancy or childbirth will inevitably amount to sex discrimination.

And it isn't only mums whose interests are looked after by the law – dads have rights too. As babies get older both parents can take extra time off to care for them and can ask to be given more flexible working arrangements to make family life easier or just so that they can spend more time with their offspring. You can read more about the rights of a father in the section 'Giving dad time off for the new arrival', and more about flexible hours in the section 'Dealing with requests for flexible working'.

Allowing time off for antenatal care

While she's pregnant an employee is entitled to reasonable time off to attend *antenatal appointments* (appointments that the doctor or the midwife recommends that the mother-in-waiting attend, such as medical examinations and relaxation or parent-craft classes). You must pay mum at her normal hourly rate when she is taking time off for these appointments. If you wish to make sure that an employee really is taking the time off to go to an antenatal appointment, ask her to show you her appointment card each time she needs time off (or ask for medical proof that she's pregnant).

The right to time off for antenatal care exists from day one of someone's employment. If you don't give her the time off, with pay, she can complain to an Employment Tribunal within three months of the date of the appointment that you refused to let her attend. The tribunal may award her compensation, which you would have to pay. See Chapter 15 for more information on Employment Tribunals.

Some women will sail through pregnancy needing very little antenatal care, but others will have more complicated pregnancies and need more time off. If you want to find out more about how pregnancy can affect your employees, pick up a copy of *Pregnancy For Dummies* by Sarah Jarvis, Joanne Stone, Keith Eddleman, and Mary Duenwald (Wiley).

If you refuse time off for antenatal care your employee may decide to leave and bring claims against you for automatic constructive unfair dismissal, unlawful detriment, and sex discrimination – hopefully you won't end up in this situation but Chapter 4 covers dismissal and Chapter 13 deals with discrimination if you'd like to find out more.

Coping with sickness during pregnancy

If the employee is sick during the run up to the birth, the period of illness should be treated the same as any other period of illness (see Chapter 8 for more details on illness).

She should get normal sick leave and sick pay – unless her illness is pregnancy related and within four weeks of the week in which she expects to give birth. If she's sick within four weeks of her expected week of childbirth but before the date she intended to start her maternity leave – and the illness is to do with the pregnancy – then her maternity leave will automatically start.

If she's sick at the end of her maternity leave, the normal sick leave and sick pay rules in your workplace apply.

Taking Maternity Leave

Two types of maternity leave exist:

- ✔ **Ordinary maternity leave.** This consists of 26 weeks of leave, and an employee is entitled to this regardless of how long you have employed her.

- ✔ **Additional maternity leave.** This is an extra period of 26 weeks of leave, added on to ordinary maternity leave, and employees are entitled to this so long as they've completed six months of service with you.

Your employees may qualify for one or both kinds. Both types of maternity leave are described in more detail in the following sections, but before taking this leave, your pregnant employee has to give you proper notification.

She has to tell you by the start of the 15th week before the expected week of the birth that she intends to take maternity leave. This 15th week before the *Expected Date of Childbirth* (to give the baby's due date its official legal title) is known as the *Qualifying Week* – the week in which the employee qualifies for statutory maternity pay (which she may be entitled to, and about which you can read more in Chapter 18) and for additional maternity leave, which is explained later in this chapter in the section '26 weeks more: Additional maternity leave'.

A pregnant employee has to give you the following details (in writing if you want her to) by the start of the Qualifying Week:

- ✔ Confirmation that she is pregnant

- ✔ The expected week of childbirth – the week in which the Expected Date of Childbirth falls

- ✔ The expected start of her maternity leave

You can also ask her for a certificate *MAT B1* from her doctor or midwife verifying the expected week of childbirth.

After she has given you all the necessary details about her pregnancy, your employee can change her mind about the date she wants to start her maternity leave. She might decide that she's coping so well she'd rather put her leave back to nearer the time of the birth, or that she's coping less well than she expected and would like to start her leave earlier than she'd planned. She just has to give you at least 28 days' notice to change the date on which her leave starts.

Maternity leave can't start any earlier than the 11th week before the week in which the baby is due. And it can't start any later than the day of the birth itself!

When an employee tells you she's pregnant and gives you notice of when she intends to start her maternity leave, you have to respond, in writing, giving her the date on which you expect her to return to work if she takes her full entitlement to maternity leave (see the following sections for more on the length of leave).

26 weeks and counting: Ordinary maternity leave

A pregnant employee is entitled to 26 weeks off work, known as *ordinary maternity leave*, regardless of how long you have employed her. Whether or not she's entitled to *statutory maternity pay* – the minimum amount you must pay an employee on maternity leave – depends on whether or not she has worked for you long enough to qualify. You may of course have made more generous provisions than the legal minimum for paying for maternity leave in your employees' contracts. You'll find details about statutory maternity pay in Chapter 18.

If an employee is off on 26 weeks' ordinary maternity leave, her contract of employment with you continues. So she's entitled to all the benefits set out in her contract. Her holiday entitlement will continue to build up. She has the same rights if she's made redundant – see Chapter 5 for more on this (but be careful not to make her redundant rather than someone else just because she's on maternity leave, as that will be unfair treatment). She's entitled to pension contributions, private medical insurance, permanent health insurance, use of a company car, and any other benefits while she's off if she's entitled to them when she's at work.

Some women will want to get back to work as quickly as possible – even before the 26 weeks of ordinary maternity leave is up – especially if they aren't entitled to any maternity pay. Their rights are explained in the section 'Returning to Work' later in this chapter. But compulsory maternity leave must be taken into consideration. *Compulsory maternity leave* applies to all employees no matter what their other terms of employment are; under this rule, a new mother is not allowed to come back to work until 14 days after she gives birth.

No matter how much she's missing you and all her friends at work and no matter how hard she pleads, you can't allow a new mother to come back to work any sooner than 14 days after the day the child is born. That's the law!

26 weeks more: Additional maternity leave

If an employee has been with you for 26 weeks continuously by the qualifying week (refer to the section 'Taking Maternity Leave' to find out what week this is), she will also be entitled to take *additional maternity leave* for up to another 26 weeks, starting immediately after her ordinary maternity leave. Statutory maternity pay (explained in the section '26 weeks and counting: Ordinary maternity leave') doesn't apply during additional maternity leave, so unless you're a very generous employer (and have promised her maternity pay in her contract beyond the first six months) she won't have any money coming in.

Despite not being entitled to statutory maternity pay, some employment rights continue during a worker's additional maternity leave (as do some of her obligations to you as her employer):

- ✔ She carries on accruing statutory minimum holiday entitlement.

- ✔ She's still entitled to the notice period in her contract if you end her employment.

- ✔ She must give you the period of notice stated in her contract if she wants to leave.

- ✔ Whatever her contract says about disclosure of confidential information concerning your business, accepting gifts, and taking part in other business still applies.

- ✔ Disciplinary and grievance procedures still apply.

- ✔ You still have an obligation to treat her with trust and confidence, just as she is still obliged to treat you in good faith (see Chapter 3 for more on this).

Giving dad time off for the new arrival

Despite not being the one doing all the pushing, dad has the right to some leave when his child is born! An employee can have up to two weeks off to support mother and baby, known as *paternity leave*. The rules are more or less the same as for maternity and adoption leave, as explained throughout this chapter.

To qualify for paternity leave, an employee has to have worked for you for 26 weeks continuously at the beginning of the 15th week before the baby is due (known as the qualifying week). He must be responsible for the child's upbringing, and be either the biological father of the child or the mother's partner. Leave can start on the day the child is born or days or weeks afterwards . . . maybe once mother-in-law has been packed off home. But dad has to take his paternity leave within 56 days of the date of the birth or up to 56 days after the expected date of childbirth if the baby made its appearance earlier than planned.

New fathers can take either one week or two consecutive weeks of paternity leave, but not odd days or one week here and one week there. This is what the law says, but as an employer you may be altogether more flexible.

Most men will qualify for statutory paternity pay (dealt with in Chapter 19) while they're off work, although you may decide to do better than that and pay your new dads their normal pay.

If an employee intends to take paternity leave, he must to let you know by the qualifying week and must tell you when he wants the leave to start. He can – as mums can – change his mind about the date and should give you 28 days' notice if that's possible (but it's not always possible, as babies tend to be fairly unpredictable). You can ask your employee for a completed self-certificate as proof of entitlement to paternity leave.

Even if your employee has just become a father to more than one new baby, he still only qualifies for one period of paternity leave.

Adapting to Adopting

Some employees who are adopting a child are entitled to adoption leave. To qualify, an employee must be newly matched with a child for adoption by an approved adoption agency and must have worked continuously for you for 26 weeks at the week in which they receive notification of being matched with the child.

Adoption leave applies to employees who are adopting as individuals or to one partner of a couple adopting jointly. Either partner can take it – mother or father. The partner who chooses not to take adoption leave is entitled to take paternity leave. Again that can be the father or the mother. Step-parents adopting their partner's child don't qualify.

Adoption leave is like maternity leave – a 26-week ordinary adoption leave period followed by up to 26 weeks additional adoption leave. Most employees who qualify will also qualify for statutory adoption pay for the first 26 weeks they're off (see Chapter 18 for more on this).

Adopters can choose to start their leave from the date of the child's placement or from a date up to 14 days before the expected date of placement. Employees have to let you know that they intend to take adoption leave within seven days of being notified by the adoption agency that they have been matched with a child. You need to respond in writing to your employee, within 28 days of hearing of their plans, with the date you expect them to return to work if they take their full entitlement to leave.

Like expectant mothers, adopters can change their minds about the date they want to start adoption leave, as long as they give you at least 28 days' notice if that is at all possible.

You can ask for a matching certificate from the adoption agency as proof of your employee's entitlement to adoption leave.

All the normal terms and conditions of the employee contract carry on applying during adoption leave apart from being paid their salary – they get Statutory Adoption Pay instead. You can't sack an employee or treat them unfairly for taking adoption leave.

Returning to Work

When an employee informs you she's taking maternity or adoption leave, you have to respond in writing and put in your letter the date you expect her to come back to work if she takes her full leave entitlement. If she then takes her full leave entitlement, she won't have to do anything other than turn up on the prescribed day.

If your new mum or new adoptive parent (read more about adoption in the section 'Adapting to Adopting') intends to return to work before the end of her ordinary or additional maternity leave or adoption leave, she must give you at least 28 days' notice of the date she intends to reappear in the workplace. However, she can't come back straight after giving birth – see the section '26 weeks and counting: Ordinary maternity leave' for more details about this.

If an employee who is entitled to additional maternity leave decides to come back to work at the end of her ordinary maternity leave, again she has to give you 28 days' notice.

If you don't get the correct period of notice you can postpone an employee's return from maternity leave to a date 28 days away, so long as that isn't later than the end of the full leave period. So if someone is due to return on 1 October but decides to come back on 1 August, she must tell you her intention by 4 July. If she doesn't tell you until 11 July, you can in turn give 28 days' notice that you're postponing her return until 8 August.

You can take disciplinary action against an employee who doesn't give you the correct notice of returning to work, but you can't make her give up her maternity rights.

If an employee is off sick at the end of her maternity leave, her return to work isn't postponed. Instead, the normal rules about sickness apply (see Chapter 8 for more about sick leave).

Coming back to the old job

And so back to work for mum! An employee returning from maternity leave is entitled to return to the same job on the same terms and conditions as when she started her leave. It's as if she's never been away. Anyone who filled in while she was on maternity leave has to go back to their old job or back to the temp agency they came from, unless you have something else to offer them.

New mums returning to work quite often want to work part-time, at least for a while, or even to work some of their hours from home. No legal right exists to go back to work on a part-time basis: the right is to return to the same job on the same terms and conditions. It's down to the employer to decide, but you do have a duty to give such a request careful consideration. If you can accommodate the request, maybe through a job share, that's fine by law and won't break the employee's employment contract.

If you reject a request to work fewer hours or from home without a good business reason, the employee can bring a claim against you for sex discrimination on the grounds that, because women usually have primary childcare responsibilities, a refusal to allow her to work fewer hours or from home has more of an impact on her life than on a man's.

You may decide you'll be doing everyone a favour if you bring in a policy in your workplace of allowing all women returning from maternity leave to work part-time. But be careful . . . what if a new father asks to be allowed to work part-time? If you refuse to grant his request he can also successfully claim sex discrimination at an Employment Tribunal.

Offering another job

If taking an employee back in her original job isn't practicable – perhaps because the workplace has been restructured in her absence and her original job no longer exists – she has to be offered suitable alternative work of equivalent status and responsibility.

This has to be suitable and appropriate in the circumstances, so you can't make the head of marketing redundant and offer her the receptionist's job just because the receptionist happens to have left. And you have to give the returning employee terms and conditions that are no less favourable than her original contract.

 A job is redundant – never a person. You can't dismiss someone by reason of redundancy if the job they've been doing still exists or if you have a suitable alternative job for them. If a suitable vacancy exists and you don't offer it to her, you've just made an unfair dismissal (see Chapters 4 and 5).

Working conditions for new mums

As her employer you have legal duties to make provision for a new mother to breastfeed her baby. Unless you have genuine business reasons why you can't allow her to work different hours you have to be flexible about her hours and conditions so that she can breastfeed. If you refuse she can take a case against you for indirect sex discrimination (see Chapter 13).

You have to have somewhere suitable in the workplace she can go with her baby. Guidelines from the European Commission recommend that she should have access to a private room with a clean fridge to store breast milk and time off to express milk or breastfeed.

You have to make sure you protect her from health and safety risks – just as you did while she was pregnant. She has to notify you in writing before she comes back to work that she intends to breastfeed so that you can carry out the necessary risk assessment.

You also have to make sure women who've given birth in the past 6 months or are breastfeeding have enough breaks for rest, meals and refreshments.

 If you feel there's no way you can accommodate a working mother who wants to breastfeed because there's nowhere suitable for her to go with the baby in your workplace is there another boss nearby who also has new mums on the staff? Perhaps you can share facilities. Or perhaps she can do the majority of her work from home. There are always ways to be flexible if you think laterally.

Requesting time off during the first five years as parents

Employees who are natural mums and dads and those who are adoptive parents can qualify for *parental leave* – time off work to look after a child, make arrangements for the care of the child, or that parental leave can be used just spend more time with the child.

Each parent can take up to 13 weeks' parental leave for each child in the first five years of that child's life. If more than one child is involved, that becomes 13 weeks for each one.

Parental leave is unpaid and a 'week' is the number of hours the employee normally works in a week (so an employee working a 28-hour week will be entitled to 13×28 hours).

Qualifying for parental leave depends on the date of the child's birth and the employee's length of service:

✔ Employees who have children born or placed for adoption on or after 15 December 1999 must have worked for you continuously for a year by the time they want to take parental leave. The leave has to be taken by the time the child reaches their 5th birthday or the 5th anniversary of the placement date for adoption (or their 18th birthday if that's sooner).

✔ Parents of a disabled child can take up to 18 weeks' parental leave at any time up until the child's 18th birthday, as long as they meet the qualifying requirements above.

While on parental leave, an employee still works for the company and has to come back to the same job if a period of leave is four weeks or less. If an employee takes a longer period of parental leave, you still have to allow them to come back to the same job or, if that's not reasonably practicable, offer a similar job with the same or better status and terms and conditions.

To keep track of parental leave within your business, you should put in place a parental leave scheme so that everyone knows where they stand – including you. The scheme has to include all the parental leave rights shown in this section . . . and you can always be more generous than the law requires (but not less). Your scheme may cover how much notice has to be given for leave, when you can postpone the requested leave if the business can't cope, or what time blocks leave should be taken in (from individual days to separate weeks, one long block, or even as reduced hours in several working weeks). You can have individual agreements with individual employees, and ask for evidence to support a request for leave. Because parental leave has to be taken over a period of five years, and employees may work for more than one employer in that time, they may already have taken some of their 13 week entitlement before they get to you. You can also check with previous employers how much parental leave someone has already used up and if you find someone has been cheating you can take disciplinary action. If it's problematic agreeing the terms of your parental leave scheme with your staff, take a look at the nearby sidebar 'Parental leave – the government way'.

Employees can complain to an Employment Tribunal if you unreasonably postpone their parental leave or prevent them from taking it. If you dismiss a member of staff on the grounds of parental leave, that automatically becomes unfair dismissal, as explained in Chapter 4.

Dealing with requests for flexible working

Employees who are parents, adopters, guardians, or foster parents of children under 6, or of disabled children under 18 – or partners of people who fit any of those categories – have the right to ask to work flexibly and the employer has to take the request seriously. Flexible working can involve starting later and finishing later; or working extra hours one day and fewer on another; or working some of the time at home instead of at the workplace. You can read more about flexible working in Chapter 6, but this section contains information relevant for parents' requests.

Employees may request parental flexible working if:

- They have worked for you continuously for at least 26 weeks on the date they apply for flexible working.

- They make their application at least two weeks before her child's 6th birthday or a disabled child's 18th birthday.

- They have or expect to have responsibility for the child's upbringing.

- They haven't made another application to work flexibly during the past 12 months.

Employees have no automatic right to have their flexible working wishes granted, because you may not be able to accommodate their request without throwing your business into chaos. Nevertheless you have to consider the request, discuss it, and try to find a solution that works for you both.

Parental leave – the government way

If you and your workforce can't or don't come to an arrangement for operating a parental leave scheme or you don't agree one with a recognised union that has the right to negotiate with you on behalf of your staff, don't worry! The government sets down a fallback position, saying the following:

✔ Parental leave must be taken in one-week blocks up to a maximum of four weeks a year for each child.

✔ Parental leave may be taken a day at a time if the child is disabled.

✔ The employee must give 21 days' notice before taking a period of parental leave.

✔ Employers may postpone parental leave (but not for more than six months) if their business will be seriously disrupted.

✔ Employers can't postpone parental leave if the employee has given notice that they want to take it immediately after the time the child is born or placed for adoption.

Take the opportunity of an employee requesting child-related flexible working to have a long hard look at the way your team or company works overall. Having someone in earlier or there after everyone else goes home can mean calls getting answered by a real person rather than an answering machine. Just because the place has always worked one way doesn't mean it's the only way to operate or even the best way. Refer to Chapter 6 for more details about operating flexible working schemes, and for the procedures that both employers and employees need to follow.

Applying for a promotion while on maternity leave

Sometimes a job opportunity comes up while an employee is on maternity or adoption leave. If that employee might normally have applied for the job and is seen as a suitable candidate, you should give her the chance to apply. You can't treat an employee unfairly just because she's on maternity or adoption leave. Tell her about the post and take her application seriously if she does apply. You should make it possible for her to get to an interview – taking into consideration her childcare responsibilities as you would for any other candidate – and if she's the best person for the job you should offer it to her. The starting date will then coincide with her return to work. Anything less might be seen as unfair detriment on the grounds of pregnancy.

New rules in the pipeline

In April 2007 the right to paid maternity leave for those who are entitled to it will be extended from 6 months to 9 months, and the government propose to increase it to 12 months. Legislation is also to be introduced to allow a mother the right to transfer to up to three months of her paid leave to her partner, so that a father may spend three months with his child in the first year of its life.

To find out more about maternity and paternity pay, flick through to Chapter 18.

Part III
Keeping Your Workers Healthy and Safe

"There's certainly a lot more tension in the office since we brought in the smoking ban."

In this part . . .

You have a legal obligation to look after the safety, health, and welfare of people working on your premises – and visitors too. You have to provide a safe working environment. If you are negligent in any way and that negligence leads to an accident or illness, you may find yourself facing a big bill for compensation.

The chapters in this part explain your responsibilities and how you can make sure that your workplace is as safe and healthy as it possibly can be. Small business employers often complain that they can't afford health and safety measures, but the truth is that you can't afford to be without them.

Chapter 10

Applying TLC

. . . .

In This Chapter

▶ Understanding your obligations to care for your staff

▶ Getting to grips with health and safety regulations

▶ Coming up with a health and safety policy

▶ Spotting the hazards and risks around your workplace

▶ Involving all your staff in the health and safety process

. . . .

*H*ealth and safety are sometimes afterthoughts for small businesses – a commonly heard misbelief suggests that putting all the necessary policies and safeguards in place is too expensive. The truth is that if you have an accident in your workplace the cost of dealing with it (and the aftermath) is much higher. According to the Health and Safety Executive (the government body that regulates such things), health and safety problems cost the UK's economy around £6.5 billion a year. Health and safety should be as important in your business as your pay system or your marketing.

Quite apart from the financial cost, you will damage your reputation and the morale of the workforce if something goes wrong. Customers don't want to use firms that don't look after their staff, good potential employees may choose to work for more careful bosses, and companies don't want to do business with firms that have had accidents or occupational health problems.

The law says you have to have a health and safety policy if you have five or more employees. You also have a duty to protect the environment. The regulations are often lumped in with the Health and Safety Regulations, but they aren't discussed in this book because they don't come under the remit of employment law Your local Business Link, for which you can find the number in your phone book or on the Business Link Web site (`www.business. ink.gov.uk`), has further details.

Health and safety should to be an integral part of your business plan, not just a bolt on. Look after your employees and they'll look after you and your clients. The best way to do this is to get good advice and support from the outset. The Health and Safety Executive does have an enforcement role (see below) but the department wants to help employers to avoid health and safety problems. They are very happy to help and you shouldn't hesitate to contact them. Around the time of the publication of this book they plan to launch a new helpline service for small businesses called Workplace Health Direct. Look out for ads which will tell you how to contact the service.

Caring for Your Staff – Your Duty of Care and the Regulations

The obligations on employers to care for their staff come from common law as well as from specific legislation and regulations. *Common law* is the unwritten law of custom based on decisions made over the years by judges in court cases.

Court cases are going on all the time making decisions that can affect you and your business, so checking with the Health and Safety Executive or your local Business Link every so often is a good idea.

Abiding by common law

You have a duty under common law to take all reasonable steps to keep your employees safe. If an accident occurs because you haven't taken all reasonable steps to avoid something that a judge decides was 'reasonably foreseeable', you can be sued for damages and found liable for being negligent.

'Reasonable' is a word you'll come across a lot referring to health and safety, but the test in court is whether you should have foreseen that something could go wrong and whether you did what any 'reasonable' employer would have done to avoid the incident happening. If the judge thinks you should have seen it coming and didn't do enough to stop it, you will have been negligent and will have to pay damages.

Under common law, you have to provide your employees with:

✔ **A safe place to work.** A safe place of work means a safe building, in good repair, and well maintained. If something happens to make it dangerous – even only temporarily – you have to be quick off the mark to make sure an accident doesn't happen. If, for example, some oil gets spilled that someone can slip on, you need to make sure it's cleaned up quickly and properly. If you send an employee to work somewhere else, you have to make sure that place is safe to work.

✔ **A safe means of access to that place of work.** If employees have to walk along footpaths on your property, the paths should be well-kept. You don't want to have employees breaking ankles because you haven't repaired potholes. You should consider outside lighting if shifts end after dark, and you should clear away ice in the winter (in case someone falls).

✔ **A safe system of working.** This means coming up with a method of doing the work that's safe, and making sure your employees stick to it. Make sure your employees don't take short cuts that can put them at risk and don't encourage them to do something that can make the system unsafe even if it improves productivity and your profits. Make sure enough people are available to operate the system and provide enough supervision for them.

✔ **Adequate equipment and materials.** Having safe equipment and materials means making sure that everything you provide for your employees to do their jobs is safe to use and that you check anything delivered to your workplace for dangerous defects.

✔ **Safety-competent fellow employees.** You have a duty to make sure that your employees are all well-trained, qualified, experienced, and not likely to do something careless or idiotic that may cause one of their colleagues to be injured. You need to recruit sensibly and provide good training.

✔ **Protection against unnecessary risk of injury.** If your employees use heavy machinery, you must know that it's safe, well-maintained, and working well. If risks such as sparks, noise, or moving parts occur, you have a duty to try to cut down the risks as far as possible. If the risks can't be done away with completely, you have to make sure employees have safety equipment (such as goggles, ear protectors, or heavy-duty gloves) to protect them and that they use this equipment properly.

Under common law not only do you have to be on the ball yourself when it comes to keeping your employees safe and healthy, you are also liable for accidents, injury, or damage caused by one of your employees if they're being negligent while at work. If someone is larking about while he's doing his job and drops something heavy on another employee's foot, for example, the injured person can sue you. This is a legal principle called *vicarious liability* – you are liable for accidents caused by the negligent actions of your employees where they are acting in the course of their employment. But there's no vicarious liability if the negligent act committed by the employee was so far removed from what he was authorised to do that he could be said to be on a 'frolic of his own'.

If someone sues you for negligence, the court will consider how negligent you've been but also whether the person suing you was in some way negligent and contributed to their own injury. Maybe he didn't use the safety equipment you provided despite all your warnings and safety training. The amount he is awarded in damages can be reduced if that's found to be the case.

You have to have insurance to cover any liability you have to your employees if they are injured or damaged at work because of your negligence. Insurance policies are explained later in this chapter, in the section 'Insuring Yourself'.

Following the regulations

The principles you must follow to safeguard the health and safety of your employees are set out in the *Health and Safety at Work Act (HSWA) 1974.* In effect the Act:

- ✔ Secures, as far as possible, the health, safety, and welfare of employees at work

- ✔ Protects other people against risks to health and safety arising out of activities of employees

- ✔ Controls the storing and use of explosive, highly flammable, and other dangerous substances

- ✔ Controls the emissions of noxious substances from premises

The Act is pretty much equivalent to the common law duty of care you owe your employees (described in the section 'Abiding by common law' earlier in this chapter). On top of this duty, the Act says you can't charge your employees for anything you do or supply in order to comply with the regulations. So if your employees need to wear masks because they're working with chemicals, you can't charge them for those masks.

The HSWA just gives the general outline of what's expected of you as an employer. A whole raft of other detailed and specific regulations are approved by parliament and can be legally enforced. You can get full details of all the regulations that affect you from the Health and Safety Executive by calling the Infoline on 0845-3450055 or through the Web site www.hse.gov.uk. Your local Business Link can also give you a wealth of information. Your find your nearest office in the telephone directory or take a look at the Web site www.businesslink.gov.uk. I list the most important/common regulations for small businesses here:

- ✔ **The Management of Health and Safety at Work Regulations 1992.** These regulations requires you to make an assessment of the health and safety risks that your employees are exposed to at work and of the risks that other people not in your employment may face as a result of your business. Risk assessment is discussed in the section 'Assessing the risks around the workplace', later in this chapter.

- ✔ **The Workplace (Health, Safety and Welfare) Regulations 1992.** These regulations cover maintenance of the workplace, ventilation, temperature, lighting, cleaning, waste materials, room dimensions, space, and conditions of floors and traffic routes. They also cover falls, falling objects, washing facilities, escalators, and gates.

- ✔ **The Manual Handling Operations Regulations 1992.** These regulations say that you must, as far as is reasonably practicable, not ask your employees to do any manual handling jobs that will put them at risk of being injured. *Manual handling* is lifting, carrying, pushing, and pulling. *Reasonably practicable* means that you take all steps you can until the costs get such that you can't afford to do any more. If manual handling operations can't be avoided, you have to assess the risks of all manual handling operations that need to be done in your workplace. See Chapter 12 for more details.

- ✔ **The Provision and Use of Work Equipment Regulations 1998.** These regulations cover the condition and maintenance of work equipment. This equipment must be suitable for the job, well-maintained, and in good working order and state of repair. You have to give your employees proper information and training, and they have to be protected from the risks associated with using that equipment.

- ✔ **The Personal Protective Equipment at Work Regulations 1992.** These regulations state that employees who may be exposed to risks to their health and safety while at work should be provided with suitable personal protective equipment and that you have to ensure that it's properly used. Other people using your premises (including visitors) have to be protected too. Chapter 12 fills you in on this.

✔ **The Health and Safety (First Aid) Regulations 1981.** These regulations set out the first aid provision you have to make. See the section 'Arranging First Aid', later in this chapter, for more details.

Chapters 11 and 12 go into the details of some of these specific regulations: Chapter 11 looks at the health issues and workplace hazards, and Chapter 12 looks at accidents . . . and what you're expected to do to avoid them.

Health and safety have to have a high priority in any workplace and the organisations that have the job of making sure you stick to the rules will offer plenty of help and advice. Their role is explained in the next section. Don't be afraid to ask for their help right from the start. These organisations are more interested in preventing accidents and ill health in the first place than in having to punish you later for letting accidents happen.

Enforcing the rules and regulations – The HSE

The Health and Safety at Work Act also established and set out the powers of the *Health and Safety Executive* (HSE), the main enforcing authority for health and safety regulations, which inspects premises, enforces the law, and prosecutes negligent employers. Local authorities also have enforcement powers for some workplaces and premises such as shops, offices, sports centres, pubs, and restaurants.

You have to register with the HSE if your premises are a

✔ Factory, workshop, or other manufacturing or processing site

✔ Building site

✔ Railway

✔ Mine or quarry

✔ Your company carries out installation, maintenance, or repair work related to electricity, water, or gas

To register with the HSE, you must contact the organisation on the Infoline – 0870-1545500 – and they will send you form F9 to fill in and send back.

If your business operates from an office or shop you need to register with the local authority instead of the HSE. Phone the Environmental Health Department at your local council offices and they will send you form OSR1. If you're unsure which to register with call either office for advice. After you've registered, the relevant body – the HSE or the Environmental Health Department at the local authority – gets in touch with you for more information about your business and gives you any advice and information you need. They may decide to visit you. Don't be wary of them – their advice is there to help you get the health and safety aspects of your business right. Treat these advisers as an asset to the business and a good source of valuable, free assistance.

Some businesses come under both the HSE and the local authority – such as funeral directors – so it can be difficult to know which to register with. If you need advice, get in touch with the environmental health department at your local council.

You usually hear about HSE inspectors when an accident's happened and they're called in to investigate, such as with high-profile rail crashes, but the HSE can also go into premises to inspect them without an accident having taken place. They can take samples, carry out tests, and talk to employees. They may issue a notice that you must act on:

- ✔ An *improvement notice* will be issued if you're breaking the law or have broken the law and the inspector thinks that's likely to continue. You have 21 days in which to put things right.

- ✔ A *prohibition notice* is issued when the inspector believes a real risk of serious injury exists to someone in your workplace, and identifies what is responsible for the risk. This notice orders you to stop that unsafe practice or activity.

If you don't comply with an improvement or prohibition notice you can be prosecuted. You can also be prosecuted for intentionally trying to stop the HSE inspector doing his job. You can be fined or even go to prison.

Drawing Up Your Health and Safety Policy

Under the Health and Safety at Work Act regulations, unless you have fewer than five employees, you must have a written health and safety at work policy for your workplace and employees and you must make arrangements for that policy to be carried out all day and every day. Your policy must include:

- ✔ A general statement of your approach to health and safety

- ✔ Guidelines showing how your organisation goes about implementing the policy

- ✔ An assessment of specific hazards in your workplace and a statement of the rules put in place to deal with them

The Health and Safety Executive publishes a range of books and leaflets that can help you comply with the health and safety laws. You can buy *The Health and Safety Starter Pack* or *Essentials of Health and Safety at Work*, for instance, through the HSE Web site www.hsebooks.co.uk, from bookshops or from HSE Books, PO Box 1999, Sudbury, Suffolk, CO10 2WA or by calling 01787-881165. There's also a free leaflet called *Starting your Business* – guidance on preparing a health and safety document for small firms. These will help you to draw up your written policy and carry out your risk assessments.

You have to make sure your employees know about the policy. You can't just write it, put it in the back of a drawer, and forget about it. Your employees have obligations too. They must

- ✔ Take reasonable care of their own, and their colleagues', health and safety at work.

- ✔ Co-operate with you to make sure that all the health and safety requirements are met. If, for example, they work on a building site and you have provided hard hats, they have a duty to wear them.

- ✔ Not deliberately or recklessly interfere with any health and safety measures you have put in place or they may be guilty of a criminal offence and be fined.

You can sack someone who ignores his legal health and safety obligations but you must have instructed him properly on the safety measures in place and previously made him aware that interfering with those measures may result in dismissal. You also have to make sure you follow all the right procedures for dismissal – see Chapter 4 for more details.

Assessing the risks around the workplace

The main tool of your health and safety policy is the risk assessment. In order to carry out a risk assessment you have to identify the hazards and draw up plans to deal with them. The HSE defines a *risk* as 'the chance, great or small, that someone will be harmed by a hazard', and a *hazard* as 'something that may cause harm'.

A *risk assessment* involves going around your workplace and looking for the hazards that may cause harm; thinking about who they
might cause harm to; deciding how high the risks are; trying to
remove them or reduce them to as near nil as possible; recording
what you've done; and checking up regularly to see if anything
more can be done.

Risk assessment sounds easy, but of course the degree of difficulty
depends on your workplace. In some places hazards are few, obvious, and straightforward. If so, don't complicate the issue – just
apply a liberal dose of common sense. But in a bigger, more indus-
trialised workplace, risk assessment may well be a complicated
issue. You may not be the best person to carry out the assessment
because you're probably so familiar with the place that you may
well no longer spot the hazards. It can be a good idea and money
well-spent to pay a professional risk assessor to do the job for you.
Talk to the HSE for advice.

Hazards can be anything from lorries and forklift trucks to heavy
machinery to cables running across the floor. The bigger hazards
are more obvious. Some things like dangerous chemicals will be
immediately spotted, but what about the dangers of water? If
someone has their hands in water for most of the day it can cause
skin problems. Uneven flooring or carpets, badly stacked shelves,
boxes that are just a bit too heavy to lift, badly positioned desks
and chairs, poor lighting above computer screens, frayed wiring –
all these may cause damage over the long-term but are harder to
spot as hazards. Talk to your employees – they work in different
areas of your business and may well already know where most of
the hazards lie because they're always trying to dodge them.

 Don't forget risk assessment around the outside of the workplace.
For example, delivery lorries coming in across the staff car park
may present a risk, or forklift trucks that aren't separated off from
people walking around a warehouse. Plenty of potential exists for
accidents outside.

Eliminating hazards

When you've identified potential hazards in your workplace, act to
eliminate them. All workplaces will have their own specific requirements, and both you and your employees will probably have your
own ideas about making the necessary changes. For example, if
your employees need to shift boxes around, is there a way to avoid
having to ask them to lift and carry those boxes? Perhaps you can
install a machine or conveyor belt to take the strain your employees are currently under? Other possible ideas include making sure
transport vehicles and people are kept separate, having electrical

cables running around the walls instead of across the floor, or coming up with a different process that doesn't use dangerous chemicals. As an employer you are expected to do everything reasonably practicable to make the working environment safe and healthy, which means doing all you can up to the point where the necessary changes become prohibitively expensive or would make it impossible to carry out your business.

Cutting down the risks

In many cases eliminating hazards completely isn't an option because your business simply can't operate if you try that.

If this is the case in your workplace, you need to think instead about ways of cutting down the risks. For example, you can mark out lanes along which forklift trucks have to drive in the warehouse and where people aren't allowed to walk, making sure that you post suitable warnings at any intersections. In this way you can cut down the risks and the forklift hazard then poses less risk to fewer people. Similarly, making sure delivery lorries don't drive across areas of car park where staff may be walking cuts down on risks – even if the lorries do have to go the long way round. If you work with hazardous substances, make sure that all dangerous chemicals are clearly labelled and stored under lock and key and that only the people who really need to use them are allowed access. And organising materials deliveries in lighter loads and smaller boxes cuts the risks of back injury from lifting and carrying.

Sometimes reducing the risks only goes so far before it becomes prohibitively expensive to lower them any further. In such instances, you have cut the risks as far as is reasonably practicable: Maybe a new machine can do the same job and be much safer in terms of moving parts. If your business just can't afford to buy one and eliminate the hazards, you have to reduce the risks on your existing one as far as possible with guards, rails, notices, and training. The Health and Safety Executive Web site www.hse.gov. uk, Infoline (0845-3450055) and publications are very helpful.

Providing safety equipment

If you've done all you can to eliminate the hazards and reduce the risks and there are still hazards to be dealt with, think about what protection you can give your employees against the remaining risk. This can include

- ✔ Rubber gloves when working with hands in water
- ✔ Ear protectors in noisy environments

✔ Masks where you can't cut the dust down any further

✔ Goggles where there are still sparks flying

✔ Heavy gloves and metal aprons for heavy machinery

Chapter 12 gives more advice on kitting out staff safely.

Housekeeping Your Way to Safety

You can't get away from the housekeeping just because you're at work! Under the Workplace (Health, Safety and Welfare) Regulations 1992 (see the section 'Following the regulations' earlier in this chapter) you have specific duties to maintain the workplace. If you don't and employees are adversely affected they can claim damages.

You have to make sure that your work premises:

✔ Are clean and well maintained

✔ Aren't overcrowded

✔ Are at a minimum temperature (Chapter 11 has the details)

✔ Are well ventilated, drained, and lit

✔ Have fresh drinking water and washing facilities

✔ Have room for clothing and seating

✔ Are safe from dangerous substances, and that machinery is well fenced

The housekeeping is the first thing anyone notices when they come into your workplace. If the place looks bright, neat, and clean, it's likely that people will go away with the impression of a well-run business where it is safe to work. If it's dirty and seedy, neither prospective employees nor customers may feel confident about doing business with you. There's a good business case for putting health, safety, and welfare high up your agenda. See Chapter 11 for more on these aspects of the workplace.

Arranging First Aid

You have to make sure that there's adequate first aid for your employees. What's adequate will depend on your workplace, how many employees you have, and the kind of work that goes on there.

The first aid box and what should be in it

You have to provide first aid boxes. The boxes should contain only the items that your first aiders have been trained to use. Don't include medication of any kind – not even a few aspirin – because you aren't qualified to give medication and even an aspirin can be dangerous if given in the wrong circumstances. The kind of first aid boxes you can buy in the shops will be suitable to put the various items into.

What you put in the boxes depends on the types of hazards you've identified in the workplace that you've not been able to eliminate. So if you think there's a chance that people may get cuts, you need the kind of bandages that can be applied to cuts and antiseptic creams or washes to clean them out with until they can be properly treated. Any special equipment needed to deal with a specific hazard should also be in the box or beside the box. Make sure the box is kept well-stocked.

If there isn't any accessible tap water to wash eyes with, you need to have sterile water or normal sterile saline in the box in sealed containers holding at least 300 ml.

Make sure first aid boxes are strategically placed to be as near as possible to any potential hazard and that everyone knows where they are. The more employees you have and the more risks there are in the workplace, the more first aid boxes you should have.

First aiders and their responsibilities

You need an appropriate number of employees trained as first aiders to deal with accidents and emergencies or someone appointed to take charge if there's no first aider available.

A *first aider* must have a current first aid certificate issued by an organisation approved by the Health and Safety Executive or be someone who is properly trained or approved by the HSE. If no first aider is available, you have to have an appointed person on hand who's authorised to deal with the situation – someone who can make decisions such as calling for an ambulance or a doctor.

The number of first aiders you need depends on how hazardous a place your business is to work in and how many staff you have on the site at any one time. If you're running an office where risks are low and you have fewer than 50 employees, one appointed person is likely to be enough on each shift. But if you have more than

50 employees during normal working hours, you should have at least one first aider for every 50. The more hazardous the environment, the more first aiders you'll need.

Some situations require you to have staff trained to deal with specific hazards. Make sure that enough specially trained people are around to deal with the situation if you have a danger of:

✔ Poisoning by certain cyanides

✔ Burns from hydrofluoric acid

✔ Oxygen needing to be used to rescue someone in a confined space

Talk to the Health and Safety Executive about the hazards and training available.

If you have a enough employees to merit it and your workplace carries plenty of risks so that injuries may be fairly frequent and bigger than just the minor scrapes that a first aider with a well-equipped first aid box can cope with, you should consider whether you need to provide a first aid room that's fully equipped and staffed to deal with injuries and emergencies.

You have to display information about your first aid arrangements in the workplace with the names of the first aiders and the locations of first aid equipment. First aiders need to keep records of all the cases they deal with, giving the name, date, time, place, and details of what happened and what treatment they gave. You need to keep these safe along with records of the first aiders' qualifications and any training or refresher courses they go on.

Your records of accidents, incidents, injuries, or near misses can be very useful. They can give you a lot of information about the health and safety provisions you've made and whether or not they're adequate, and help you to identify hazards. All of this can help you review and improve your risk assessment and health and safety policy. The fewer incidents first aiders have to deal with the better your policy is working.

Posting Health and Safety Notices

You have to put suitable health and safety signs up in your workplace. You can either give all employees copies of the leaflet 'Your health, your safety: A guide for workers' or put up the poster 'Health and safety law: What you should know'. You can get both posters and leaflets from the HSE – through the Web site – www. hse.gov.uk or call 01787-881165.

You have to have your certificate of employer's liability insurance on display, somewhere prominent for employees to see. That's the insurance policy that covers you if employees claim compensation for personal injury or illness caused by their work. See the section 'Insuring Yourself' later in this chapter. As part of your risk assessment you also need to think about where you should put notices to bring people's attention to any hazards you've identified, such as moving vehicles or chemicals in storage. If you can't eliminate hazards you have to make sure that people know about them – not just your employees but anyone else who might visit your premises. In some cases that may mean marking off whole zones as areas of risk.

Make sure the notices are in suitable places. There's no point in having a notice in reception saying forklift trucks are a risk in the warehouse if the danger areas in the warehouse aren't clearly marked.

Appointing Safety Reps

If there's a recognised union in your workplace (see Chapter 7) you have to appoint safety representatives. These reps must be allowed time off, with pay, to carry out their duties. These duties include

- ✔ Investigating potential hazards, dangerous incidents, and accidents.

- ✔ Investigating complaints from employees about their health, safety, and welfare.

- ✔ Representing other employees in any health and safety negotiations with you.

- ✔ Carrying out inspections at least every three months and after a notifiable accident, dangerous occurrence, or a notifiable disease has been contracted – see Chapters 11 and 12 for more details.

- ✔ Consulting with and receiving information from the HSE on behalf of members.

- ✔ Attending meetings of the safety committee – made up of all of the people in the workplace whose role it is to ensure the workplace is kept safe and healthy.

Treat safety representatives as an asset, to help you meet your obligations and to avoid injuries and health and welfare problems, rather than as a threat. You have to make sure that they have the right training to carry out their duties. You have to give them time off to train, and you have to pay for the training. Representatives have the right to complain to an Employment Tribunal if you don't allow them the time off, with pay, required to fulfil their role.

Even if you don't have a recognised union, you still have to consult your employees on health and safety matters. You can consult with the whole workforce, individually or as a group, or allow them to elect their own reps. This consultation process is particularly important when it comes to making changes around the place. The employees who'll be working with new equipment or new work stations may well spot any potential problems before you do.

Work together with your safety reps on any proposed changes. That way health and safety considerations remain an integral part of running your business.

Training for Staff

Consider having your appointed people trained in emergency first aid too. If the workplace is particularly hazardous with specific, well-identified hazards like those associated with certain chemicals you use, they need training to deal with those specific emergencies.

If you don't provide appropriate training and something goes wrong – and an employee sues you – a court may find you guilty of negligence. That includes giving your employees appropriate training to make sure they can do their jobs safely. Review training needs for all your staff regularly.

Working Away

Just because an employee is working away from your workplace doesn't mean your duty of care for that employee stops. If they're working for you it's your duty to see that their health, safety, and welfare are taken care of.

Working outside the workplace

Your duty of care to your employees means that if you send them to another place to work, maybe to a client's or third party's premises, you still have to – as far as is practicably possible – make sure that those premises are safe. That may mean visiting the premises yourself or sending someone else who is competent to check them. Or you can ask for a copy of the other party's risk assessment and health and safety policy. If you aren't happy that the premises are safe for your employee to do whatever he has to do there, you shouldn't ask him to go.

If an employee sues you over an accident at the third party's premises, the court will look at whether you did what any reasonable employer would have done in the circumstances to protect your employee.

Working at home

Most of the regulations that apply to employees at work apply to homeworkers – people you employ to work from home – as well. You have a duty to look after their health, safety, and welfare.

You have to do a risk assessment of the work that people do at home and decide whether or not anything needs to be done to make sure that they or anyone else affected by their work comes to no harm. If, for example, employees working at home have to handle goods as part of their work, you need to decide whether to give them training and supply them with lifting equipment such as a trolley to cut down the risk of back injury. If you do give people equipment to use at home, you need to make sure that it's the right equipment for the job, that they have all the information or training they need to use it properly, that it has any protective attachments like guards that it requires, that any personal protective equipment like gloves that should be used with it are provided, and that you check it regularly to make sure that it's in good condition and does not present a danger. IT equipment is the most often used at home and you have to take all reasonable steps to make sure that it's safe, that the employee uses it properly, that he takes the right breaks from work, and that it doesn't affect his health.

Homeworking and pregnancy

When assessing risks to someone working at home you have to pay special attention to women who are pregnant and new mothers who have given birth in the past six months (which includes having delivered a stillborn baby after 24 weeks of pregnancy) or are still breastfeeding. The Health and Safety Executive guide *A Guide for New and Expectant Mothers Who Work* sets out the risk in detail and gives advice on how to make sure that you're complying with the law. Get it from www.hsebooks.co.uk or ring the publications line on 01787-881165.

It's difficult to keep an eye on homeworkers and what they get up to, but that's why training and information are so important. Good employers take time to see for themselves how work stations are set up in people's homes.

You have to provide appropriate and adequate first aid, investigate, report, and keep records of any accidents, injuries, and illnesses that are work related. HSE inspectors have the right to visit homeworkers and your workplace safety reps can represent homeworkers' interests.

Insuring Yourself

Despite all your best efforts, things can and do go wrong. Unless you're prepared to face complete ruin, you need to be insured against a successful claim. Insurance costs worry small businesses and some bosses take risks by cutting back on the policies they buy (or breaking the law and not buying any at all). This section explains why you don't want to cut corners on Employers Liability Insurance.

Carrying out a risk assessment is one way of keeping your insurance costs down. It's an important first step to making sure all the right measures are in place to prevent injuries and accidents or ill health, so it can play a part in reducing your premiums. If you can show you've really got to grips with health and safety issues, over and above what the law expects of you, then your insurers may be able to offer you a better deal. A good safety record and good training can help.

On the other side of the coin, your insurer may reduce, delay, or even refuse to pay out on any claim if something that has caused the problem hasn't been maintained or checked regularly. Good, effective risk management will pay dividends.

Covering yourself with employer's liability insurance

You must have employer's liability insurance in case you are found liable to pay damages to an employee who has been injured at work because of negligence on your part or because you have broken the law. The only employers who are exempt run some family businesses where employees are all closely related. But even that exemption doesn't apply if your business is a limited company. You have to be insured to the tune of at least £5 million for any one incident. If an employee does bring a claim she brings it against your insurance company and it's up to that company to defend the claim. The insurer can't refuse to pay out if you have failed to comply with certain conditions or if you have been negligent. However, if it does have to meet a claim against you the insurer may impose conditions on continuing to offer you cover. It can insist on inspecting your premises and demand that you make improvements in your risk management.

You have to display your insurance certificate in your workplace, a new one each year, and you have to keep old certificates for 40 years. Some insurance companies offer business policies, or you can get them through specialist brokers.

Insuring visitors to the workplace

As the occupier of your business premises you owe your employees and anyone else who comes into your workplace a duty of care under the *Occupiers' Liability Acts of 1957 and 1984.* These acts require you to take all reasonable steps to make sure that employees and visitors are reasonably safe using the premises for the purposes for which you invite them or permit them to be there. That goes for everyone, including the postman. *Owner's liability insurance* protects you against a claim for an injury to someone inside your premises.

Where members of the public and customers can be affected by your work activities, you need *public liability insurance*. This type of policy protects you if someone is injured or there's damage outside your premises as a result of your business. It covers things like someone tripping over something you've left lying around or where someone working for you causes damage to a house he's working on. If an injured person sues, public liability insurance will cover your legal costs and compensation claims.

If an employee or visitor is injured by an independent contractor working on your premises, you won't be liable if you can show that you:

- ✔ Acted reasonably in giving the work to the independent contractor
- ✔ Exercised reasonable care in selecting that contractor
- ✔ Checked to make sure the work was properly carried out

If you make food or drink products or supply goods to a consumer, consider buying *product liability insurance* to cover you in case any harm comes to someone because of your products.

Another sensible option for some small businesses is *professional indemnity insurance*, providing cover in case someone claims for damages as a result of any advice you've given or decisions you've made.

Remembering Disabled and Older Workers

Don't forget that older or disabled workers may have different health and safety needs to other employees. Consider whether your workplace is fully accessible and suitable for them. Doing so makes life so much easier for everyone – all employees who stay with you will get older and may acquire some disabilities related to age.

 Sometimes older and disabled employees are determined to show they can cope and are less likely to complain or admit to not finding their working conditions as easy as they once did. Give them the opportunity and encourage them to talk to you about any worries they may have. If you make informal chats about the working environment a routine event and talk to them individually, employees can be more forthcoming.

Making Everyone Responsible for Health and Safety

Everyone in the workplace has to play their part to make sure they and all their colleagues, as well as anyone else who comes into the workplace, are safe. Discuss your health and safety processes with staff and make sure they know that they need to report to you any problems they have, no matter how small. It's all very well making sure that no one is going to get dragged into a dangerous machine or be run down by a forklift truck, but you have to know about the little things too, such as the hot water that's scalding and may cause burns, or the torn carpet that may trip someone up and break an ankle. The more involved and aware employees are of how much attention you're paying to their safety, the more they will also take care of their colleagues and visitors. As an added bonus, your safety record can enhance your reputation as a good employer and a good company to do business with.

Chapter 11

Proceeding with Caution

*I*n 2003, 2.2 million people suffered from what they thought to be work-related ill health. When you are drawing up the health and safety policy for your workplace, you have to give as much emphasis to the 'health' as to the 'safety'. Where the greatest risks lie depends on the type of work you do, but sometimes in businesses where there are potentially big safety risks from transport or machinery, people forget about health. It's easier to spot the hazards posed by lorries than to spot the hazards presented by the less obvious problems like poor ventilation, lighting, exposure to chemicals, or the harmless-looking computer keyboard. And the biggest hazard of all in many workplaces is the one that's hardest to spot until the damage has been done – stress. It can creep up on people and its cause can be very hard to find.

You have to safeguard employees' welfare by identifying risks, considering their needs when you plan their work, giving them all the advice, information, and training they need, and monitoring and keeping records of their health issues. Some aspects of occupational health management are just about good practice and common sense, but you do have a legal duty of care to your employees – so you have a legal responsibility for health and safety issues at work even it they don't come under specific laws or regulations. Refer to Chapter 10 for more details.

Quite apart from keeping your employees happy, a healthy environment has big business benefits. It cuts absenteeism and staff turnover, improves productivity, and boosts your reputation as a good employer and therefore a good person to do business with.

This chapter concentrates on the health issues. Chapter 12 deals with safety and the accidents that can happen.

Attending to the Detail – Things to Keep an Eye On

Assess the risks from the hazards around the workplace and try to eliminate the hazards. If complete elimination's not possible you must reduce the risks as far as possible, and as a last resort offer employees protection against those that still exist. Chapter 10 deals with risk assessment and handling the risks.

The hazards and risks that affect occupational health depend very much on the kind of work you do. If you have people working alone a lot, perhaps in agriculture, they face particular safety risks from machinery, but a more serious risk may be that to their health because of the isolation. In offices people are more likely to suffer because of poor heating, insufficient lighting, ill-designed workstations, or overuse of the computers.

Also remember to take your employees' needs into consideration when planning their work. You need to establish their capabilities and make sure that you don't expect too much from them or that they don't get frustrated because you're not giving them sufficient to challenge them. People who don't feel they are getting enough out of their work may become unhappy, as may those who feel snowed under and unable to cope. Unhappy people get sick and take time off work. Make sure they have someone to talk to about their worries and can make suggestions about improvements to their own working environment and the workplace in general. Think about what advice or training they might benefit from and monitor their workloads and health carefully.

Apart from making your employees feel valued, you need to have an eye for detail around the workplace.

Temperatures

You have to keep your workplace above a certain temperature – 16 degrees Celsius if employees are sitting most of the time and 13 degrees Celsius if they are moving around all day. If you can't guarantee that your heating system can rise to those heights, you have to have extra heaters around to boost the temperature as and when needed.

No maximum limit is set for temperatures, but if staff are too hot they are going to feel sleepy and lethargic. They may get less work done and be in danger of making mistakes that can cost your business dear, as well as putting themselves at risk of having accidents.

Make sure that the place is well ventilated and, if windows can't be opened to let in fresh air, think about installing air-conditioning. There probably aren't many days in the year when you'd need a full-blown system, but you can buy portable temporary units or electric fans.

Smoking

Set out a clear policy on smoking. You have a legal obligation to ensure, as far as practicably possible, the health of all your employees and to protect non-smokers from discomfort caused by tobacco smoke in rest rooms and rest areas. If you have a written policy on smoking, that shows how you're meeting those responsibilities.

The government recommends that smoking should not be allowed in enclosed workplaces and you should give priority to the needs of non-smokers. If you don't want to ban smoking altogether you can make special provision for smokers – such as a smoking-room. You can make people leave the premises to smoke, but it doesn't look too good to have smokers hanging around on the doorstep and you may find they take longer breaks than they would if they go to a smoking-room. If you simply designate smoking areas, make sure that the ventilation is good enough to protect non-smokers.

Consult your employees and come to an agreement on your policy. That usually stops disputes between them. You also need to think about what happens if your employees are out and about – perhaps working in customers' homes. You may need to ban them from smoking there too so as to avoid upsetting clients and to help the image of your business.

Drinking and drugs

Alcohol and drugs present a whole set of hazards around the workplace. How serious a risk they pose and how you deal with them depends on the kind of work you do. Legally you can't allow employees to take illegal drugs at work or to drink and drive, so you can't just bury your head and ignore the issues, but sacking someone isn't always the best policy.

If you have a business where people operate machinery or drive, you may decide on a complete ban on drinking during work hours. If that's not the case, you may not have a problem with the odd drink at lunchtime. Be very clear about what is and isn't accepted. Think about the risks that someone's drinking can pose not only to themselves but also to their colleagues. You can be sued if you allow someone's drinking to go on to the point where they cause an accident in which another employee is injured. If you can't allow drinking, then make sure that people know what the disciplinary procedures will be and that violators can ultimately be dismissed.

More of a problem for you can be the employees who don't drink during the working day but have a drink problem that affects their work. Look out for the signs:

✔ Coming in late and hung over.

✔ Being off sick more than the average for your workplace.

✔ Not getting as much done as colleagues in similar jobs.

✔ Having minor accidents.

✔ Customers complaining.

 Keep records so that you can build up a picture of the problem, but when broaching the subject bear in mind that no matter how sure you are there may always be another explanation. People don't always want to talk about their problems, especially with a manager, so think about offering them confidential help outside work, perhaps with a counsellor. You can't just dismiss them on the spot – you must go through the fair procedures (refer to Chapter 4).

Drug use presents you with similar problems and again, just because you think you've identified the signs don't forget that there may be another reason. Perhaps the employee is acting the way she is because of prescription drugs. Be as supportive as possible while making it clear that you can't accept any behaviour that puts the employee herself or her colleagues at risk of an injury. Be clear about what disciplinary procedures you will take if you do find that an employee is misusing drugs, but again, offer counselling as the best way to deal with the problem.

 Both alcohol and drug problems may be the result of stress – either stress related to the workload or stress because there's too much work and not enough time for family life. If you can remove the stress or prevent it in the first place, this goes a long way to sorting things out.

Keeping the noise down

Noise is covered by the Noise at Work Regulations 1989. Your business may be a relatively quiet office where noise levels aren't in danger of doing your employees any harm. But they don't have to be excessively loud to cause health problems. Check how people feel about working in open-plan areas, for example, because just the background noise of many people making and taking phone calls can be distracting and cause stress for some. Discuss the working environment and think about possibly adding screens at strategic points, offering people headsets so that they can hear their callers better, and if there's room adding a private office where people can retreat if they have something they really need to concentrate on away from the hubbub. The danger is that if people can't concentrate they don't get through their day's work and end up staying late or taking it home – affecting their home life and causing mounting stress all round.

If you have to shout to make yourself heard by someone two metres away from you in your factory, workshop, or even bar or nightclub, then you probably have a noise problem. And if people's ears are still ringing when they come out of your premises or leave a particular noisy area, you probably have to take steps to protect anyone going into that environment. Continuous noise can be a hazard, but so can sudden sporadic noises.

Do a noise risk assessment to try to eliminate or at least reduce noise levels. There may be ways of muffling or silencing machines; adding noise-absorbing screens or soundproof barriers around machines; moving them further away from workers; or changing working patterns so that people aren't exposed to the noise for such long periods of time. Assess the impact of the noise on you, your employees, and other people who do work for you. There's much more information on assessing the risks around the work-place in Chapter 10 and the HSE Web site www.hse.gov.uk has all the information you'll need or call the Infoline on 0845-3450055.

The more obvious problems associated with noise are ringing in the ears and loss of hearing. If you use machinery or equipment that can be noisy, very strict rules apply about levels of noise and exposure to noise:

✔ If employees are exposed to noise at or above 85 decibels every day, you have to do your risk assessment and check the level of the noise; provide information and training about noise risks; and provide ear protection to anyone who asks for it.

✔ If the noise is 90 decibels or above you have to take steps to reduce it or to reduce exposure to it; supply hearing protection to everyone working in the area rather than just those who ask for it; and mark the affected areas so that everyone knows they need ear protection inside that zone.

✔ If noises in your workplace are above 90 decibels or peak at 200 pascals, you have to take all reasonably practicable steps to reduce noise exposure over and above providing ear protectors. Can you get rid of the source of the noise or change your working practices?

If you use ear protectors, put up notices showing where in your workplace they have to be used.

The type of protection you have to provide is covered by the Noise at Work Regulations. The protection should:

- ✔ Fit and be used properly
- ✔ Reduce noise to below 90 decibels
- ✔ Be kept in good condition
- ✔ Work with any other protective gear that people have to wear or use

It's your job to make sure that people use their ear protection properly, so think about doing spot checks and make it a disciplinary matter if the protection you supply isn't worn.

Dealing with hazardous substances

Hazardous substances come under the COSHH regulations – Control of Substances Hazardous to Health. Find out more about COSHH from the HSE Web site or Infoline. Check if anything in your workplace can cause your employees harm if they breathe it in, get it on their skin, swallow it, or get it splashed into their eyes. Any of those events can cause short-term or long-term health problems, such as dermatitis, asthma, or even cancer – you are dealing with a hazardous substance.

Hazardous substances include:

- ✔ Adhesives, solvents, paint, cleaning agents; the suppliers should have labelled them hazardous if they can cause harm and they have to give you safety data sheets with them
- ✔ Fumes generated by the work you do
- ✔ Natural products such as blood or grain dust that you work with or that result from your work
- ✔ Biological agents like bacteria or micro-organisms

At first glance you may think that nothing around your workplace comes into those categories, but even everyday cleaners and chemicals can pose problems over the long run. For example, in a hairdressing business dyes and bleaches can be hazards and cause dermatitis or asthma or make existing conditions worse. Your business may include delivering hazardous substances and if so, your employees need to be protected too. Some people working for you may be more vulnerable than others, such as those who already have allergies.

As with any aspects of health and safety, you have to do a risk assessment. Don't forget about materials that have been supplied to you, things that can cause fires or explosions if they're not stored properly, and waste products that your business produces.

Try to eliminate the hazards. Think about whether you can use different, non-hazardous materials instead or change your processes to avoid using hazardous materials completely. Control or reduce the risks by cutting down the number of people who come into contact with the hazardous substances, train those people, and make sure that your ventilation keeps the substances away from people who may breathe them in.

If you can't eliminate or reduce the risks, provide protection such as clothing, masks, eye protectors, or suitable gloves. Personal protective equipment is covered by the COSHH regulations. Make sure that you dispose of the waste safely and don't forget that you have a duty to protect people outside your workplace too.

Abolishing asbestos

If your employees can come into contact with asbestos, the Asbestos at Work Regulations 2002 apply to you. Asbestos is only a risk if the fibres get into the air and people breathe them in. If that happens they can cause cancers of the lungs and chest lining. Around 3,000 people die every year in the UK because of exposure, at some time in the past, to asbestos. It can take anything up to 60 years before asbestos-related diseases make their appearance. You may be aware of various court cases in which patients or their families have been fighting for compensation from employers.

The law says that you have to prevent the exposure of your employees to asbestos and if you're in any doubt about whether asbestos is present in something, you have to treat the materials as if they do contain asbestos to be on the safe side. It's now illegal to use asbestos when building or refurbishing, but a lot of it was used in the past for construction and some materials containing asbestos were still used as recently as 1999. Asbestos still exists in many premises. If you know that asbestos is in your premises you have a legal duty to manage the risks or to cooperate with whoever has the job of managing the risks, such as the landlord of the building.

Unless someone else has responsibility for repairing and maintaining the premises you work in, the Asbestos At Work Regulations say that you have to:

- ✔ Inspect the premises to find out if asbestos is there, where it is, and what condition it's in.

- ✔ Keep records of the locations with plans and drawings and the condition of the materials.

- ✔ Do a risk assessment and plan how to manage any risks.

- ✔ Take any action that you decide is needed and keep the situation under constant review.

- ✔ Make sure that anyone who may work on the material knows where it is and not to disturb it.

If someone else is responsible for repairs and maintenance, you have to make sure that they do all that and you have to co-operate with them. In the search, don't damage any materials you think may have asbestos in them or you put yourself and your employees at risk. Check with surveyors, architects, builders, and anyone else who may know about the building. Builders' plans and invoices can give you useful information. You can hire specialists to do the investigation for you, but if you're not planning any repair work on the premises and they're fairly small you can do it yourself. Sometimes the only way to be sure is to take samples and have them analysed, but that has to be done by properly trained people.

If the age of the building and the information you gather give you strong evidence that no asbestos materials are present, you don't need to do anything other than record that and your evidence. But if the building is old enough and there are areas you can't get access to, you have to assume that asbestos exists and act accordingly. You can't ignore it unless you have strong evidence that it isn't there.

Three types of asbestos exist, usually called blue, white, and brown. They're all potentially dangerous, but white is the most so.

After you know where the asbestos is and what type it is:

- ✔ **Check its condition and whether or not it's likely to be disturbed or get damaged.** If the asbestos isn't likely to be damaged or disturbed and it's in good condition, it is probably safer to leave it where it is. If you do leave it be, check on its condition regularly and keep records of your checks. If it's likely that the materials may be damaged or disturbed or they're in a poor condition, you have to decide whether to repair or remove them.

- ✔ **Keep records, including drawings of the locations.** Mark the area with a warning sign. If anyone does come into the premises to do any work that might disturb asbestos, you have to make sure that they first receive all the information they need. The best way is to set up a system where no repair or maintenance work goes ahead without your approval.

If your asbestos is beyond repair, someone who is trained in how to do the job safely has to remove it. Use a contractor who is licensed by the Health and Safety Executive.

You have a legal duty to tell anyone who may work on the repair or maintenance of your premises about the location and condition of any asbestos. That means not just your own employees but also contractors who come in to do work for you. If employees or contractors are working on the asbestos, you have to make sure that they take all necessary precautions to keep themselves and everyone else safe:

- ✔ Keep everyone who doesn't need to be there out of the areas they're working on.

- ✔ Take care not to create any more dust than they have to and keep the material wet to keep down the dust.

- ✔ Don't break up large pieces of asbestos and don't use power tools that would create a lot of dust.

- ✔ Make contractors wear protective clothing and masks or respirators.

- ✔ Ensure that contractors don't take protective clothing home to wash.

- ✔ Don't expose anyone who isn't in protective clothing to the asbestos.

- ✔ Clean up with a suitable industrial vacuum cleaner.

You have to handle asbestos waste properly for the safety of your employees and the whole of your local community. Double bag it in heavy-duty bags, clearly label the waste, and take it to a licensed disposal site. Your local authority can tell you where the nearest one is. Don't be tempted to dump it outside your premises and forget about it. Asbestos is very dangerous stuff.

Minimising dust and fumes

Dust and fumes can cause allergic reactions, skin conditions, eye, brain, or liver damage, and serious illnesses ranging from breathing problems and asthma to cancer. Dust is any dry particles in the air and fumes are gases, vapours, smoke, and even smells. It may not occur to you, but even in an ordinary office chemicals can exist in some of the equipment that can be hazardous, especially over a long period of time with poor ventilation.

You have to make sure that you protect not only your employees but anyone else who may come into the premises, such as customers and members of the public. You must monitor the level of dust and fumes and make sure that you have ventilation systems that are up to the job of keeping the air free from both and that they are in the right places.

Follow the same procedures as for other hazards: do your risk assessment, and try to eliminate the hazards. You can use special equipment to monitor levels of gases and fumes such as carbon monoxide and ozone, or get specialists in to do it for you. The best way to eliminate the hazard is to take away the cause of it, but that may not be possible if it's part of your business process. If dust and fumes can't be entirely eliminated, reduce them or control them. Good cleaning and maintenance, updated machinery, extractor fans, good ventilation, and windows and doors that open to let dust and fumes escape (as long as they can't harm people on the outside) can all help. If a risk is still present because the dust or fumes can't be fully controlled, give employees protection such as masks and protective overalls.

Working with water

What can be less hazardous than life-giving water? But if you have your hands in it all day water can be very hard on the skin and can make some skin conditions worse. It's a good idea to give employees suitable protective gloves. If you spill water on a floor it can be slippery, so you need to make sure that you clear up any spillages quickly. If your workplace has hot water taps, check that the water isn't too hot in case it scalds someone. Make sure that water can't mix with any chemicals where it would react and give off dangerous fumes.

Ventilation

Good ventilation is the best defence against health problems relating to dust and fumes and other hazardous substances in the air like cigarette smoke. Under the *Workplace (Health, Safety and Welfare) Regulations 1992* you must keep your premises well ventilated. With good ventilation clean air is sucked into the building from outside and circulated. Depending on your business and the levels of dust and fumes or any chemicals you use, doors and windows may be enough to ventilate the place; but don't forget to make sure that they work properly. If you need additional ventilation, desk-top fans and stand alone air-conditioning units may be useful, as well as the bigger ventilation systems.

Some of your employees may work in the open air. It's tempting to think that means they will have all the ventilation they need. But they may still be at risk from dust and fumes that the fresh air can't take away. Check, and if need be make sure that they have protective masks and clothing.

Lighting

The type and level of lighting you need to work safely will depend on the premises and the type of work that people are doing under it. It has to be bright enough and placed correctly to make it easy for people to see their work without glare. Employees may need to have individual lamps for some types of work in addition to ceiling lighting, and they should have control over the lighting so that they can adjust it to cut glare. Make sure that lights are kept clean or the power will be reduced. Windows will need adjustable curtains or blinds where it's possible there may be glare from the sun.

Facilities

You must provide a minimum standard of facilities for anyone working in your business. Whatever work you do, people have to have enough room to move around without bumping into things. The rule is that if you take the volume of the room when it's empty and divide that by the number of people working in it, they should each have 11 cubic metres of space; if that isn't enough for the kind of work they're doing, they should have more.

Toilets and washing facilities

Your employees have to have adequate toilet and washing facilities, which must be:

- ✔ Separate for men and women unless they are in a room that can be locked and is used by one person at a time

- ✔ Well lit, ventilated, and clean

- ✔ Have toilet paper and sanitary-disposal facilities

- ✔ Have hot and cold running water and soap

- ✔ Have a washbasin and some way of drying hands

- ✔ Have showers if yours is a dirty business

You have to provide a certain number of toilets depending on how many employees you have. Table 11-1 shows the figures for mixed-use or women-only toilets.

Table 11-1 Minimum Staff Toilet and Washing Facilities

Number of Employees	Number of Toilets	Number of Wash Stations
1–5	1 toilet	1 wash station
6 – 25	2	2
26 – 50	3	3
51 – 75	4	4
76 – 100	5	5
Over 100	An additional toilet and wash station for every 25 employees	

You have to make sure that you provide toilet facilities suitable for disabled employees.

Food and drink

You have some legal obligations to provide eating and drinking facilities. If employees regularly eat in the workplace they should have:

- An area where they can eat away from anything that can contaminate the food (such as dust and fumes)
- Chairs and tables for eating and drinking at
- Facilities to make hot drinks
- A way of heating food if they can't get hot food from somewhere nearby
- Facilities that are kept clean and well maintained to prevent sickness

If people can eat in the work area and it's clean and has space for the food, you don't need to provide a specific area. But you do have to provide free drinking water and cups in all workplaces.

Rest areas

Provide suitable, clean rest areas for staff. If you have a staff canteen, that can count as a rest area as long as employees can use it without having to buy food or drinks. Rest areas must be:

- Big enough to accommodate the maximum number of employees you expect to use them at any one time
- Furnished with tables and seats with backrests
- Somewhere where there's no need for protective equipment
- Arranged so that non-smokers aren't irritated by smoke

Storage areas and changing facilities

If your employees have to wear special clothing you have to provide them with a big enough changing room that is kept clean. This changing room should:

- Have or be close to storage for workers' clothes and provide some way of stopping personal clothing coming into contact with dirty, wet work clothes

- Have or be close to washing facilities

- Have seating

- Have hangers or pegs for hanging up clothes

- Allow privacy

- Allow for drying clothes, if possible somewhere well ventilated

Remote workers

You must look after employees who are working away from your premises or at home. If they work somewhere without water and toilets, you may have to provide chemical toilets and washing facilities. If they work from home, you need to do a risk assessment or make sure that they're trained to do their own. Identify any hazards they may face and work out how to cut down or remove the risks. (See Chapter 10 for advice on spotting hazards.)

Using Computers

Although computers look harmless, they can cause a whole array of problems. You have to minimise risks to staff working on what's correctly called *display screen equipment* (encompassing the screen, keyboard and mouse, and hard drive unit).

Under the Health and Safety (Display Screen Equipment) Regulations 1992 – amended in 2002 – computer screens should:

- Tilt and swivel

- Be adjusted to the correct height

- Not flicker

- Adjust easily for brightness and contrast

- Not have reflected glare

- Have a suitable screen size

Keyboards should:

✔ Have a tilt adjustment

✔ Be separate from the screen so they can be moved to a comfortable working position

✔ Have enough space in front of them to allow for resting arms and hands when not typing

✔ Have a matt surface that doesn't give off glare

✔ Be easy to read

Computer hard drives shouldn't be so noisy as to distract the people using them and shouldn't give out so much heat as to make people uncomfortable.

The best way to reduce risks with screens and keyboards is to make sure that your staff know the dangers and are trained in how to minimise them. You have a duty to make sure that they use the equipment properly, but you can't be expected to stand looking over your employees' shoulders every minute of the day or nobody would get any work done – so good training is the key. Make sure that employees know:

✔ What the risks are of using the equipment without enough care

✔ How to adjust the screen, keyboard, contrast, and brightness controls

✔ How to adjust the print size on the screen so they can read it easily

✔ To keep their wrists straight when using the keyboard

✔ Not to strike the keys too hard or overstretch their fingers

✔ That they must take frequent breaks (see the following section on 'Repetitive strain injuries')

The Health and Safety Executive produces leaflets on using computers; look at its Web site for more details (www.hse.gov.uk). You can view the leaflets *Working with VDUs* and *The Law on VDUs – An Easy Guide* on the Web site as PDF files. You can buy copies from the HSE by calling 01787-881165 or through hsebooks.co.uk. Make it possible for employees to look after themselves and encourage them to do so by making sure that they see these leaflets.

Give employees a mix of work, some of which takes them away from their screens, and make sure that they aren't overloaded and feeling chained to their desks. The section 'Taking Breaks' in Chapter 6 explains more about the breaks people working on computers must have during the working day.

What's true for desktop machines is also true for laptops. Employees shouldn't use laptops if there are bigger desktop machines available, but if they're out and about and laptops are a must, make sure that they are as easy to use and as light and easy to carry as possible. You have to provide training for employees using laptops so that they know how to use and adjust the screen and keyboard, how to reduce the risks from lifting and carrying them, and the importance of taking breaks. This training should also include advice on reducing the risk of getting mugged – one of the biggest health and safety risks for a laptop user.

Make sure that all staff using any computer equipment know that they need to report any problems as soon as they crop up. Problems may arise if people are constantly moving between desks – you have to make sure that all the relevant elements are easy to adjust, and that employees know how to and that they must adjust them.

Repetitive strain injuries

People working at their screens for long periods can be at risk of *repetitive strain injuries* – aches and pains in the back, neck, arms, and hands caused by undertaking the same tasks with the same muscles, over and over again. These aches and pains can cause long-term problems if you don't deal with them immediately and you have to take all possible steps to try to prevent them (by using breaks from the screen and correct training).

 A lot of repetitive strain injury problems stem from the use of the mouse, trackball, or some other pointing device where the same finger is used over and over again to click the device.

The best defence against repetitive strain is taking a break. The length and frequency of the breaks that people need depend on the kind of work they're doing. If they usually work at their screen for long periods non-stop, then more, shorter breaks are better, say 5 to 10 minutes in every hour rather than 15 minutes after 2 hours. Let the employee choose – she'll know better than you how often she needs to get away from the screen. A break doesn't mean that she stops working but that she has a break away from the screen, possibly doing some other kind of work. But it's important that she moves away from her desk and moves around if she has been constantly sitting down.

If someone does develop aches and pains, she should report it straight away and you need to check that her workstation is adjusted to suit her and review the work she's doing to try to stop whatever is causing the pain. Make sure that she sees a doctor straight away. If she can carry on working while the condition is being treated, you should give her different tasks or offer her alternative work. If more than one person gets repetitive strain injuries, there may be something wrong with the way you have set up the workstations. You probably need to review your risk assessment and whether or not you're doing all you can to eliminate risk. Maybe you need to have an expert look at your work setup or organise more training for your employees.

Eye tests

If employees use display screens frequently they are entitled to eye tests, and you have to pay for them. You don't have to pay for glasses unless an employee who needs them can't use ordinary ones and needs special ones for the work you need her to do.

Space

Your employees need enough space to work in comfortably and change position without getting in one another's way. When you're laying out workstations don't forget the space the chair takes up and that people have to push chairs back to get comfortably out and in without banging into people around them.

Your employees are entitled to a minimum working space. Take the volume of the room when it's empty and divide that by the number of people working in it. Each employee must be allowed 11 cubic metres of space.

The minimum 11 cubic metres may not be enough depending on the type of work that has to be done – a desk or work surface for computer work needs to be big enough for the monitor, keyboard, and any paperwork to be moved around to suit the person using them. It has to have a surface that doesn't glare and be steady on its legs.

Ergonomics

Ergonomics is all about posture, how people sit while they're working, how they position their chairs, and how they organise their workspace to avoid over-stretching.

Chairs have to be stable and adjustable, both for height and for the tilt of the chair back. Check out the design of your chairs: the arms shouldn't get in the way of the person's arm movement and shouldn't stop the chair getting under the work surface. The chair also has to be wide enough to be comfortable and the back of it should give support to the user's back. If people can't rest their feet flat on the floor, you may have to give them foot rests. Make sure that they all know how important it is to adjust their chairs to suit themselves and that if they do use different desks they need to adjust whatever chair they're using and adjust the height of the screen.

Posture is very important for people sitting for long periods working at a computer because poor posture can lead to all sorts of problems with the back, neck and shoulders, arms and hands. Make sure that your employees know the importance of sitting properly. Remind them to:

- ✔ Change position regularly and take regular breaks.

- ✔ Keep their arms roughly horizontal and their eyes at the level of the top of the display screen.

- ✔ Keep the things they use most within easy reach.

- ✔ Keep the mouse close enough so they can use it with a relaxed arm and a straight wrist.

 If employees have problems with keeping wrists straight, you can offer them wrist supports, which sit on the desk for the wrist to rest on.

Training

 Under the health and safety laws you have to train your employees how to use display screen equipment. Good training is well worth the time and cost because it cuts down on health problems and days off work.

The training has to include:

- ✔ Outlining the potential health and safety risks of working with computers

- ✔ Positioning and adjusting all the equipment and software

- ✔ Understanding the importance of good posture, changing position frequently, and taking breaks

- ✔ Picking up good keyboard and mouse techniques

- ✔ Spotting symptoms of any strain injuries that might result from computer use and the importance of reporting them

- ✔ Maintaining and cleaning the equipment

- ✔ Knowing about a worker's entitlement to eye tests

If you upgrade or replace computer equipment, employees may need retraining. Homeworkers can carry out their own risk assessments and adjust their own workstations, but you have to provide them with training too.

Knowing the Fire Drill

Your business must meet all the necessary fire safety standards – you can find out about these by visiting the HSE Web site or www.odpm.gov.uk (the Office of the Deputy Prime Minister, which has responsibility for fire regulations). But the first port of call should be the fire safety officer at your local fire station. To conform to the standards, you have to do a risk assessment to work out where the risks are and eliminate as many of the hazards as possible. The number of possible hazards is virtually endless – chemicals, badly maintained machines, frayed electrical cables, badly positioned heaters, and careless smokers are just a few, not to mention arson! What you have to do to meet the fire safety standards will depend on the building and the kind of work you do.

Under the Fire Precautions (Workplace) Regulations 1997 you need a fire certificate from your local fire authority if:

- ✔ Your premises are open to the public (such as a shop or restaurant)

- ✔ Your business occupies a building where more than one business operates

- ✔ You employ more than 20 people

- ✔ You employ more than 10 employees working below or above ground level

You should discuss your premises with the fire safety officer at your local fire station. You may need to make changes to your premises to bring them up to scratch. You should test alarms regularly and have fire drills at least twice a year to make sure that everyone knows what the fire alarms sound like, how to get out of the building as quickly as possible, and where to gather. New employees should get all that information as part of their induction when they first arrive.

Fire safety issues you have to consider are:

- ✔ Escape routes and a safe place for employees to gather if you have to evacuate the building

- ✔ Fire doors and walls

✔ Fire alarms

✔ Fire-fighting equipment

✔ Emergency lighting

✔ Safe places to store any flammable materials and chemicals

✔ Staff training and fire drills

Appoint one or more *fire marshals* to take charge in the event of a fire breaking out. The training of marshals is covered in the Fire Precautions (Workplace) Regulations 1997. Everyone should have instruction and training on what to do if there's a fire and how to get out of the building. Fire marshals make sure it happens smoothly, so they must have additional training to enable them to take the responsibility for marshalling the workers. Small fires may well be tackled with the fire-fighting equipment you have on the premises, but if the fire threatens to get out of control and endanger employees, someone has to make the decisions about when to evacuate the building and call the fire brigade as well as make sure that everyone gets out of the building. If you have several departments, make sure that each department has its own fire marshal. The more employees you have, the more fire marshals you need to jump into action when the fire alarms go off. If you have lifts in your premises make sure that you post notices warning people not to use them in the event of a fire.

Creating a Stress-Free Environment

Stress is a big problem even for small businesses, causing more lost working days now than even that old faithful the back problem (but then again, a fair proportion of back problems are probably really stress). So the multimillion-dollar question – sometimes quite literally – is: Is stress a problem in your workplace? Many small business owners think that just because they have few employees stress can never be an issue; others think that because they have few staff they all just have to accept that stress is part of keeping the show on the road. Don't ignore stress or your business will suffer.

 Talk to your staff (individually, in groups, or via a questionnaire) to find out about stress levels in your workplace. Make sure they know that any information they give you will be kept confidential and that they are not at risk of losing their jobs. Ask them about:

✔ Working hours – whether they can do their jobs in normal working hours and if they get home on time

✔ The kind of work they're doing – whether they enjoy it or it's merely a means to pay the bills

> ✔ What they expect to get out of their work – development, training, promotion
>
> ✔ What's best and worst about their jobs
>
> ✔ How they get on with bosses and colleagues
>
> ✔ How they feel about the amount of information you give them and how well you listen to them
>
> ✔ If they'd change anything in their physical environment

You may not like all the answers, but the information you get is useful in helping you think about changes you can make to avoid stress building up and in recognising where future problems may lie. You can't just sack someone for being stressed (see Chapter 4 on Unfair Dismissal) and you have a legal duty to look after their welfare (see chapter 10).

You may prefer to keep your door shut and your head below the parapet, but discussions with employees can give you clues about possible problems and how to prevent them; employees' ideas can be invaluable.

Stress usually builds up because the workload is too heavy to fit into the hours and so work accumulates, or the employee works too long in order that it doesn't; or due to clashes between colleagues or employee and boss, which can sometimes amount to harassment or bullying. Signs when someone's stressed include:

> ✔ Tiredness, grumpiness, and having less of a sense of humour than usual
>
> ✔ Work not being up to scratch, failing to make decisions, and making mistakes
>
> ✔ Headaches, back problems, stiff neck, or other pains and stomach problems
>
> ✔ Sleeping badly and taking time off sick
>
> ✔ Arriving late, staying late and taking work home
>
> ✔ Having disagreements with colleagues

A high turnover of staff is another sign of stress in the workplace.

A stress-free working environment is one that benefits from employees who take fewer days off sick, are more productive, have fewer drink- and drug-related problems, and better morale. Preventing stress in the first place is the holy grail and is more effective than having to cure it. After you put some measures in place to relieve stress, you may find that you are happier to go to work in the morning too.

Beating stress

If you've identified stress in the workplace, you have to tackle it and if possible eradicate it. You can't ignore stress, because you have a duty of care to your employees to look after their health and welfare.

Make sure that employees are in the right jobs and know exactly what those jobs are. Sometimes they are doing jobs they aren't fully trained to do and a bit of additional training can make all the difference.

Often people are not passing on work to the people they can delegate to. If they are simply overworked, take steps to reduce the workload – sharing it with other people who are under less pressure; giving employees time-management training; or even employing an extra person.

If you can give employees leeway to determine their own work schedules, that choice can help stress levels, especially if employees can work flexibly around their family obligations. Encourage a better work–life balance by making sure that people don't work later than they should and that they take all their holiday entitlement. Make sure that they know that you are sympathetic if they have family problems and need time off at short notice.

Employees worry less if they know what's going on and what your business plans are, so tell them about any changes you're thinking of making. They will also appreciate knowing that they can talk to you about problems and ideas. Reviews of their work, feedback on it, and appraisals are all good opportunities to talk.

If the problem appears to be bigger than you can handle, think about some training for the employee such as time management, assertiveness, communications skills, anger management, or even relaxation, yoga, or keep-fit classes. Counselling can help, especially if stress has resulted in, or exacerbated, alcohol or drug problems, or if outside influences such as family, relationship, money, or bereavement problems are causing the stress.

Watching your own stress level

Are you the one who's stressed and allowing it to affect the rest of the workforce? Ask yourself all the questions you ask your employees and check yourself out for all those same symptoms. Bosses who run small businesses are often quite isolated. Maybe you don't have a management team to discuss business decisions with and are always the one employees look to for direction and guidance. You owe it to them to look after your own health.

Balancing work with the rest of life

Work isn't the be-all and end-all of most people's lives. If things are going wrong in the rest of their lives, your employees may be more prone to health problems than usual. It's often very hard to tell if it's work or life that's causing a health problem.

Employees may have family, relationship, or money worries, be under pressure because of divorce or moving house, or be dealing with the death of someone close. That in itself may not be enough to make an employee ill, but it can be enough to make their work suffer or lead to accidents at work, which in turn can add to the stress and push them into ill health.

The more you know about employees' problems outside work, the better you can deal with out-of-work stress affecting performance, but remember to avoid being intrusive. Offer a sympathetic ear to problems and time off to deal with them. Work out flexible working patterns that may take the pressure off, at least temporarily. That can involve coming in and going home at different times for a while, doing some work from home, or perhaps going part-time. Take care of your employees and they'll take care of your business and your customers.

Think about joining an organisation that enables you to meet other business people; finding a coach or a mentor; or getting advice on specific problems from your local Business Link. Look in the telephone directory or at the Web site (www.businesslink.gov.uk). Maybe you can take some time out to get additional training that would make life easier for you. Your work–life balance and family life can suffer too.

Dealing with Bullying and Harassment

Bullying and harassment can be hard to get to the bottom of. Someone who is guilty of either is unlikely to own up and may sometimes not even be aware that her behaviour amounts to bullying or harassment, or that the employee on the receiving end perceives it that way. The employee may be too worried about her job to complain, especially if it's a superior who is meting out the treatment. The first you know of it may be when you notice signs of stress.

You should have a policy in place for dealing with bullying and harassment (see Chapter13). Those situations should be dealt with in your grievance and disciplinary procedures (see Chapter 15). People should know that you won't tolerate them in your workplace and that those being bullied or harassed can expect your sympathetic support, while those handing it out can expect to be disciplined and possibly even sacked.

If you have an open-door management approach where employees know they can talk to you in confidence about their problems, they will come to you. You have to investigate any claims fully before tackling the culprit and get the employee to keep a record of incidents as they occur. It's not an easy situation to deal with, but you have a legal obligation to look after the welfare of your employees so you can't shirk your duty.

Chapter 12

Accidents Do Happen

· ·

In This Chapter

▶ Facing the consequences of an accident at work

▶ Avoiding the most common accidents

▶ Cutting down the risks of accidents

▶ Protecting your employees from harm

· ·

*M*any owners and bosses of small businesses lament the cost of putting all the essential health and safety measures in place in their premises and take short cuts with their employees' safety, so accidents and even deaths do happen. But if you think health and safety is expensive, you should think about the costs of having an accident.

In 2003 – the last year for which we have figures from the Health and Safety Executive – 235 work-related deaths occurred. That was up 4 per cent from 2002. Half those deaths were in the construction and agricultural industries. And 30,666 major injuries were reported – up by 9 per cent on the year before. The fact that the figures are increasing is very worrying.

You have to have employer's liability insurance (see Chapter 10) in case someone gets killed or injured while working for you.

If you are sued and found to be at fault, the insurance policy pays out, but it may not cover all the claim or all your costs. It's likely that your insurer may want to review your risk assessment and put other safeguards in place before renewing your policy. Your premiums are likely to go up and some insurers may refuse future insurance.

But you pay in more ways than just financially. Big firms are increasingly doing business only with other firms that have a good safety record. They can't afford to be sued on the grounds that they were negligent in hiring a subcontractor with a poor safety record. An accident may cost you contracts and customers. The community in which you work will be angry that one of its members has been killed or injured and bad news travels fast. Your employees will be devastated at the loss of a colleague and morale will plummet. People then start re-evaluating their lives and looking for other jobs or employers where they can feel safer. They may lose trust in you as a good boss and probably suffer from stress, which leads to illness, days off, and lost production. It can take a long time to recover from an accident and rebuild a shattered reputation.

Avoiding Accidents

The majority of accidents are slips and trips. One third of all major injuries reported in 2003 were caused by slips and trips. Falls, falling objects, workplace transport, and machinery with moving parts are other potential dangers. The best way to avoid accidents is to create an environment where doing anything that may cause an accident is unacceptable and in which everyone is involved in the process of reducing risks.

The biggest weapon in your armoury is your risk assessment (refer to Chapter 10). After you've worked out where all the hazards are and taken all possible, reasonably practicable steps to get rid of them, you're left with the risks. You have to reduce or control these as far as possible and then, as a last resort where risk still exists, make sure that you protect employees from those risks with information, training, and protective equipment. Preventing an accident is a lot easier than dealing with the aftermath of one, which is why health and safety has to be a business priority and part of your business plan right from day one, rather than something that you add on later.

If you have more than five employees you have to write down your risk assessment findings and make sure that your employees know about them.

The other big weapon in your arsenal is your staff. Involve them in every aspect of your safety planning and risk assessment. They can help to identify hazards and ways to eliminate them. They can come up with ideas for controlling or cutting down the risks and can tell you what kind of safety equipment and protection they need. Employees can act as an early warning system as long as they are encouraged to talk to you about potential problems, and they'll look after each other better if they're fully informed and involved. Establish a safety culture in your workplace – train your staff to use the machinery, equipment, and safety gear properly, and to be continually aware of the hazards and risks. Set an example yourself and it will soon become second nature.

Slipping and tripping – the biggest bugbear!

Slips and trips don't sound too serious, but they're renowned among health and safety specialists. About a third of all serious accidents reported in the workplace are in this category and they cost the economy almost £800 million a year in lost productivity and days off sick. Make sure that they don't happen.

Be sure to assess the likelihood of slips and trips as part of your overall risk assessment. The things that are likely to pose hazards are uneven floors or floor coverings; things left lying around like rubbish or tools; spillages that make the floors slippery like oil, water, or food; or trailing cables without warning notices. I've even heard of someone being injured by tripping over a safety notice left in a silly place. And remember to check the outside of your premises too. If people are working away from your premises you can't do a lot, but make sure that they are always aware that there can be risks and that they're well trained for their jobs. Making safety part of your work culture means that employees will take the same approach when they're working elsewhere.

Having identified the hazards and assessed the risk that they will harm someone and who they're likely to harm, you have to set about reducing the risks by:

- ✔ Making sure that the premises are well lit and that potential danger spots have particularly good lights that are well positioned, always working and kept clean.

- ✔ Filling in any cracks in the floors.

- ✔ Nailing down any curling carpet and evening out any bumps.

- ✔ Stopping the floor getting wet and slippery – or at least fitting a non-slip floor covering or paying for special shoes for employees.

- ✔ Making it policy that any spillages have to be cleared up immediately.

- ✔ Putting up notices warning people of wet floors.

- ✔ Ensuring that everyone knows where the cleaning stuff is kept and whose job it is to use it.

- ✔ Ensuring that cables don't trail across where people are likely to walk and are stored properly when they're not being used.

If you've reduced the risks as far as possible but areas where people may slip or trip up and hurt themselves are still present, use plenty of warning notices and warning strips.

Lifting – a pain in the back

Lifting, carrying, pushing, or pulling – *manual handling* – is another big cause of injuries, lost working days, and compensation claims. Manual handling caused two thirds of all three-day injuries reported in 2003. There aren't many businesses which don't do some manual handling. Even in the offices someone has to shift all those boxes of photocopy paper from time to time. You must assess manual handling risks to your employees as part of your risk assessment. As with slips and trips, your staff can help with the assessment and working out how to get rid of or reduce the risks.

You have to provide equipment (such as trolleys or forklift trucks) that does away with the need for employees to do much of the lifting and carrying if it's *reasonably practicable*. A judge in court expects such equipment to be in place unless the cost of the equipment is so prohibitive that it would outweigh any of the benefits of having it.

Think about ordering deliveries in smaller boxes so they're lighter to handle. Organise your workplace so that materials that are delivered are stored next to the machine or areas where they're going to be used.

If you can't eliminate the need to lift and carry, then you have to provide training so that people know how to do it safely. They need to learn things like the right posture for lifting – to lift with knees and hips partly bent and then stand up, rather than squatting and standing up or bending over from the waist and lifting with the back. The HSE gives advice on training courses, and can be contacted through the Web site www.hse.gov.uk.

Using equipment safely

Under the *Provision and Use of Work Equipment Regulations* (PUWER) you have to make sure that your work equipment is safe and used safely. *Equipment* is machinery with moving parts (anything from welding tools and machine tools, photocopiers and printers, to vehicles like forklift trucks). The rules cover all types of businesses, from factories to shops and offices.

Equipment must be:

✔ Suitable for the job it's used for.

✔ Well maintained and clean.

✔ Inspected before it's first used and regularly after that.

If, when you do your risk assessment, you spot threats to employees' safety, you have to make sure that you minimise the risks. If any chance exists that someone may have a hand or even a finger cut off in a machine, you have to make sure that you fit protective guards and rails. Machines with moving parts should have emergency stop buttons. Employees should be given training before they use the equipment and then retraining or refresher courses as needed. You may need to offer special courses for specific bits of equipment. They need instructions for use, and you need to put up warning notices if necessary on or near the equipment.

Vibrations

Hand-held tools are the most likely equipment to cause vibrations. People who use them regularly can get what's known as *hand–arm vibration syndrome*. This syndrome can cause pain and loss of feeling in the fingers and arms. A less severe condition is *vibration white finger*, where the fingers go white and lose feeling. All sorts of tools can be responsible, from the big power drills used to cut up pavements to chain saws and lawnmowers. Keep the use of these tools to an absolute minimum and make sure that employees don't use these tools for long periods of time and that they take breaks. If possible, have a team of people working on jobs where hand-held tools are used so they can swap roles.

Driving forklift trucks and other transport

Whether your business is transport or you just use some forms of transport around your workplace, vehicles and people can be a lethal combination. Not only do dangers arise from vehicles moving around, but risks are also involved in loading and unloading materials from vehicles and with vehicles like forklift trucks.

Your risk assessment should look at:

✔ Keeping pedestrians and vehicles not involved in loading or unloading away from loading areas.

✔ Making sure any vehicle onto which things are loaded is stable and never overloaded.

✔ Separating vehicles from other equipment that may be damaged by vehicles, possibly with guard rails.

✔ Considering what would happen if a vehicle overturned or the brakes weren't on properly.

✔ Determining where vehicles reverse and park.

One of the main causes of injury is reversing trucks. A quarter of all workplace deaths involve a reversing vehicle. Try as far as possible to keep employees, apart from those involved in the operation of the vehicles, away from any area where these turn, park, or reverse. Vehicles should have appropriate mirrors and warning alarms to alert people that they are reversing and they shouldn't reverse where there are blind spots. If people do have to use an area that vehicles also use, mark off routes that the people on foot should use to separate them as far as possible from moving vehicles, and where the pedestrian routes cross traffic routes put up warning signs. People falling, literally, off the back of a lorry constitute another common cause of injuries. If you provide a loading platform that risk is almost eliminated.

Exhaust emissions come under hazardous substances (see Chapter 11). They can cause health problems, but they can also kill. You have to stop people being exposed to them as far as possible. That may mean fitting extractor fans in areas where lorries come and go and where fumes can build up, insisting that engines are turned off when the vehicle isn't moving, and making sure that all vehicles are regularly serviced to keep exhaust emissions as low as possible. In enclosed or small spaces you must use electric vehicles or ones that operate on liquid petroleum gas so that fumes don't build up.

Forklift trucks are notoriously unstable if they aren't loaded carefully and they can turn over. One in five deaths is caused by an overturning vehicle. Legally most vehicles have to be fitted with a roll-over protection system, but drivers have to be properly trained and you must make sure that they use the vehicles safely and don't drive them unsafely or in dangerous conditions. Keep all the routes they are likely to use clear of any obstructions.

Using protective clothing

In some businesses no amount of risk assessing, risk managing, process planning, or training can reduce all the risks to zero and so employees will need protection. The *Personal Protective Equipment Regulations 1992* (PPE) say that workers must use protective equipment if their health and safety can't otherwise be adequately protected. Because the effectiveness of protective equipment depends on people using it properly, it should be employed as a last resort.

Think about whether your employees need protection for the head, eyes, ears, body, arms and hands, feet, or a combination. Keep records of all the protective equipment you've got and of checks, repairs, and replacements. Make sure that employees know that the law says they have to tell you if any equipment is lost or damaged.

If you don't comply with the Personal Protective Equipment Regulations you can be fined up to £5,000 in the Magistrates Court or much more in the Crown Court. Protect yourself by protecting your employees!

The regulations about protective equipment don't apply to:

- ✔ The crews and masters of sea-going ships

- ✔ Ordinary work clothes and uniforms that don't protect the health and safety of employees

- ✔ Equipment used for playing competitive sports

- ✔ Portable devices for detecting risks (like those that detect electrical cables)

If your legal obligations to provide protective equipment are covered by other more specific regulations, the Personal Protective Equipment Regulations don't apply. Six other regulations also cover protective equipment for different types of work:

- ✔ The Construction (Head Protection) Regulations 1989

- ✔ The Noise at Work Regulations 1989

- ✔ The Control of Lead at Work Regulations 2002

- ✔ The Control of Asbestos at Work Regulations 2002

- ✔ The Control of Substances Hazardous to Health Regulations (COSHH) 2002

- ✔ The Ionizing Radiations Regulations 1999

The Health and Safety Executive can give you all the information you need about these regulations, and you should check your legal obligations with them.

Where the PPE regulations do apply you have to provide your employees with personal protective equipment where necessary. You have to pay for it and make sure that people know how to use it correctly. A whole range of protective clothes is available, from steel-toed boots and hard hats to heat-resistant gloves and aprons, overalls, and reflective suits. And items of protective equipment like earplugs, goggles, safety harnesses, masks, and respirators may also be required.

You need to be sure that separate protective items can be used together without interfering with the effectiveness of any one of them and you have to make sure that the equipment meets the set standards. Protective clothing and devices have to be:

- ✔ Suitable for the risks and workplace conditions
- ✔ Suitable for the employee and fit correctly
- ✔ CE marked if bought after 1995 (showing that it meets key health and safety standards)

Working with electricity

All businesses use electricity and most of us tend to take it somewhat for granted – which can cause accidents. For example, water and electricity don't mix, and a frayed cable is a real danger.

When doing a workplace risk assessment:

- ✔ Check that the cables are all in good condition.
- ✔ Separate electricity and water as far as possible.
- ✔ Re-route cables that run across floors where someone may trip over them.

Work areas where water and electricity can't be separated, such as hairdressing salons, need careful planning to avoid water being spilled where hairdryers are used and to avoid hairdryers coming anywhere near wash-basins. You should clean up spillages immediately and set up an area for wash-basins well away from electrical equipment.

Reporting Accidents

Some workplace incidents have to be reported under the *Reporting of Injuries, Diseases and Dangerous Occurrences Regulations 1995* (RIDDOR). You can either report direct to the Health and Safety Executive (HSE) or your local authority – whichever enforcing authority you have registered your business with (see Chapter 10) – or you can report to the Incident Contact Centre by phone 08453-009923, fax 08453-009924, post to Incident Contact Centre, Caerphilly Business Park, Caerphilly CF83 3GG, or e-mail to riddor@natbrit.com.

The following accidents must be reported under RIDDOR if they involve any of your employees:

✔ Death as a result of an accident related to work

✔ Major injury, such as fractures, amputations, loss of sight, or consciousness

✔ Dangerous occurrences – incidents that didn't cause injury but certainly could have; this may be an explosion, something falling, a building or crane collapsing, or a fire, for example

✔ An injury that keeps someone off work or unable to do their job for more than three days, known as a *three-day injury*

✔ Reportable diseases. If an employee goes to the GP the GP has to let you know if he has one of these diseases. Reportable diseases include:

- Poisoning

- Skin diseases such as occupational dermatitis or skin cancer

- Lung diseases such as occupational asthma or pneumoconiosis

- Infections such as hepatitis, TB, anthrax, or Legionnaire's disease

- Conditions such as occupational cancer or hand–arm vibration syndrome

If a self-employed person (rather than one of your employees) has been injured while working for you, you must report the incident if it's a death, major injury, or three-day injury.

In the case of a death or major injury to someone working on your premises, you have to report it immediately by phone and fill in and send in accident form F2508 within ten days. You can find the forms on the HSE Web site, www.hse.gov.uk. You have to report dangerous occurrences without delay and again follow that up by a completed F2508 within ten days. A three-day injury only has to be reported within ten days of it occurring, again using the F2508 form. If a doctor tells you that one of your employees has a reportable disease, you have report it on form F2508A without delay, to the same enforcing authority.

Keeping the Accident Book

The RIDDOR regulations say that you have to keep a record of injuries, diseases, or dangerous occurrences, and that you have to keep this record on your premises for at least three years. It can be kept in an accident book, on forms in a file, or on your computer. If the enforcing authority – the HSE or the local authority with which you've registered your business – asks to see the records, you have to produce them.

Safety representatives appointed in your workplace (refer to Chapter 10) or the safety committee members, if there is a committee, have the right to see the records, but can't see anything relating specifically to individuals unless those individuals have given their consent. The information in the records must include:

- The date and time of the accident
- Details of the injured person – name and occupation if an employee, or customer or contractor details
- Details of the injury
- Where and how it happened
- The date you reported it to the authorities and how you reported it

If your premises are a factory or you employ ten or more people, you have to provide an accident book for them to write in details of accidents that caused injuries. You can purchase an HSE-approved accident book – known as BI510 – through the HSE Web site, www.hse.gov.uk, or go direct to HSE books, PO Box 1999, Sudbury, Suffolk CO10 2WA.

Learning from Near Misses

The temptation with dangerous occurrences that don't lead to injuries and with smaller accidents where no one's hurt is to dismiss them. That was a near miss! But you can learn a lot about your business operation, risk assessment, and risk management from near misses. Carry out a full investigation, just as you would for a death or major injury. You may discover that equipment is inherently unsafe, badly maintained, or in need of repair or replacement. You may find that you haven't done all you can to separate people from risks from traffic or machinery. You may come to the conclusion that some employees are doing jobs they aren't fully qualified for, or that they need training. Maybe you have upgraded machines or equipment but not provided enough retraining.

You may discover that your risk assessment hasn't been reviewed and updated often enough or your risk management has become complacent and slipshod. You can't afford to have many accidents in your workplace, so you can't afford to ignore all the clues and indications a near miss can give you.

Investigating the Causes

With any incident – no matter how trivial it seems – investigate it fully. It's no good having all the safety procedures in place and then employees seeing you shrug incidents off as unimportant. Talk to everyone involved or who might have witnessed what happened. Check out any machinery or equipment involved. Get an expert in to check it over if necessary. Be sure that there can't be a repeat occurrence. Do a review of your risk assessment and make any changes you think are necessary. If the incident is more major you may have to report it, and the Health and Safety Executive may also have to carry out an investigation. The Infoline will give advice on any aspect of health and safety – 0845-3450055 – and the HSE Web site www.riddor.gov.uk gives help with reporting accidents.

Calling In the Health and Safety Executive

If a death occurs in your workplace, the Health and Safety Executive (HSE) will investigate. As with other situations you have to report (see 'Reporting Accidents', earlier in this chapter), the HSE may well visit your premises, depending on what's happened. The HSE uses most of the resources it has available for investigations for the most serious cases. When deciding what incidents to investigate, it considers:

- ✔ The severity and scale of the situation.

- ✔ How serious any potential breach of the law may be.

- ✔ Your past health and safety record.

- ✔ Its own enforcement priorities.

- ✔ What results it's likely to achieve by investigating.

- ✔ How relevant the incident is to the wider community and whether it's of serious public concern.

The investigation works out the causes of the accident, whether action needs to be taken to prevent the same thing happening again or to make sure that you are complying with the law, what lessons can be learned, and what should be done if you've broken the law.

Getting Advice

From setting up your business until the day you sell it or wind it up, your enforcing body – the HSE or your local authority – will help you keep a good safety record. It can give you information on everything from risk assessments to the right organisations to turn to for training courses. The HSE Web site (www.hse.gov.uk) is packed with information and the HSE Infoline is a very valuable source of help – 0845-3450055.

HSE inspectors would really rather not be inspecting your premises to investigate a death or a dangerous incident and they don't want to prosecute you. They'd much rather help you to prevent accidents, so use them as a source of information and advice.

Part IV
Respecting and Consulting Staff

"Why can't people in this company write a letter of resignation like they do in other companies?"

In this part . . .

I look at the steps you have to take to keep personal information about your employees secure and the ins and outs of monitoring telephone, e-mail, and Internet use at work. Employees have the right to expect some privacy at work, and they also have the right not to be discriminated against when applying for jobs – or after they leave – as well as while they're in your employment.

However good an employer you are, a chance always exists that disputes will crop up from time to time and that employees will have complaints. We look at the necessity for a good policy for dealing with disciplinary matters and grievances and at the consequences for you if disputes turn into claims against you.

Chapter 13

Saying No to Discrimination

· ·

In This Chapter

▶ Turning to help with these complicated laws

▶ Understanding what discrimination is

▶ Knowing who the discrimination laws protect

▶ Preparing for new regulations coming up for older workers

· ·

*A*s an employer you have a duty not to discriminate against an employee on the grounds of race, sex, sexual orientation, disability, religious or other beliefs, and by the end of 2006 age discrimination laws will be in force too.

Some of the governing legislation has been on the statute books for over 30 years, but we're still seeing reports of men being paid more than women for the same jobs, and black people being treated less fairly than white people.

The best way to avoid discrimination in your workplace is to have an Equal Opportunities Policy in place so everyone knows that you don't tolerate such behaviour. One of the first things an Employment Tribunal will ask to see in any claim for discrimination is your Equal Opportunities Policy, so it is very important to have one. ACAS – the Advisory, Conciliation and Arbitration Service – can give advice on the drawing up of policies. Contact ACAS through the Web site www.acas.org.uk or through Equality Direct at ACAS (0845-6003444). The Equal Opportunities Commission, the Commission for Racial Equality and the Disability Rights Commission can also help employers and all their contact numbers are given in the relevant sections later in this chapter.

If an employee does take you to a tribunal for discrimination at any stage of her employment, from recruitment through to dismissal, be warned that no limit exists on the amount the tribunal can award in compensation. You can face a very big bill indeed, so it's worth taking time to understand what discrimination means and how you can get on the wrong side of the law.

Discrimination cases are being brought and being decided on regularly and those cases are important in clarifying the law. That means that the law is forever changing, so if someone does take a case against you, you need to get good advice from a lawyer who specialises in discrimination.

Clarifying Your Position – Getting Advice

Discrimination is a very complicated area of law. If you're facing a claim or, better still, if you want to get it right from the outset and avoid the possibility of a claim, get advice.

Have a look at the Access to Work programme on the Job Centre Plus Web site (www.jobcentreplus.gov.uk), or talk to the Disability Employment Adviser at your local Jobcentre about employing people with disabilities. The Disability Rights Commission Helpline on 0845-7622633 can also assist. ACAS is always helpful and its Equality Direct Helpline number is 0845-6003444. The Women and Equality Unit Web site (www.womenand equality.gov.uk) can help on equal pay; the Equal Opportunities Commission (www.eoc.org.uk) and the Commission for Racial Equality (www.cre.gov.uk) may also be able to offer advice.

The big three commissions – Equal Opportunities, Racial Equality, and Disability Rights – are to become one: The Commission for Equality and Human Rights. The government has not yet decided when the change will happen, but this may be around the end of 2006.

Understanding Discrimination

Some forms of discrimination are quite easy to understand. Others are more difficult to explain. In theory the principles behind the different pieces of legislation are fairly straightforward, but in practice the law is extremely complicated. The law says that employees have the right not to be discriminated against at work, but discrimination itself can take different forms. While some forms are easy to recognise, some are a lot harder to pin down.

It's your duty as an employer to make sure that no-one – manager or worker – is guilty of discrimination and to protect your employees from that kind of behaviour by their colleagues. If you don't, you can have a discrimination case taken against you even though members of your team are discriminating and not you.

If a person takes a discrimination case against you, your motives for discriminating won't come into the decision at tribunal. If the tribunal members find that you made the decision on the grounds of race, sex, disability, religion, or sexuality, you'll be guilty of unlawful discrimination. By the end of 2006 the same will apply to decisions made on the grounds of age. You also have to take care not to discriminate against people who no longer work for you by giving them less favourable references on any of the above grounds. Anyone can bring a claim against you if they think you're guilty of discrimination, regardless of how long they've worked for you.

Discriminating directly

If you treat one employee less favourably than you treat another, you're guilty of direct discrimination. You may think that you have the very best of motives for turning down someone for a job on the grounds of sex, race, religion, disability, or sexuality. You may believe that the person wouldn't get on with the rest of your team or that your customers would not be comfortable with him, but that's no defence.

Direct discrimination may be because of:

- ✔ Sex
- ✔ Race
- ✔ Sexual orientation
- ✔ Disability
- ✔ Religious or other beliefs

Discrimination can occur in many different decisions regarding employees. For example, if you offer training to a man but don't offer it to a woman who does the same job and has the same experience and qualifications because she may leave to have a baby, that's a clear-cut case of sex discrimination (because only women can have babies and by refusing them training you are treating them less favourably on the grounds of sex). If a man and a woman both apply for a promotion and there's only one job available, you have to give it to the person who is best qualified, experienced, and suited to the post. If that's the man then that's not discrimination, but it would be direct sex discrimination if he got the promotion although the woman was better qualified, experienced, or suited to the post. The same principles apply to the other categories. For example, if a gay man applies for a job but is told it's gone and someone else later applies and gets it, that's direct discrimination on the grounds of sexual orientation.

Discriminating indirectly

Indirect discrimination is much harder to recognise and you may be doing it without realising it. If you put an ad in the paper for a new employee and you set out a requirement that isn't vital to the job, but that excludes whole chunks of the population, that is indirect discrimination whether you intended to discriminate or not.

For example, if you have a job in a factory and you advertise for someone who can speak good English, that may rule out all sorts of would-be applicants whose first language isn't English. If the job involves the employee giving instructions to other workers in the factory and the common language is English, then you can justify asking for good English skills, but if it isn't needed for the job you're likely to be indirectly discriminating.

Discriminating positively

In the UK *positive discrimination*, where you decide you will only hire a minority ethnic group, or only hire women, isn't legal but positive action is. You can set targets so that you balance up your workforce. For example, if historically only men have been hired and you want a better balance of men and women, you can take positive action to reach your targets. The same goes for all the other categories of discrimination.

Victimisation

If someone complains about being discriminated against and you then treat them less favourably as a result, that's *victimisation*. For example, suppose a black employee is claiming against you in a discrimination case after a less well-qualified white man was promoted over her head. If you sack her, demote her, or transfer her, you're likely to be guilty of victimising her (regardless of the outcome of the original discrimination claim).

Tribunals view victimisation as a form of discrimination so the penalties are the same. For example, if you refuse a reference after an employee's left because the employee has taken a discrimination claim against you, that's victimisation . . . and therefore discrimination.

Harassing behaviour

Harassment is anything that violates a person's dignity or creates an intimidating, hostile, degrading, humiliating, or offensive environment for an employee. That includes racist jokes, language, or graffiti, or employees being picked on or ostracised by other employees because of their ethnic origins or colour. The same goes for disability, beliefs, and sexual orientation.

Race discrimination laws specifically mention harassment and make racial harassment illegal. So do disability discrimination laws and the laws on sexual orientation and religious or other beliefs. Sex discrimination laws don't specifically mention harassment, but the number of cases of sexual harassment that employees have brought through the courts and won is legion. *Sexual harassment* is the kind of offensive behaviour that makes employees feel humiliated and intimidated, such as inappropriate remarks, jokes, or touching. It can happen to men as well as women.

You have a duty to protect your employees. Harassment is bad for business. It affects not only the individual concerned but also other employees who see it happening whose morale is likely to be affected and whose productivity and performance will suffer. Employees who dislike the harassment they see around them lose confidence and respect for you because you aren't doing anything about it. They feel that they may be next and that they have no protection. Such concerns lead to stress, which leads to more days off sick.

The best way to deal with harassment is to have a policy in place so everyone knows that you don't tolerate it in your workplace; Chapter 15 discusses this policy. Apart from taking a case against you for discrimination, employees can claim that you didn't provide a safe and healthy working environment (see Chapter 10) or that they were unfairly constructively dismissed (see Chapter 4) because they had no choice but to quit.

Hiring and Firing without Discriminating

Discrimination isn't just something to be aware of with current employees. It can creep in before you've even hired someone and it can play a big part in the decision to get rid of someone through redundancy. Just as discrimination at work is against the law, so is discrimination before and after employment.

Job ads, application forms, and the selection process offer opportunities to discriminate unintentionally. Most employers realise that they can't get away with advertising that specifically requests applicants of a particular race or sex. But if you say that you want someone young, energetic, and English-speaking you're ruling out older people, some would-be applicants with disabilities, and those whose English isn't very good. If you say you're looking for someone with a minimum of 10 years' experience, you're ruling out younger people. Look very carefully at what the job is and what skills, qualifications, and abilities someone would need in order to do it and stick to those. Not only will that keep you on the right side of the law, but you've got more chance of getting the best employee.

You must not suggest in job ads that any particular section of the community is not welcome to apply or that you won't make reasonable adjustments for people with disabilities.

You can be taken to an Employment Tribunal by someone who believes you turned him down for a job because you were discriminating against him. Make sure to stick to job-related questions in application forms and interviews. You shouldn't ask for information about sexual orientation, religious or other beliefs, and don't ask about whether someone is married and intends to have children. It doesn't make any difference if they're married and as women are the ones who have the children you can be seen to have turned them down on that basis, which is sexual discrimination. Make sure that you ask everyone at interview the same questions and that any questions you ask about a person's disability are absolutely necessary from the point of view of knowing how you may make reasonable adjustments so he can do the job.

When firing employees you have to go through the correct dismissal procedures (flick back to Chapter 4 for more details). You need a fair reason for giving someone the boot and you must do it in a fair way. If you fire someone or, more usually, select someone to be made redundant because of their race, sex, or sexual orientation, because they're pregnant or have had a baby, because they're disabled, you don't like their religion or beliefs, or they join or refuse to join a trade union, that is unfair and you can be taken to an Employment Tribunal on the grounds of unfair dismissal or discrimination.

Recognising Discrimination in All Its Guises

Discrimination legislation has generally come about because certain groups of people have been discriminated against historically, and those groups have required protection from different kinds of discriminating workplace practices. This section explains in more detail the kinds of discrimination that the law specifically protects against.

Gender

Sex discrimination can be direct or indirect. If you sack an employee, select her for redundancy, turn her down for a job, or refuse her a promotion for which she is the best qualified on the grounds of her sex, that's clearly discrimination. But the same applies if you do any of those things because she's pregnant, has had a baby, is a mother, asks for maternity leave and pay, or asks for parental leave in the first five years of the child's life (see Chapter 7). Sexual harassment isn't specifically mentioned in the sex discrimination laws (but see the section on 'Harassing behaviour').

Sex discrimination cases apply to both women and men. Refusing to consider requests for parental leave by men can be seen as discriminatory if you are sympathetic to requests from women. Discriminating on the grounds of gender reassignment is also ruled out under the sex discrimination laws.

Race

You're breaking the law if you discriminate against someone on the grounds of race, colour, nationality, or ethnic origins. If you're an English employer and you refuse to take someone on just because they are Scottish, Welsh or Irish (or Welsh refusing to employ a Scot etc.) that can get you into just as much trouble as refusing to employ someone just because they are African, Caribbean or Asian. This goes for harassment, too.

Disability

You can't discriminate against someone on the grounds of their disability unless you can fully justify your actions. The Disability Discrimination Act 1995 (the DDA) has been coming in, in bits and pieces, since1995. All small businesses now have to comply with the DDA.

The *Disability Discrimination Act 1995* applies to people with a physical or mental impairment or medical condition that has substantial and long-term effects (lasting 12 months or more) on their ability to carry out day-to-day duties. These may be to do with mobility, manual dexterity, ability to lift objects, eyesight, hearing, speech, memory, ability to concentrate or learn, or awareness of danger. The DDA covers mental illnesses such as schizophrenia or manic depression. It doesn't apply to people who, for example, are misusing drugs or alcohol, or who are abusive. From December 2005 the protection of the act will be extended to people with cancer and HIV, and other mental illnesses such as stress and depression. The disability Rights Commission will be able to advise you on the changes.

You must not treat a person with a disability any less favourably than any other employee. You can't refuse her an interview or turn her down for a job because she has a disability. You have to give her the same opportunities to have training or get a promotion as anyone else. Harassment on the grounds of disability is against the law.

You have to make reasonable adjustments to enable a disabled person to work for you or to go on working for you if she became disabled while she is your employee. Most reasonable adjustments won't mean big costs for your business. They can include providing an induction loop for someone who has a hearing impairment to allow them to go on using the telephone, or moving someone who uses a wheelchair to a ground-floor office. You are expected to make those reasonable adjustments to remove the barriers that put a disabled person at a disadvantage. Altering your premises or changing to more flexible working hours, providing extra training, or even just allowing a person with a disability a parking space nearer to the front door may be enough. If the adjustment that's needed is just too expensive or impractical, you may be able to justify refusing. Nevertheless, don't forget that an employee can bring a discrimination claim against you under the DDA even though you are employing her, and no limit exists on the amount of compensation a tribunal can award her.

Sexual orientation

Discrimination against an employee or someone applying for a job on the grounds of sexual orientation became unlawful in December 2003. The Employment Equality (Sexual Orientation) Regulations apply to discrimination against lesbian, gay, heterosexual, and bisexual people. As with the other forms of discrimination I've mentioned, it can be direct or indirect and includes harassment and victimisation.

The rules cover discrimination on the grounds of perceived as well as actual sexual orientation. So, for example, if you don't appoint someone because you thought she was lesbian, whether she actually was or not, that is discrimination.

Religion or belief

The Employment Equality (Religion or Belief) Regulations also came into force in December 2003. They apply to discrimination on the grounds of religion, religious belief, or other philosophical belief. As with sexual orientation, discrimination applies to perceived as well as actual religion or belief. If you treat someone unfairly because you think they are of a particular religion, whether they are or not doesn't matter. It's still discrimination. If you run a seven day a week operation and employ people whose religion doesn't let them work on a Sunday you must make arrangements so that they do not have to work on Sundays. You must also allow people of other religions to have a day off that fits in with their religious faith. Orthodox Jews, for example, will need to be away from the workplace from sundown on Fridays until sundown on Saturdays. If you don't take this into account, you can be accused of discrimination.

Union membership

You can't refuse someone a job or sack her if she joins a trade union or refuses to join one. And you can't treat her unfairly for carrying out her trade union activities at an appropriate time. That may be in breaks and lunch hours or at times you've agreed. There are instances when you have to give people time off for union work (refer to Chapter 6). Industrial action such as striking doesn't count.

Paying Fair

Apart from the laws covering discrimination, you need to take into account the *Equal Pay Act* (providing equal pay between men and women). This Act covers everyone who works for you whether they're part-time or full-time, temporary or permanent, working on your premises or at home. Even apprentices are covered. A woman is entitled to be paid the same as a man who is:

- ✔ Doing *like work* (meaning work that's the same or more or less similar)
- ✔ Doing work that is rated equivalent under a job evaluation survey
- ✔ Doing work of equal value

Employees have to bring equal pay cases while they're still working for you or within six months of the end of their employment. Be aware that many employees with unfair pay cases don't act until after they've left in case it makes their lives more difficult.

Knowing it's hard for an employee to bring a case against you is no reason not to pay equal pay for equal work. Successful cases have been brought. Although the law was brought in to protect women workers it can work for men too, and anyone else who feels they're being discriminated against by being paid less.

Remembering the Part-Timers

Anti-discrimination legislation applies to part-timers (and anyone on a fixed-term contract) just as it does to full-timers. No definition exists of what is part-time. It's just something less than your full-time working hours. Everyone, whether they are employees or anyone else working for you part-time as well as full-time, is entitled not to be treated unfairly.

The Sex Discrimination Act 1975 and the Equal Pay Act 1970 don't mention part-time workers, but most part-time workers are women and so discrimination against part-timers can be indirect sex discrimination (see the section 'Discriminating indirectly'). You may be imposing a condition or requirement that affects more women than men. If you don't allow part-time workers any additional contractual sick pay (see Chapter 18) on top of their Statutory Sick Pay, for example, but you do give it to full-time employees and most of your part-time people are women, that may be discrimination. If you exclude part-time workers from the pay-related benefits such as private medical insurance or bonus schemes that full-timers are entitled to, or pay them lower hourly rates, that can be discrimination.

Coming Up – New Laws on Age Discrimination

New laws on Age Discrimination should come into force by October 2006. Estimates as to how much age discrimination costs the UK economy vary – anything from £16 billion to £31 billion depending on which surveys you believe. But even at the lower end of the scale that's a huge amount of money going down the UK PLC plughole, all because employers don't take on older workers or are keen to let them go early – sometimes as early as 45.

No details of the Act are available yet, but it will generally make it unlawful to treat employees unfairly on the grounds of age. It will give older workers the same protection as everyone else in the workforce. For example, at the moment people 65 and over aren't entitled to redundancy payments. The government has said that may change. It may also become unfair to dismiss someone over 65 in the same way that it can be unfair to dismiss younger people.

Existing codes of practice

A *Code of Practice on Age Discrimination* already exists, set out by the Department for Work and Pensions. What it basically says is that employers should do everything in their power to make sure that age isn't a factor and that they don't put up any barriers to employees because of their age – younger or older. More and more employers are signing up to it. Many have realised that they simply can't afford to let good people go. Not only do they take their skills, qualifications, and training with them – much of which the employer has paid for over the years – but they take away a lot of knowledge about how the company is run. That kind of experienced know-how may not be recorded in any job procedures and can't be easily handed on to a new employee. You can read a copy of the code by going to www.agepositive.gov.uk and reading a leaflet called *Being Positive About Age Diversity at Work – a Practical Guide for Business*. You can also get copies by calling 0845-7330360.

The code of practice covers:

- ✔ **Recruitment.** You need to recruit on the grounds of skills, ability, and potential, so you don't advertise jobs with age limits in them. You need to advertise in all sorts of places, not just in the press that younger people typically read. Don't ask for qualifications that older people are unlikely to have. If you ask for a GCSE in English, for example, you're ruling out people who sat their exams before GCSEs were introduced. It's easy to unintentionally rule out a whole age group through something in an ad and then wonder why so few people have applied.

- ✔ **Selection.** Some employers use application forms from which they can remove all the personal detail such as age and age-related information. What they are left with to make their selection from is details of skills and ability. Always ask job-related questions in interviews. By selecting people on those grounds you're less likely to miss out on good people simply because of age.

- ✔ **Promotion.** Select on ability, skills and potential rather than age. Make sure the opportunities for promotion are open to all your staff; that interviewers ask only job-related questions and don't make decisions based on their prejudices and stereotypes, and if possible make sure there are people of different ages on the interview panel.

✔ **Training and development.** Give all your employees the same chances for training and development. If you don't offer training you won't have an up-to-date workforce. More importantly, don't look on training of older workers as a waste of time and money – they can learn new tricks. Talk to people about how they like to learn. Some won't like the idea of going back into a classroom-type situation, but would be willing to take a course online. Others may prefer it to learning from books on their own.

✔ **Redundancy.** When it comes to making people redundant, don't go for a selection process that gets rid of people just because they are older and costing you more, or younger and less experienced. You may be losing many of the skills that are most essential to your business. It is very important to be fair when selecting who should be made redundant. See Chapter 5.

✔ **Retirement.** Some bosses have dropped retirement ages and encourage people to work as long as they choose. The government certainly wants to encourage us all to work longer. When you're thinking about your own policy on retirement, you need to think about your business as well as the needs of your individual employees. If someone knows they're going to have to retire at 60 whether they like it or not, they can end up simply sitting it out for the last few years and give very little of value to the company. If employees have the choice of when and how to retire, they usually feel more in control and more motivated.

Provide as much support to retiring employees as you can, perhaps getting outside organisations in to talk to them about pensions or other work they can do. The better you handle it the more work you'll get out of them for longer.

Preparing for the new laws

Although the new age discrimination legislation doesn't come in until 2006, there's no reason why you shouldn't get ahead of the game. Whatever the details, the principle will be more or less the same as the other pieces of legislation. You simply won't be able to treat employees unfairly on the grounds of age – any age, young or old. For many employers that will necessitate a whole shift in culture. Many have simply always got rid of older workers at the first opportunity, believing that they are more expensive and less energetic and enthusiastic than younger ones and therefore less productive. But increasingly bosses are realising that you can throw an awful lot of babies out with the bath water and that they've been getting rid of some very valuable people, leaving only the younger and less experienced ones.

If you have employees who are going to reach your retirement age before the legislation is in place, talk to them now about how they feel about retiring and whether they'd like to stay on longer.

You shouldn't put pressure on employees nearing retirement age to stay longer, but you should give them a choice. If they do want to stay on, discuss with them what would make the working relationship better and more profitable for both of you. What you ideally want is a mixed workforce where older and younger workers can learn from each other.

Chapter 14

Minding Your Own Business

*Y*ou have a right to know what's going on in your business. You can legally monitor your employees' phone calls, e-mails, and visits to the Internet under certain circumstances. You can even install CCTV cameras. You can act like 'Big Brother' – but before you do, think about the various laws that cover privacy at work and the effect your actions may have in your workplace. And remember that workers have the right to keep their personal lives to themselves and to expect some privacy at work.

Respecting Your Staff's Privacy

The problem for employers regarding staff privacy is that the relevant laws can conflict, so it's the cases that come to court that are gradually clarifying the situation. The laws influencing what you can and can't do are:

> ✔ **The Human Rights Act 1998,** giving people the right to privacy and respect for family life.

> ✔ **The Data Protection Act 1998,** protecting employees and giving them rights to see any data that you hold about them either electronically or on paper.

> ✔ **Lawful Business Practice Regulations,** giving you the right to read some communications without your employees' consent.

The best way to stay out of trouble is to have a policy in place telling everyone what types of communications you may monitor and why, and what is and isn't acceptable in terms of private use of phone, e-mail, or the Internet.

Protecting Data

Under *The Data Protection Act 1998* you have a legal responsibility to process personal information in a fair and proper way. If you don't, you can be guilty of a criminal offence. *Personal information* is any information about anybody who is still living who can be identified by that information – in this case staff records. It applies to customer data too.

The Data Protection Act requires you and everyone who works for you to handle all information about individuals properly and fairly. You can't pass on personal information to anyone who is not involved in whatever you collected it for. For example, if you collect personal information on application forms or CVs you can use it as part of your recruitment process, but you can't then pass it on to the receptionist without the consent of the person concerned. You can't pass it on to someone outside your business or use it for your own purposes that have nothing to do with your business. You have to use the information for the reason it was originally collected. Anyone who does disclose personal information outside your business without your consent, or the individual's consent, can be committing a criminal offence.

Collecting and holding information

You have to comply with the Data Protection Act, and following the Employment Practices Code (set out in Section 51 of the Act) helps you to do that. The code's aim is to strike a balance between the right of employees to have their personal details handled properly and your rights to run your business. It covers information you have about anyone who may work for you, currently works for you, or has worked for you in the past. You have to respect people's rights to have their personal details treated in confidence. Do not give such details to anyone else unless it's really necessary and you have the individual's consent, and always keep them securely so they don't fall into the wrong hands.

You can read more about the Data Protection Act on the Business Link Web site, www.businesslink.gov.uk or go direct to the Web site for the Office of the Information Commissioner, which enforces the act (www.informationcommissioner.gov.uk). There you'll find more about the act and the code. The Information Commissioner Helpline is the place to talk to someone about your responsibilities under the act – 01625-545745.

Although the code isn't compulsory in itself, it sets out best practice and by following it you'll know you're complying with the law. You may have other ways of meeting your legal requirements, but if you do nothing you risk breaking the law.

The Employment Practices Code of the Data Protection Act 1998 covers most information you collect and keep about your employees, such as:

✔ Completed application forms, CVs, and interview notes

✔ Salaries and bank account details

✔ Individual files

✔ Staff appraisals

✔ Any details about incidents involving named workers

✔ Supervisors' notebooks holding details of individuals' work abilities

The code doesn't cover information about the workforce as a whole where no details can be used to identify individuals. But it does include most work-related information about individuals who want to work for you, currently work for you, or have worked for you including employees, agency workers, casual staff, and people on contracts. Even volunteers and work experience people are covered by some parts of the code.

The code applies to information held on paper, in filing cabinets, on microfiche, and on a computer. And it applies to how you get the information, store it, use it, give access to it, disclose it to someone else, and eventually get rid of it.

Having a policy

You need to have processes in place for storing information securely. All employees should know who can have access to what information, and in what circumstances, and should have given their consent to this access. For instance, people who work for you should know that the person who deals with their salaries has their bank details but keeps those details in such a way that no one else can get hold of them without the employee's say-so. It doesn't engender confidence if all personal files with individual names on them are in an unlocked filing cabinet in the main office where anyone staying late at work can have a good search through them. Similarly, anyone applying for a job with you and filling in an application form should be able to be confident that that form won't fall into the hands of the people he may eventually be working with or anyone else outside the business without his permission.

Following the Employment Practices Code (outlined in the section 'Collecting and holding information') has business advantages apart from helping you stay on the right side of the law. If everyone knows that you handle personal information with care, trust will grow in your employment practices and the organisation as a whole. People are also more likely to treat everyone else's information with the same respect, including information about customers. Following the Employment Practices Code encourages good house-keeping where everything is kept securely and safely and you get rid of out-of-date material, making the rest easier to deal with.

Handling sensitive issues

You can't collect certain sensitive pieces of personal information about employees without very good reason. These include:

- ✔ Racial or ethnic origin
- ✔ Political opinions
- ✔ Religious beliefs
- ✔ Details of physical conditions or mental health
- ✔ Information about someone's sex life
- ✔ Information about criminal convictions (but see Chapter 2)
- ✔ Trade union membership

The key to collecting such information is having good reason. You can have health information on file as part of sickness records; trade union details because of deducting union subscriptions from salaries; racial origin because of equal opportunities recruitment policies; information on disabilities so that you can make changes to your workplace.

This kind of sensitive information has to be treated with great care otherwise you can leave yourself open to charges of discrimination. If it fell into the hands of someone who used it against the individual concerned, that person may bring a case for victimisation, harassment, or bullying.

Monitoring at Work

If you monitor your workers by collecting or using information about them the Data Protection Act still applies, and you have to able to justify monitoring as an appropriate response to a particular problem. You may want to monitor staff to:

    ✔ Check the quality of work and see if they're up to the job or need training

    ✔ Make sure that health and safety laws aren't being broken

    ✔ Keep workers safe

    ✔ Make sure that no one is breaking the law

    ✔ Make sure that no one is ignoring company policy

    ✔ Stop thefts or fraud

Make sure that this monitoring is justified and appropriate to a particular problem, that everyone is fully aware of it, and that you only do it when and where necessary. You can get employees' consent to monitoring by putting it into their contracts, but any time you do decide to do some monitoring you still have to make sure that it's justified.

Under the Act individuals also have the right to a copy of any personal information about them collected through monitoring, and you have to make sure that they're aware of why and how your monitoring takes place.

The Regulation of Investigatory Powers Act 2000 also covers monitoring. It sets out the reasons why you might monitor staff and the principles for carrying it out. If you don't monitor properly you can fall foul of that Act, the Data Protection Act, and the Human Rights Act.

The Regulation of Investigatory Powers Act 2000 covers monitoring through CCTV; recording phone calls, checking telephone logs, and listening to voicemails; monitoring e-mails or checking Internet use; even searching staff and their workspaces and putting tracking devices into vehicles. These are all legally acceptable if you do them properly and under the right circumstances.

Any kind of monitoring is likely to cause a stir among your staff and make them feel insecure and mistrusted. Do all you can to avoid damaging relations by consulting them about monitoring and why you feel you need to do it. Think carefully about other possible ways of dealing with any problems before you go down the monitoring route.

Making a monitoring policy

When it comes to monitoring, having a policy is your best defence. Make sure that everyone reads a copy of this policy, get them to sign to confirm that they have, and keep it somewhere it can be re-read. You may want to make it part of your company contract or handbook (see Chapter 3). Set out clearly what activities are acceptable, and what the consequences are of not sticking to these guidelines. You may take the view that using the company phones for private calls in emergencies is fair enough, but that libelling someone in an e-mail or downloading porn will be a disciplinary offence and may even result in dismissal for gross misconduct (see Chapter 4).

Your policy should cover:

- ✔ Why monitoring is needed
- ✔ What is and isn't acceptable in terms of phone, fax, e-mail, and Internet use
- ✔ Whether or not personal use is OK, when and to what extent
- ✔ What your rules are for opening or downloading incoming e-mails and files
- ✔ How business e-mails are to be written
- ✔ What kind of messages and material are not to be circulated by e-mail
- ✔ What monitoring you undertake
- ✔ What the consequences are if anyone gets it wrong

If you don't make it clear what is and isn't acceptable and what may result in dismissal and then you sack someone, you may face a claim for unfair dismissal.

If anyone does ignore the terms of the policy, deal with it in the same way as any other problems in the workplace, by investigating fully first and deciding whether to use your disciplinary procedures (see Chapter 15).

Justifying monitoring

Don't monitor if you don't have to. Serious intrusion into workers' privacy can only be justified if a risk of serious damage to your business is present, and monitoring may itself do serious damage to your business, making your employees feel untrusted. Think about:

- ✔ Your reasoning for monitoring and what the benefits will be
- ✔ The impact on the workers weighed up against your reasons
- ✔ What confidential information might come out into the open

> ✔ Being as fair as possible to all your workers
>
> ✔ Consulting with unions and workers
>
> ✔ Making sure that you can keep all the records you collect safe and secure

If serious crime goes on around your workplace, you may be able to justify monitoring without your workforce knowing about it. But be careful, as covert monitoring is rarely justifiable. If you think that the matter is serious enough for you to call in the police, for example, but you don't want to involve them yet and you think that making people aware of the monitoring would hamper your investigation, you will be on fairly safe ground. But only monitor as part of a specific investigation and stop as soon as that investigation ends.

Watching CCTV – pros and cons

Workers have the right to keep their personal lives private and to have a degree of privacy in the workplace. CCTV can be very intrusive. It should be used only for security reasons and for your staff's security. Make sure that everyone knows that you are installing CCTV and why, and make sure that the cameras are set up in such a way that they aren't simply spying on people while at work. Talk to staff about where they feel most vulnerable and therefore where they think the cameras can be of most use, such as in dark areas of the car park or the footpath leading to the main road. If you want to deter someone from breaking into the company safe or the office where confidential records are kept, place the cameras so you can see people coming and going and keep them trained on the safe. Don't secretly monitor in private offices, staffrooms, or toilets.

If you don't place CCTV cameras correctly, employees will just feel that you're watching them. That will make them feel insecure and demotivated – as if you are watching their every move. You'll also be breaking the law if you have continuous audio or video monitoring or if you do either in private places.

Monitoring telephone calls, e-mails, and Internet use

Probably the biggest bugbear for employers is keeping a check on what employees are using the phones and computers for. The misuse of either can cause problems inside and outside your business.

You can monitor calls and e-mails, check on Web sites visited, listen in to voicemail messages, and intercept faxes. But you can only do that if you make all reasonable efforts to let workers know that that's what you'll be doing and if you can justify it as being necessary or relevant to the business. You may have to monitor to make sure that your business is complying with regulations, to prevent or detect crime, or to check for business communications while an employee is on holiday.

In some workplaces, such as call centres, all phone calls will be recorded. If it isn't necessary for the work, don't continuously record calls. Think about less intrusive ways of monitoring such as spot checks and checks on stored e-mails instead. Think too about who needs to have access to the Internet and who doesn't.

Prevention is always better than cure. Working on that principle, it's better to have a policy in place that tells everyone how, where, and when they can use the phones, faxes, e-mail, and Internet around the workplace.

Phone calls and faxes cost you money, so you may restrict their use to business only. But bear in mind that eight hours a day under your roof is a long time and people may simply not be able to run their lives without making the odd call or sending the occasional fax. Be reasonable. Perhaps you can make it clear in your policy that you expect staff only to use the facilities if they have to, or with your permission and preferably in their work breaks. Most people do have work to get on with and don't abuse your hospitality, especially if they feel you trust them.

E-mail and Internet use are a bit different in that they won't usually be increasing your bills. If they're done in employees' own time they aren't costing you anything. You have to get a balance between being able to monitor business e-mails to make sure that they are the written in the right way and are not too informal for business purposes, and allowing staff free rein and getting you into deep water. The problems arise if people are sending personal e-mails and surfing the net booking their holidays during work time. They may also be clogging up the system sending large attachments to all their friends. More problematic is that you can get viruses in your system or someone can be downloading or sending offensive or pornographic material.

Monitoring business vehicles

It's all very James Bond, but company vehicles can be monitored with satellite tracking devices. If you go to those lengths, make sure that any employees who drive them know exactly what private use they are allowed, and if possible get a device that can be disabled when the vehicle is in private use.

Getting your monitoring wrong

If you use monitored information for reasons other than those you collected it for, you can get into trouble. If you set up blanket recording of call and e-mails, have continuous video or audio monitoring, or record in private areas, you are breaking the law. If you don't fulfil all your legal obligations, you may face claims against you by your staff. You must protect the data you collect, make everyone aware of the monitoring, take steps not to intrude on workers' privacy, and set out your rules on private use of telephones, e-mail, and the Internet – and the consequences of breaking those rules.

If you breach the implied terms of trust and confidence in employees' contracts (see Chapter 3), they can claim constructive dismissal on the grounds that your actions left them no choice but to resign (see Chapter 4). If someone suffers damage or distress because you didn't safeguard personal information under the Data Protection Act or because of your monitoring practices, you can face a claim for damages. And if an employee is unhappy about the way you go about the monitoring process, he can ask the Information Commissioner, who is responsible for the data protection legislation, to make an assessment of how you're going about things.

Giving References

You don't have to give an employee a reference. A lot of employers are so concerned that an employee may sue them for saying something in a reference that adversely affects a career that they give only the bare facts such as start and finish dates, length of employment, and job title. If you can't give a positive reference, stick to those bare facts.

Whatever you say in a reference has to be true. You have a duty of care to your employee when writing a reference – you may ask colleagues what they think, but you should check that their claims can be substantiated. You can only say what you believe to be accurate and fair and you must be very careful not to say anything discriminatory.

Even if you give a positive reference, you've still got to tell the truth, so don't overflow with praise if it's not accurate. If you lead a prospective employer to believe they're hiring someone better than they really are and the new employer suffers as a result, the other employer can sue you.

Refusing to give a reference on someone who is bringing a claim against you for discrimination may be considered victimisation (see Chapter 13). If you do give a reference, remember that the employee may eventually see it. Under the Data Protection Act an employee can ask his current employer for access to references held about him. That means that after he leaves you he can ask to see the references you supply to his new boss.

When an employee is leaving and asks you for a reference, you can agree the wording of that reference with him. It still has to be truthful, but you can discuss with him what you can and can't say.

Appraising Employees' Work

You don't have to do staff appraisals, but they're a very important management tool. Appraisals help you to give employees feedback on their work, set goals for them to achieve in the coming year, see where training might help, talk to them about their career development, and find ways to improve their performance. Employees shouldn't dread appraisals as meetings in which they get pulled to pieces by the boss. They should look forward to the chance to put their point of view and discuss the opportunities they'd like to be given.

Small business managers may feel that appraisals just take up valuable time, but they can have big benefits for the business if you do them well. You get an idea of how the employees think the business is doing and give them a sense of belonging. If nothing else, appraisals give you and your employees the chance to talk on a one-to-one basis and get to know each other and the business a bit better (but keep the conversation strictly business unless it's relevant to the job).

You can do appraisals on an informal basis without too much form filling, but it's a good idea that employees know when their appraisals will be so they can be prepared to talk about what works for them and what doesn't and how they think they can be helped to do their jobs better. Some employers ask employees to fill in forms beforehand to make the review easier, but it's the discussion that's important.

Appraisal documents, like any other information you hold about your employees, should be kept safe and confidential. The Data Protection Act applies to appraisal documents in the same way as to any other information held about your employees. If anyone in the company other than you has access to them, you should tell employees and get their consent beforehand. Keep confidential documents securely locked away from prying eyes.

Whistleblowing

If you or someone working in your business is up to something illegal and one of your employees reports it (known as *whistleblowing*), that employee may be protected under the Public Interest Disclosure Act.

The *Public Interest Disclosure Act* protects whistleblowing employees who:

- ✔ Make a *Qualifying Disclosure* showing that:
    - A crime has been committed
    - Legal obligations haven't been complied with
    - Someone's health and safety is at risk
    - Something damaging to the environment has been done – dumping industrial waste in a river, for example
    - A miscarriage of justice has taken place (not so likely to apply to small businesses)
    - A cover-up has taken place to stop information about any of these situations getting out
- ✔ Follow the correct procedures (explained below)
- ✔ Have been dismissed or suffered a detriment by reporting this incident

An employee may make a qualifying disclosure and be protected under the Act in several ways. He has to make the disclosure in good faith believing that the information he has is true. He may:

- ✔ Tell you that a qualifying disclosure is happening in the workplace
- ✔ Take legal advice and tell a lawyer about it
- ✔ Tell a *prescribed person* (a regulatory body such as the Health and Safety Executive)
- ✔ Tell someone outside your business (such as a union official or a journalist) if he:
    - Thinks reprisals against him will take place if he reports the incident internally
    - Thinks you won't act on his report
    - Thinks you'll destroy the evidence

- Has no prescribed person to tell

- Has told you and a prescribed person and nothing has been done about it?

✔ Bypass all of the above and make an exceptionally serious disclosure direct to the police for example.

You can't put a clause in employees' contracts to stop them whistleblowing. Even if you require members of staff to sign a confidentiality clause, this doesn't apply to whistleblowing covered by the Act's protected disclosures.

If someone working for you does comes to you with tales of illegal goings-on, you have to take him very seriously. You certainly can't sack him or do anything that would leave him worse off just because he's brought the subject up, or you can face a bill for compensation running into hundreds of thousands of pounds.

If you fire a whistleblower, even if he's only worked with you for a short while, he can claim unfair dismissal (see Chapter 4). The normal upper limit on the amount of compensation that he may be awarded for unfair dismissal doesn't apply in these circumstances. Awards of over a quarter of a million pounds have been made in whistleblowing cases. Apart from not being able to dismiss the whistleblower, you can't take reprisals against him or do anything that's to his detriment. It isn't just employees who are protected by this law – consultants, contractors, or self-employed people working for you can all blow the whistle.

Chapter 15

Resolving Differences

● ●

In This Chapter

▶ Drawing up your disciplinary and grievance procedures

▶ Putting these procedures into practice

▶ Defending your position if your differences escalate

● ●

*I*nnocent until proven guilty is a good legal principle and it applies in employment law just as it does in the wider legal system. You can't go around punishing people with black marks on their files or by sacking them for something they haven't done or weren't responsible for. You have to follow the correct procedures before you can take disciplinary action. If you don't do that and just sack someone, your employee can make a claim against you at an Employment Tribunal for unfair dismissal provided she's been employed by you continuously for one year.

So you have to have a *disciplinary procedure* to resolve differences within the workplace.

New Dispute Resolution Regulations came into force in October 2004. They fundamentally changed the way employers have to deal with disputes, and with disciplinary and grievance procedures. If you dismiss someone and get those procedures wrong, the employee can bring a case against you at an Employment Tribunal. The tribunal will find that you have automatically unfairly dismissed the employee, and can order you to pay greatly increased compensation. You can't ignore these new rules and procedures. More and more cases are being brought against employers who don't know the law has changed, or who have ignored the changes.

Statutory guidelines set out the minimum you must do to resolve differences between members of staff if matters can't be settled amicably. A disciplinary procedure helps you to be consistent in the way you treat your employees and allows you to have an influence over the way employees conduct themselves around the workplace, because they all know the score from the outset and what will and won't be tolerated. It also helps you to deal with problems such as poor performance. You set down the rules, and you then have a process to enforce those rules and give you a fair way of dealing with people who don't stick to them. By making sure your employees have seen the disciplinary procedure, everyone knows where they stand and what to expect.

Even with disciplinary procedures in place, a tribunal may still decide that you did not act reasonably.

ACAS (The Advisory, Conciliation and Arbitration Service) has produced a code of practice on how to resolve disputes with details on how to draw up and operate disciplinary and grievance procedures. The code is used as the yardstick to judge how reasonable an employer has been if an employee brings a claim for unfair dismissal to an Employment Tribunal, so get a copy of the code from ACAS and incorporate it into your own procedures. Contact ACAS at 0845-7474747 or through the Web site at www.acas.org.uk.

You must also have procedures in place to deal fairly with employees' complaints. Again, these procedures help you to deal with all employees consistently and quickly and the employees know that they can use this procedure to ensure that someone listens to their complaints.

Handling Employee Disputes

Some bosses have separate procedures for dealing with the conduct of their employees around the workplace and for dealing with someone whose work performance is under par. Some use the same procedure for both.

Be clear about what rules you think are necessary for the workplace to function efficiently and safely. You probably can't cover every conceivable situation that may arise and the rules naturally vary depending on the kind of work you do, the number of employees you have, the working environment, and work processes. Whatever rules you do set down, make sure they aren't so general that nobody really knows what you're getting at. For example, your rules may say that smoking isn't allowed on the premises or that you won't tolerate people drinking during working hours.

Everybody you employ should know what the rules are and giving them a copy in writing is a good idea. You can go through them in a meeting with employees so that your members of staff can ask you to clarify anything they don't understand.

You should have good reasons for the rules you want obeyed. If you explain the reasoning behind them you're much more likely to get employees' support than if you simply say this is the way it is because this is the way it is.

After setting out the rules, include what happens if these rules are broken or if someone's work isn't up to scratch. Employees need to know what can get them dismissed. Be clear about what amounts to gross misconduct. Examples include:

- ✔ Hitting a colleague

- ✔ Stealing company property, theft, fraud, or some other dishonest behaviour

- ✔ Bullying or harassment

- ✔ Putting someone else's safety at risk by careless behaviour

- ✔ Deliberately damaging your property or premises

- ✔ Bringing the business into disrepute

- ✔ Being drunk or under the influence of drugs at work

Chapter 4 explains these points in more detail.

Clearly spell out all the steps you take when you find that someone is breaking the rules. They need to know what warnings and interviews they can expect; what chance they will be given to improve; what will happen if they don't; and what the ultimate sanction will be. You should also, as far as possible, give a timescale for the whole process.

Your attitude to discipline matters. When you see your processes as being a way of helping people to behave well at work and encouraging them to improve if they aren't behaving well or pulling their weight, rather than giving you a big stick to beat them with, your employees are more likely to respect the rules. The best disciplinary procedures:

- ✔ Are in writing

- ✔ Explain to whom they apply

- ✔ Make sure that problems can be dealt with quickly

- ✔ Don't discriminate against any particular workers

- ✔ Make sure that no action is taken without fully investigating the problem first

- ✔ Keep the investigated information confidential

✔ Spell out the disciplinary action to be taken, and in what circumstances

✔ Make it clear who has the authority to take that disciplinary action

✔ Ensure that employees will be told what the complaints against them are and get to see all the evidence

✔ Give employees the right to present their side of the story

✔ Give them the right to have someone else with them at disciplinary hearings

✔ Makes sure that nobody is sacked for a first offence unless it's on your gross misconduct list

✔ Makes sure that any punishment you decide on is fully explained to the employee

✔ Give the employee the right to appeal

Putting Your Disciplinary Procedure into Practice

When an employee does break the rules or isn't performing up to par, investigate the situation straight away. Following a few basic tips will help:

✔ Don't ignore it for a few weeks – by that time everyone you talk to about it will have forgotten some of the details.

✔ Get witness statements if appropriate – and get them in writing so that no-one can claim they've been misquoted.

✔ If you have a meeting with the employee as part of the investigation, make sure she knows what it's all about and that it's not a disciplinary hearing at this stage.

If you're dealing with a serious matter and you're fairly sure that there's been gross misconduct, consider suspending the employee for a short time while you investigate. Again, emphasise to her that this is part of the investigation process, not part of the disciplinary process.

Disciplining informally

After you've completed your investigations and are sure that you have all the facts, you may decide just to drop the matter because you feel it was a one-off or an aberration on the part of someone who is usually good and reliable. You may decide that the best way forward is to suggest to the culprit that some counselling or coaching may help – such as anger management or help with an alcohol problem. If you do talk to an employee about her behaviour at this point, suggest ways in which she can improve and make it clear what will happen if she doesn't. Also make it clear that these verbal warning aren't part of a formal disciplinary procedure. If you do decide on a verbal dressing-down instead of getting formal, you have to make sure the employee understands that.

Minor infringements of the rules are usually better not dealt with formally and the situation will improve without the need to get heavy.

Disciplining formally

If you decide that the informal approach won't bear fruit or that the matter is too serious to be treated informally, you have to start the disciplinary process.

The law requires you to write to the employee notifying her of allegations against her and invite her to a meeting to discuss the matter. You must hold that meeting (at which a colleague or union representative can accompany her) and let her know your decision. You must also let her know that she has the right to appeal against that decision. If she wants to appeal hold an appeal meeting – she can again be accompanied during this – and then give her your final decision. If you don't follow this statutory procedure, or a better one, an employee who has been with you for a year or more can claim automatic unfair dismissal. A tribunal can decide to increase her compensation award by 10–50 per cent because you've not followed all the correct procedures.

Employment Tribunals do expect you not only to have followed the law but to have acted reasonably, so your process should be flexible with more chance for improvement on the employee's part. And you have to take into consideration:

- ✔ The employee's record during current employment

- ✔ The employee's position in the company

- ✔ The employee's length of service

- ✔ Any special circumstances that might partly explain the employee's conduct (such as trouble at home)

- ✔ How anyone else has been treated for some similar offence

- ✔ The extent of the bad behaviour

Let the employee know, in writing, what she is alleged to have done wrong and why you don't accept it. Give her copies of any evidence you have gathered. Invite her to a disciplinary hearing where she can put her side of the argument and you can discuss the problem. You have to have this hearing before you decide on any further action to take or any punishment. You also have to tell the employee that she can bring someone to that hearing with her such as a work colleague or a union rep.

At the meeting explain your complaint and go through the evidence you have. Allow her to set out her case for the defence. She can ask questions, bring her own evidence, call witnesses, and bring up points about your witnesses. You have to give her a fair hearing. When it's over, decide quickly what steps to take. Again, at this stage, you can opt to drop the investigation, but if you do decide to take it further make sure that you follow your disciplinary procedure correctly.

After the meeting, put in writing a warning setting out the misconduct and what the employee has to do to put it right. Tell her what will happen if things don't improve and by when. You may also decide to give her some support to help her improve, so tell her what that will be. You may decide that if she doesn't change she will get a final written warning and will ultimately be dismissed, and that should be in the letter. You need to let her know how she can appeal and that you are putting the written warning on her file. Tell her how long it will stay there – usually three or six months – after which it will be ignored if she has addressed your complaint satisfactorily and improved.

If the desired improvement doesn't materialise within the relevant timescale, you can issue a final written warning, which should set out the punishment that you will impose on the employee if there's still no improvement by a set date. The punishment is usually the sack, but if it says in your contracts of employment that an employee can be demoted, transferred to another part of your business, or suspended for a period of time as a result of disciplinary action, you can use those options instead. Again, you have to tell the employee about her right to appeal.

If you feel the misdemeanour was serious enough or amounted to gross misconduct, you can issue an employee with a final warning and dispense with any warnings in between or even summarily dismiss her. But beware of doing this. The employee might bring a case against you at an Employment Tribunal and if the tribunal decided the misdemeanour wasn't serious enough or didn't amount to gross misconduct you can be found to have automatically unfairly dismissed the employee because you didn't follow the correct procedures and as a result face having to pay increased compensation.

Behaving Criminally

Sometimes the problem will be not what an employee has done in the workplace but what she's done outside it. If she has been involved in something serious outside work – even something criminal – you can't just dismiss her. You have to think about whether what she's done has any relevance to her job. Has it damaged the relationship of trust and confidence between you (see Chapter 3), made her unsuitable to do the kind of work she does, or made her unacceptable to her work colleagues?

If she has done something criminal in or out of the workplace and the police are involved, you should go ahead with your own investigation and decide whether the matter affects her employment. Be very careful not to make any assumptions of guilt until it is proven in external criminal proceedings.

If the criminal charges against an employee are dropped, you won't necessarily have been wrong to make the decision to dismiss, but you still have to have gone through all the fair and proper procedures.

If you really do think that an employee can eventually improve and you want to give the process a bit more time, you can add in extra written warnings. After a final warning has been issued it usually stays on the employee's file for 12 months.

If nothing changes you can go ahead and dismiss the employee or carry out whatever other disciplinary threat you put in the final warning. Let her know her fate as soon as possible, in writing, giving the reasons for dismissal, the date her contract will come to an end, and her right to appeal.

If during the process the employee wants to appeal, you have to hold an appeal meeting and she can again be accompanied by a colleague or union rep. She may bring along new evidence or witnesses to an appeal meeting that can change your mind. Don't forget that all through the process you should be looking for ways to keep an employee and help her to improve rather than simply following the procedures that will allow you to dismiss her.

Overlapping disputes

Sometimes you begin a disciplinary procedure against an employee and the employee starts a grievance procedure. Perhaps you are disciplining her for poor performance and she complains that she is being bullied and starts a grievance procedure (see 'Dealing with Staff Complaints' later in this chapter). These situations are very difficult for employers to handle and you should take legal advice.

Resolving disputes

Firing a member of staff should always be the last option. A disciplinary meeting is an opportunity to find a solution rather than a first step on the way to getting rid of someone. Start the process with a determination to resolve the problem. By being open-minded you may find that it's not so much the employee as your work processes that are causing some difficulty.

A whole workforce can be affected when someone is sacked, especially if she has been there for a while, gets on well with colleagues, and you don't have many employees. If your workplace has a union you may find the union rep putting up a tough fight to get you to keep the employee on, perhaps even threatening strike action.

Don't just dismiss everyone else's views out of hand. Resolving a dispute and making things work can have a very positive effect on the rest of the employees and ultimately your business can benefit.

Calling in the arbitrators

If you can't resolve the problem yourself, think about calling in an outsider as an arbitrator. For example, if your employees belong to a recognised union (see Chapter 7 for more on unions) it may be able to send someone in to arbitrate. Various other organisations can give you advice and help you stay out of trouble (see Chapter 21). ACAS (the Advisory, Conciliation and Arbitration Service), for example, may be able to help with:

- ✔ Conciliation (where both parties are helped to come to a settlement)

- ✔ Arbitration (where someone hears the case from both sides and makes a legally binding decision in favour of one party – an alternative to going to an Employment Tribunal)

- ✔ Mediation (where an adviser suggests ways of reaching a voluntary agreement)

Dealing with Staff Complaints

Just as you have complaints about your employees, so they might have complaints about you, their working environment, colleagues, or their jobs. You have to allow them their say and have a procedure for them to follow so that their grievances can be aired and dealt with. An informal approach is best in the first instance, so make sure that employees know who to go to with their complaints if it isn't you. Usually, if they have a line manager, that's the place to start.

Using a grievance procedure

The law says you must have a grievance procedure in place for employees to follow if a member of staff's complaint can't be resolved by their manager (to cover yourself in case they ultimately take the matter to an Employment Tribunal):

1. **The employee must put the grievance in writing to you formally.**

2. **You have to invite her to discuss it with you at a meeting where a colleague or union rep can accompany her. You have to notify him in writing of that meeting.**

3. **The employee has to be given the right to appeal if she feels that her grievance wasn't properly resolved.**

4. **You then have to give her your final decision.**

If the employee then chooses to go to an Employment Tribunal, she has to allow 28 days between putting her grievance to you in writing and making her claim. This is to give the employer sufficient time to act.

Following this grievance procedure should make employees' concerns more straightforward to address. To ensure that things run smoothly:

- ✔ Keep proceedings confidential.

- ✔ Make sure that everyone knows the grievance process – give them written copies of the procedure they should follow.

- ✔ Set up a meeting as soon as you get a formal grievance letter.

- ✔ Allow the employee to explain her complaint and tell you how she'd like it resolved. You may want to investigate the situation further.

- ✔ Put your decision in writing and at the same time let her know that she can appeal.

- ✔ For appeal cases, set up another meeting. If a junior manager dealt with the first meeting, get a more senior employee to hear the appeal, or hear it yourself.

- ✔ Write to the employee with your decision as soon as possible after the meeting.

Many of the issues that employees may have grievances about, such as stress or discrimination, are dealt with in other chapters of this book. Chapters 10, 11 and 12 deal with Health and Safety and Chapter 13 deals with discrimination. Bullying and harassment are often at the root of grievance claims and they are discussed later in this chapter.

Meeting with staff and their representatives

 A member of staff may sometimes request that a third party accompany her to a disciplinary or grievance meeting, or an appeal. You don't have to allow an employee to have a lawyer to represent her unless it says so in her contract, but you do have to allow a colleague or union representative to accompany her. That person has to be:

- ✔ Chosen by the employee

- ✔ Allowed to address the meeting but not to answer questions for the employee

- ✔ Allowed to confer with the employee during the meeting

You can select dates for meetings and hearings, but if the person accompanying the employee isn't available the meetings have to be rescheduled to a date that the employee proposes within five working days. If you also employ the colleague, you have to give her time off to attend the meetings and if she's a union official you have to pay her for that time.

 If you don't allow the employee to have someone accompanying her or you don't agree to reschedule a meeting so that the companion can attend, the employee can take a claim again you at an Employment Tribunal. You can be ordered to pay her up to two weeks' pay in compensation.

Dealing with Bullying and Harassment

You can't afford to ignore bullying and harassment around your workplace. If you do, an employee can make a claim against you at an Employment Tribunal. Equally, employee morale, productivity, and performance all suffer. Employees lose confidence in and respect for bosses and managers because of their failure to address the issue, so employee relations suffer. The number of days off sick rise and you may even get some staff quitting. And to top it all, your company's reputation is likely to suffer.

Bullying is behaviour that is offensive or insulting to a colleague and makes her feel threatened, humiliated, taken advantage of, demoralised or frightened. It can take the form of verbal abuse, physical violence or violent gestures, or humiliating someone in front of colleagues. Bullying can be by letter, phone, or e-mail as well as face-to-face.

Harassment is different to bullying in that it is, legally, a form of dis-crimination. It is bad behaviour towards someone because of their race, sex, disability, religion or other beliefs, or sexual orientation. It can be delivered in the form of abuse or inappropriate remarks or jokes about any of those things or unwanted physical contact or sexual advances.

Watch out for the signs that someone is being bullied or harassed. Often people don't speak up because they fear that will just make a bad situation worse. You need to consider it a possibility if some-one is absent more often and longer than usual, or if you have a high staff turnover in a particular department or under a certain manager. If people are showing symptoms of stress – tiredness, depression, or panic attacks, for example – or if you notice a change in their performance at work or their behaviour, don't rule out bul-lying or harassment as the cause.

Bullying or harassment can be hard to recognise and so subtly done that you miss all the clues. But it can be a sign that all is not well with the way your workplace is being run. A culture may exist where racist or sexist jokes and remarks are tolerated because they've always been tolerated and no one has the nerve to complain in case they lose their job. If you don't have a procedure for dealing with complaints and resolving problems, they can fester and sour work-ing relationships. All that can do a lot of damage to your business.

The best way to deal with bullying or harassment is to have an Equal Opportunities Policy in place (See Chapter 13). Your policy should encourage anyone affected to talk to you. Put the policy in writing and include

- ✔ An explanation of what the two terms mean, with examples of what would amount to bullying or harassment.
- ✔ A statement that you won't tolerate either in your workplace and that you will suspend or sack anyone who is guilty.
- ✔ Details of who employees should contact if they want to make a complaint.

✔ Assurances that you will take any complaint seriously and details of the procedures you will go through to investigate and discipline anyone behaving in that way.

✔ The fact that you offer a right of appeal.

✔ Details of where people can get help and support – inside or outside your business.

If you don't take bullying and harassment seriously, an employee can make a claim against you because of the behaviour of another of your employees. This may be a claim for compensation on the grounds that you didn't provide a safe and healthy working environment (see Chapter 10), a claim for discrimination (see Chapter 13), or for constructive unfair dismissal (see Chapter 4) because your lack of action has left the employee with no choice but to quit.

You do have legal obligations to your staff to deal with their complaints and investigate fully, but keep in mind the chance that the complaint may be malicious.

Facing an Employment Tribunal

If the worst comes to the worst and you can't resolve a dispute or you don't deal with a complaint, if you dismiss someone without following all the right procedures, or you don't comply with the employment laws in some way, you may end up in front of an Employment Tribunal.

The government set up *Employment Tribunals* so that employees can make claims against their employers without having to pay for legal advice. Employment Tribunals are supposed to be simple, quick, uncomplicated hearings where employees can state their case and get a fair hearing without legal representation. However, the law is so complicated that employers usually pay for lawyers to represent them and employees get help from their trade union or ask the local Citzens Advice Bureau for help. The section 'Preparing for Employment Tribunals', later in this chapter, explains the processes involved.

Some small business bosses make the mistake of being so sure they're right despite not knowing the law that they don't take advice and don't prepare for the case. You can't afford to do that. You must be well-prepared and have all the documents you can to help you defend the claim and take good legal advice, even if you decide to represent yourself. Discrimination awards have no limits. The compensatory award for unfair dismissal is up to £56,800 and the basic award is £8,400: a maximum total of £65,200 although the average award made by tribunals is much lower.

That's not a bill that many small businesses can afford to pay.

Tribunals deal with disputes including:

- ✔ Equal pay
- ✔ Wages (such as claims that you haven't paid the National Minimum Wage)
- ✔ Discrimination
- ✔ Unfair and wrongful dismissal
- ✔ Written reasons for dismissal
- ✔ Dismissal for requesting statutory rights or taking industrial action
- ✔ Redundancy
- ✔ Working hours and part-time working
- ✔ Maternity, paternity, adoption and parental leave, and leave for family emergencies
- ✔ Requests for flexible working
- ✔ Written Statements of Particulars of Employment
- ✔ The right to be accompanied at a disciplinary or grievance hearing in the workplace
- ✔ The right to campaign for trade union recognition
- ✔ Time off for trade union activities or duties as a safety representative or pension fund trustee
- ✔ Whistle-blowing – an employee reporting to the authorities any kind of illegal or potentially fraudulent practice going on in the workplace

In some cases the employee has the option of taking a claim in the civil courts, for example for a wrongful dismissal (see Chapter 4) or other breach of contract (see Chapter 3). You can also be taken to court if an employee is claiming against you for a personal injury at work or because she's suffering from ill health because of the working environment. And if you've got on the wrong side of the Health and Safety Executive, you can be prosecuted in the criminal courts and fined or even sent to jail.

Even if you end up winning the case, Employment Tribunal and other court cases related to employment issues can be very time-consuming for a small employer who needs to be at the helm of the ship. They can also be costly, especially if you hire legal help; if an award is made against you, you can be seriously out of pocket. On top of that damage can be done to your business because other employees are badly affected by what's going on and because the publicity in the local press about the case can do your reputation a lot of harm. It's much less stressful and damaging to make sure that you abide by the rules in the first place. Avoid tribunals if at all possible by following the right procedures and communicating very clearly with your employees in the first place (see Chapter 21). And if you have followed all the rules and an employee still brings a case against you, that will be your best defence.

Employees who feel they've been unfairly treated are advised to get the opinion of a lawyer. If the lawyer feels the employee has a case against you she will usually have three months from the date that the incident happened to file a claim against you. The main reasons employees go to Employment Tribunals are

- ✔ Unfair dismissal and the failure of employers to follow all the correct dismissal and disciplinary procedures we've covered in this chapter and Chapter 4.
- ✔ Disputes over wages.
- ✔ Breach of contract.
- ✔ Sex discrimination.
- ✔ Working hours.
- ✔ Redundancy pay.

Getting legal advice

If an employee brings a claim against you, get advice straight away. If you're a member of an organisation such as the Federation of Small Businesses or the Forum of Private Business, the Institute of Directors, or the British Chambers of Commerce, ask it for legal advice. Chapter 21 has details of how to contact these organisations and more.

If you need the advice of a lawyer, don't simply go to the one who wrote your will. You want a solicitor who specialises in employment law. The issues are very complex and Employment Tribunals are frequently making decisions that can affect the outcome of future cases, so you need legal advice from someone who is up-to-date. It's even more important if the employee is suing you in the civil courts, where financial compensation awards aren't limited to a maximum as they are in an Employment Tribunal and you can be landed with an even bigger bill.

Spotting vexatious cases

Sometimes employees bring cases against employers because they feel very aggrieved at the way the employer has treated them, even though they don't have a legal case. Some may even make up the details of a claim against you. Legal proceedings brought on insufficient or frivolous grounds are known as *vexatious* cases.

These cases usually don't get past the first post because solicitors can see that the employee has no case or is making up claims for which no evidence exists.

Preparing for Employment Tribunals

If following your dismissal, disciplinary or grievance procedures have not provided a satisfactory outcome, matters may move on to an Employment Tribunal hearing. When an employee has filed such a claim, the Tribunal sends you:

- ✔ A copy of the claim form (named ET1).
- ✔ A form to fill in with your response (named ET3).

You have 28 days in which to send the ET3 back, saying whether or not you intend to defend the claim and why. In some cases where the claim against you is for breach of contract you may be able to counter claim that the employee was in breach of contract (see Chapter 3); if so, you have 42 days from receiving the copy of the ET1.

Don't ignore an ET3 – if you don't send this form back on time you'll lose your right to defend yourself and the Tribunal will automatically make a judgment against you. You also have to be very careful about the reasons you give for defending the claim, so don't leave out anything that you will use in your defence. Get legal advice at this stage rather than leaving it until just before the hearing.

When the Tribunal gets your ET3 reply, it sends copies to the employee and to ACAS (The Advisory, Conciliation and Arbitration Service), which gets in touch with you to offer to conciliate (see the next section, 'Conciliating before or during the tribunal'). At any time before the Tribunal hearing you can agree a settlement or the employee can withdraw the claim.

When you get the ET1 you may also get a hearing date if the case is fairly straightforward. If it's more complicated you get the hearing date after the Tribunal receives your response on the ET3. Either way, you will have at least 14 days' notice of when the hearing will be. You can apply to the Tribunal to delay it if you have good reasons and give alternative dates.

If you aren't clear about the claim that the employee has made against you, you can ask for more information. You have to agree with the employee or her solicitor which documents you are going to use at the hearing. You need to collect witness statements and let the Tribunal know who you intend to call as witnesses. If a witness won't agree to speak at the hearing, the Tribunal can send a Witness Order to make her attend. If you have any evidence that would affect the amount of compensation the Tribunal may award if the employee wins, collect that together too.

Conciliating before or during the Tribunal

As well as being able to help you before an employee brings a claim against you at a Tribunal, ACAS has to offer you conciliation if an employee does lodge a claim. This help is free and confidential. ACAS has to contact you and inform both you and the employee what the legal issues are and how the procedures will work.

The idea is that an independent conciliator, who doesn't represent either you or your employee, helps you both to come to a legally binding agreement. You can decide to opt for conciliation at any stage of the Tribunal process. The advantage of conciliation is that you end up with a settlement you've both agreed rather than one that's imposed on you, and all the time, cost, and effort of preparing the case can be cut down or avoided.

You can decide at any time in the Tribunal procedure to settle out of court with the employee, if you can both agree on what the settlement should involve.

Pre-hearing reviews and case management discussions

Employment Tribunals usually only consist of a main course, but sometimes starters are also served – such as case management discussions or pre-hearing reviews.

In *case management discussions* (or Interlocutory hearings) the chairperson of the Tribunal may organise a conference phone call to discuss what issues the Tribunal has to decide or to discuss something about the procedure.

Pre-hearing reviews are hearings to try to determine whether the employee or employer has a reasonable chance of making out their case in a full hearing. If the Tribunal is satisfied that the case stands no reasonable prospect of success or appears to be vexatious they will order the employee to make a deposit (see below) and put a costs warning on the file.

Preliminary hearings consider the preliminary issues in the case and the Tribunal chairperson usually hears them. Both sides have to explain the basis of their case.

Sometimes the parties can clear up a case altogether at one of these hearings or deal with some aspects of it. If need be, the case will then go on to a full hearing in front of a Tribunal panel – usually three people. Sometimes you or the employee may be asked at a pre-hearing review to pay a deposit of up to £500 to proceed to a full hearing.

Hearing the evidence

Employment Tribunals are courts and although they are less formal than other courts, the chairperson of the Tribunal is an experienced employment lawyer. Sometimes the main hearing is held in front of the chairperson alone, but two other members of the Tribunal usually sit also. These other two members aren't legal experts but have been appointed because of their experience as employee and employer.

The Tribunal has to hear evidence from both sides and from witnesses. As in court, everyone is under oath or affirmation and can be convicted of perjury if they tell lies. The other side and the Tribunal members can ask questions of witnesses. If you don't turn up to the hearing the Tribunal members can decide to go ahead without you, so you must be there.

Having heard all the evidence, the Tribunal members make their decision in private and usually you get their judgment by post rather than on the day of the hearing.

Appealing against a decision

You can ask for a review of the Employment Tribunal's decisions or you can appeal against it – but only on the grounds that the Tribunal misunderstood or misapplied the law or if it makes a decision that no reasonable Tribunal would have made. It's not easy to appeal on either of those grounds, but if you do wish to appeal, ask the Employment Tribunal for the reasons for its decision in writing. You then have 42 days to put in your notice of appeal to an Employment Appeal Tribunal. When the Tribunal sends out its original judgement there will also be a leaflet which explains the procedure for appealing. The Employment Appeal Tribunal doesn't usually listen to new evidence but looks again at all the evidence presented and at the decision that was made.

Being in the Wrong – What Happens Next?

Once it has heard all the evidence, the Employment Tribunal decides who has won the case – you or the employee. If you lose, you can lose either the whole claim or part of the claim. Losing part of a claim might happen in a situation where an employee made a claim on the grounds that she was unfairly dismissed and that the dismissal amounted to sex discrimination. The tribunal might decide that the dismissal was unfair and award compensation for that but reject the claim for sex discrimination.

If you lose, the Employment Tribunal also comes to a decision about your penalty. This outcome can involve you having to:

✔ Reinstate the employee

✔ Re-engage the employee

✔ Compensate the employee

Reinstating

In unfair dismissal cases the Tribunal my decide that you have to give the employee her old job back, on the same terms and conditions and with pay to cover the period since the dismissal. She should be reinstated and go back to the financial and employment positions she would have been in if she'd never been away.

It's very hard for any employee and employer to go back to working together after having been through a dismissal and an Employment Tribunal. The trust has gone, so it's not a usual outcome. If you refuse to take the employee back, ultimately she can apply to the county court and the court is likely to award compensation.

Re-engaging

You might be told to re-engage the employee. That means taking her on to do a new job on similar terms and conditions as the old job. You may not have to pay back pay that she would have earned since the dismissal if her conduct somehow contributed to the dismissal. Again, working together won't be easy and Tribunals only order re-engagement if they really think it will work.

Counting the costs of compensation

The most usual decision for a Tribunal to come to is that you should pay some financial compensation. There are upper limits to compensation awards for most types of cases. For unfair dismissal it's £65,200 – a basic award of £8,400 plus £56,800 for the unfair dismissal itself. Other types of cases have lower maximum amounts and in the case of an automatic unfair dismissal the compensation can be increased by up to 50 per cent. There's no upper limit set for the amount of compensation awarded in discrimination cases.

Compensation for unfair dismissal includes an element to make up for loss of earnings that the employee has suffered since you sacked her. If the employee has a new job, the compensation is usually reduced to take that into account. The compensation also takes into account loss of other benefits such as pension contributions. If the employee refused to go through all your disciplinary or grievance procedures her compensation may be reduced, and if you didn't follow the procedures the award may be increased.

If an employee has the option to use the civil courts – for cases involving breaches of contract (see Chapter 3) or in personal injury cases for example – the payments awarded against you can be higher than those awarded by a Tribunal; the highest awards of all are made by courts to employees who have suffered injury or ill health because an employer has been negligent and failed to provide a safe working environment. By law you must have employer's liability insurance to cover such cases (see Chapter 10) for up to £5 million for each incident.

Part V
Paying Up – Everything to Do with Money

In this part . . .

*M*oney, money, money . . . from wages to redundancy payments, overtime to retirement pensions, bonuses to sickness and maternity pay. Employees are entitled to the National Minimum Wage, minimum periods of paid holiday, and statutory payments when they're off sick, on maternity leave, or are made redundant. You can stick to those legal minimum amounts – but you can be more generous, and that may help you attract a better-qualified workforce.

Sometimes it's the rest of the package, such as the pension scheme you offer, that encourages employees to stay with you rather than the salary. This part of the book goes into everything to do with the finances.

Chapter 16

Working Out the Wages

. . . .

. . . .

*I*f you employ a member of staff to work for you, it goes without saying that you have to pay him for his work. But you need to think about more than simply how and what you pay him. One of the first things to consider is what other companies are paying people in similar jobs in your area. You need to encourage people to apply for your jobs and you want to keep them once you have employed them, so make sure that they aren't going to leave you for better pay elsewhere. Money isn't the only thing that keeps workers motivated and happy in their jobs, but it can go a long way. But above all you must comply with the law as far as pay is concerned otherwise you can end up facing a claim at an Employment Tribunal. That means paying at least the national minimum wage, paying men and women equal pay for equal jobs, and avoiding discrimination.

Paying the Minimum Wage – Who's Entitled to What

Almost all workers in the UK are entitled to the National Minimum Wage. The only people this doesn't apply to are the self-employed, volunteers, prisoners, workers living as part of a family, and school children. Everybody else qualifies, including home workers, part-timers, agency workers, and casual workers.

Three different rates apply, depending on the employee's age:

✔ **The adult rate:** anyone 22 or over must be paid at least £4.85 an hour – and £5.05 an hour from October 2005.

✔ **The development rate:** 18–21-year-olds get the development rate of at least £4.10 per hour – £4.25 per hour from October 2005. This rate also applies to people 22 and over who are getting accredited training during the first six months in a job. A written agreement must exist between you and the employee and the employee has to attend at least 26 days' training in those six months.

✔ **The young worker's rate:** Workers aged 16 and 17 who have reached the minimum school leaving age must be paid at least £3 an hour. Apprentices under 18 who are in an approved apprenticeship scheme, and those under the age of 26 who are in the first year of their apprenticeship, are exempt.

If you don't pay the minimum wage employees can claim it through the civil courts or an Employment Tribunal. And if you dismiss an employee for claiming his rights to the minimum wage, the dismissal will be unfair and that's another case for an Employment Tribunal.

What counts as pay?

Not everything an employee gets in his wage packet counts towards the minimum wage. The following list shows the exemptions:

✔ Tips (unless you take employees' tips and use them to make up part of their salaries)

✔ Allowances, expenses, and 'on-the-job' travel costs

✔ Extra wages from overtime and shift work

✔ Most benefits in kind (such as the use of a company car, fuel, or meals)

Bonuses, incentive payments, and performance-related pay do count. If you provide an employee with accommodation, the total value of that doesn't count – only £3.75 a day counts towards the minimum wage. This increases to £3.90 from October 2005. You also ignore loans and pension or redundancy payments.

What count as hours?

The number of hours for which you must pay an employee the minimum depends on the kind of work he does. Work is broken down into four legal categories:

✔ **Time workers** get paid for working a set number of hours.

✔ **Salaried-hours workers** are contracted to work a set number of hours each year for an annual salary paid in 12 equal monthly instalments.

✔ **Output work.** Paid according to the number of pieces of work produced.

✔ **Unmeasured work.** Paid to do specific tasks but without set hours.

You must pay an employee the minimum wage for his hours worked in a week or a month – whichever is the *pay reference period* (the period for which he is regularly paid – weekly or monthly) set out in his contract. A time worker paid to work a specific number of hours in a week must get at least the minimum wage for those hours. A salaried worker gets paid the minimum wage for each hour he works each week or month, and rest breaks, lunch breaks, sick leave, maternity, paternity, and adoption leave all count towards the minimum wage if they form part of the basic minimum hours. For output and unmeasured work it's a little more complicated.

You either have to pay an output worker the minimum wage for all of the hours he works or an amount for each piece of work, adding up to an effective minimum wage. So if a worker can make up two garments in an hour he should either be paid the current hourly minimum rate or £2.43 per garment he finishes – increasing to £2.53 per hour from October 2005.

If you hire someone to do certain jobs, such as a gardener who has no set hours but works when he's needed or when the work is available, you have to decide whether to pay him for every hour he works or to come to an agreement about the daily average hours he should work.

Keeping records of wage payments

You must keep records to prove that you've paid at least the minimum wage for all the necessary hours and you can be fined if you don't keep those records. You have to keep them for three years and employees can ask to see them. You have to give access within 14 days of a request or the employee can take a case against you at an Employment Tribunal.

If a dispute arises you'll need to prove that you have complied with the law. HM Revenue & Customs has responsibility for making sure that employers are toeing the line, so if a compliance officer asks to see your records you must produce them. No list exists of what records you have to keep, but you should probably have

- ✔ Details of gross pay for each employee
- ✔ Payments for overtime and shifts
- ✔ Details of absences
- ✔ Details of any agreements and contracts between you and your workers

If you pay well above the minimum wage your company PAYE income tax records and National Insurance contribution records (see Chapter 17 for more on these) will be enough to prove that you're within the law.

Although you must keep your records for three years, an employee can bring a case against you in a civil court for up to six years after he says you failed to pay the minimum wage. So it's a wise move to keep your records for six years.

Penalties for not paying

An employee can bring a case against you at an Employment Tribunal or in a civil court for wages you haven't paid. Failing to pay the minimum wage is a criminal offence, meaning that you can also be prosecuted and fined.

If an HM Revenue & Customs compliance officer suspects that you aren't complying with the law he can pay you a visit. If he then sees your records and believes that you haven't been paying the right wage, he can serve you with an enforcement notice – which will require you to start making the correct payments and pay any back pay owed. If you ignore that notice you may get a penalty notice and ultimately a fine. Failing to pay minimum wage, in fact, puts you at risk for prosecution on six criminal charges:

- ✔ Refusal to pay the minimum wage
- ✔ Failure to keep sufficient records
- ✔ Keeping false records
- ✔ Producing false records or information
- ✔ Intentionally obstructing a compliance officer
- ✔ Refusing to give information to a compliance officer

In each case the maximum fine is £5,000.

Small business owners complain that they struggle because of the minimum wage, but it will be raised above the £5 mark before the end of 2005. In any case, if your business wants to attract the best employees, you can't afford to pay less than your competitors do.

Paying the Going Rate – Competing in the Marketplace

You must pay your employees at least the minimum wage . . . but nothing stops you paying more than that. If you're thinking of taking on staff to do particular jobs and wondering how much to pay them, you need to take a look at what your competitors are paying and what the going rate for those types of jobs is in your area.

You want to attract the best possible people to work for you and although pay isn't the only factor that potential employees consider when deciding on what jobs to apply for, it is a fairly important one and can be a useful indicator of how good a business is to work for. You should pay people according to their qualifications and experience and if you don't offer good pay someone else will. Good pay is also important when it comes to keeping staff. Remember that if they leave you will have to go to all the trouble and expense of hiring someone new and possibly training them up again.

 Look at what other employers in your area, in your industry, and your direct competitors are paying. This is called *benchmarking*. Use www.benchmarkindex.com to help you, and do a review of your pay rates once a year to make sure that you stay competitive.

Another issue to consider is what pay scheme you're going to use. Basically you have two choices, both systems with their pros and cons:

- ✔ **The basic rate system.** You pay a fixed amount on an hourly, weekly, or monthly basis. Basic pay is simple and straightforward, but offers no incentives for your employees to do better.

- ✔ **The incentive system.** Part of the pay is basic and part is based on performance and results. Incentive schemes can work out more expensive, are less transparent, and if you base them on the performance of a team you may get some people doing all the work and others not pulling their weight.

You need to work out what scheme or combination of schemes is best for your business. You may think about paying employees more the longer they work for you. That encourages people to stay on – but what about the younger ones you employ who have better qualifications? They may not be so happy.

On the other hand, you may decide to pay more for people with better qualifications and that system encourages them to take training courses to get better qualifications, but that additional expertise in turn makes them more attractive to other employers – who are possibly in a position to pay more.

Pay is important, but it isn't the only way to keep staff happy and make you the employer of first choice. A good work–life balance, flexible working, training opportunities, an employer who consults with staff, and good conditions in the workplace can be just as attractive to employees as money is.

Paying the Same for the Same Job – All Things Being Equal

Under the *Equal Pay Act 1970* you must pay women and men equal pay for work of equal value. This applies to basic pay, hours of work, bonuses, and pension contributions. Your employees can ask you for information to help them work out whether or not they are getting equal pay and if not why not. They can also get advice from the Equal Opportunities Commission – see the Web site at www.eoc.org.uk or call 0845-6015901 and obtain a questionnaire to submit to you for that information. Just as you can't discriminate against people, harass them, or victimise them in any aspect of their working conditions, you must be equally fair about pay.

An employee's contract of employment implies an equality clause even if one doesn't actually exist. As women bring the majority of the cases against employers under the Equal Pay Act, this example uses a woman's perspective, but it applies equally to men. A woman can compare herself with a man employed by you if:

- ✔ she does 'like work'
- ✔ a job evaluation scheme has rated her work as equivalent
- ✔ her job is of equal value

A woman is employed on *like work* if her work and that of a man are broadly similar and any difference between the two roles isn't of practical importance. Job titles carry far less importance in this situation than job descriptions.

You don't have to carry out a job evaluation, but if you do and a woman's job is rated as equivalent to a man's when it comes to effort, skill, qualification, and responsibilities, make sure that the pay is equal too. A woman can bring a claim against you for equal pay if she can show that her work is of equal value to a man's – again taking into account effort, skills, qualifications, and responsibilities – so a job evaluation may well be worth your time!

If an employee wants to make a claim for equal pay, he can do it at any time you employ him or within six months of the date he leaves. The Tribunal can make you pay up to six years' arrears up to the date the employee started proceedings (five years in Scotland).

Interestingly, a woman can't bring a claim for equal pay if the job she's doing has more responsibility or requires more skill than a man's but is less well paid – although recent cases suggest that she can claim if the work she's doing is of greater value than a male counterpart's.

You are on fairly safe ground if you pay one employee more because of something that has nothing to do with gender. For example, if a man and a woman are doing similar jobs but the woman earns more because she earns a bigger sales-related bonus that will be fair, or if the man gets more because he's been in the job longer and you pay more for longer service that will also be OK.

Paying Extras

On top of basic pay you may have a system for paying extras to your employees. Perhaps you offer the opportunity to work more hours than the normal working week and pay for that overtime, or maybe you pay bonuses or commission. In some businesses such as restaurants and hotels tips and gratuities boost staff wages. This section gives you the low-down on these little extras.

Overtime

When employees work extra hours, you have to pay them at the rate set out in their contract. The contract can spell out any rate for overtime you want (provided you pay at least the national minimum wage, of course). You may simply pay the same for an hour of *overtime* as you do for a normal hour of work. But if you want to give employees an incentive to do any extra work as and when you need it done you may pay a little extra – perhaps one-and-a-half times the normal rate or even twice or three times the usual hourly rate.

Bonuses

You pay *bonuses* on top of basic wages and salary, and usually link them in some way to the performance of the business. The general idea is that a flourishing business benefits everyone, and that an employee who contributes to that business performance can expect a bonus that in turn acts as an incentive to him to work that bit harder. But you need to be careful that bonuses really do act as incentives and don't cause destructive rivalries. Bonuses can be counted towards the minimum wage.

Commission

Commission is a payment on top of basic salary based on performance – of the whole team or an individual. Commission is different to a bonus because it's based on the individual or team performance rather than the performance of the business. Commission counts towards the minimum wage.

Commission is common for people like sales workers, who often have lower basic salaries than other employees. Their total wage can be made up partly of a basic salary and partly of a certain amount of commission on every sale made.

The more dependent your employees are on commission to give them a decent wage, the more anxious they will be to make sales. That may be good for your business, but it can also lead to poor sales practices such as pressurising people into buying or selling customers products that aren't right for them. So pushy sales people may not do your firm's reputation much good and can be bad for business in the long run. It's important to get the balance right.

Tips and gratuities

If you let your employees keep any tips and gratuities your customers leave, they don't count towards the minimum wage. But many employers operate different ways of dividing gratuities up. Some insist that employees put all such money into a communal pot and share it out equally, and some collect all of it and pay out a share to each employee through the payroll.

If tips and gratuities go through the payroll they count towards the minimum wage.

Expenses

A member of staff has the right to recover any expenses he's run up while doing work for you. You'll need to have a system in place for dealing with expenses claims. Some employers expect employees to pay out of their own pockets and then claim the money back; others book travel tickets, hire cars, and accommodation – the bigger expenses – and pay those direct, leaving only the smaller ones for staff to pay and claim back. If you have a deadline by which employees have to claim expenses you can spread the expense more evenly through the year. Without a deadline employees are very good at forgetting to do their expenses and end up claiming a whole year's worth at once.

Make it clear what employees can and can't claim. If, for example, you will pay for meals while employees are away from their usual workplace, decide whether you want to pay the price of the meal that's eaten or want to place a limit on the amount that can be claimed for each meal. Make sure your employees know this before they order another bottle of expensive wine to wash their expenses account away with.

Paying – The Practicalities

There was a time when manual workers had the right to be paid in cash, but now the way you pay your employees is wholly a matter between you and them. Another main issue to sort out with employees is when and how often you pay them. Most employers will pay monthly rather than weekly, but the details should be set out in the contract with the date each month that payments are due. Some employers pay monthly at the end of the month in which the work has been done. Others pay in the middle of the month, when they are effectively paying two weeks in arrears and two weeks in advance. It's important to be clear how your system works to avoid confusion about what you owe when employees leave your firm. You also need to be clear about how you pay bonuses, commission, tips, overtime and any other payments due. For example, a bonus may only be paid once a year instead of monthly.

On time

Whatever system you use, always pay on the day you've said you will pay. If you don't employees may have nothing to live on until you do pay and may get into financial trouble through going overdrawn or having direct debits and standing orders cancelled and cheques bounced. You also need to let your staff know what will happen if the normal date of payment falls on a Sunday or a bank holiday. Can they expect their wages to be in the bank the day before or will they have to wait a day longer?

Into bank accounts

Employers still pay many people in cash, especially if they pay them weekly, but payment by credit transfer into your employees' bank accounts is more common. To do that you need bank account details from your employees; if an employee doesn't have a bank account and prefers not to have one, you may need to come to an agreement about an alternative means of payment (such as cash or cheque).

Make sure you keep employees' bank details safe. To do this, keep them locked up in a filing cabinet or in password-protected computer files. Make sure only the people who need to access them can.

In cash

If you pay your employees in cash and decide to change to another method of payment without their agreement, you are in breach of contract. But the courts only award nominal compensation if employees bring cases in such circumstances, so there seems to be little to stop you so long as you give reasonable notice and have a good business reason – such as increasing efficiency or security by changing over to a cashless payment system. But in the interests of workplace harmony it's best to get everyone's agreement before you go ahead. Some people are very keen to be paid in cash and some still don't have bank accounts and so will have trouble cashing a cheque.

In euros

Occasionally people want their wages in euros. They can open a euro account into which you can transfer their wages as usual and the bank will convert the money to euros and hold it in that currency.

Tax Credits

Tax credits are the way that the government provides extra income for parents and low-paid workers. Child Tax Credits support families with children whether or not any of the adults has a paid job, and Working Tax Credits help low-paid workers without children. If your employees qualify for tax credits, these are processed by HM Revenue & Customs and paid directly. You don't have to do anything and they won't affect how much you pay in wages.

Laying Off Staff – Guarantee Payments

If you decide to lay employees off temporarily, employees who you've employed for at least a month have a right to *guarantee pay* (payment to make up for some of the work they're missing out on). This means that you must pay them for up to five days' pay in any period of three months. The maximum amount you have to pay is £18.40 for any one day, and you can only pay less than that if the employee will normally earn less than that in a day. See Chapter 6 for more about this.

You don't have to pay guarantee pay if:

- ✔ The employee's contract is for three months or less.
- ✔ He isn't available for work.
- ✔ You offer him suitable alternative work and he refuses.
- ✔ He's on strike or can't work because of a strike.
- ✔ His contract of employment doesn't require him to accept work that you offer him.
- ✔ You have a collective agreement covering guarantee payments.

Going Bust

Going out of business isn't a nice prospect to contemplate, but it can happen. If it does, the chances are that you will owe your employees some outstanding pay. Your assets are sold off and any money made is given to your creditors in order of priority. Your employees are preferred creditors, so they will be entitled to any money left after your *secured creditors* (those who have some kind of security such as a mortgage on the business property, equipment, or assets) have been paid. Your employees are entitled to all wages and salary for up to four months before the company went bust and to all their holiday entitlement.

If no money is available to pay employees, the state will pick up the bills for:

- ✔ Pay arrears for up to eight weeks at a maximum of £280 a week.

- ✔ Holiday entitlement for up to six weeks at the same maximum weekly amount.

- ✔ The statutory minimum notice period at a maximum of £280 a week.

- ✔ Any statutory maternity pay owed.

- ✔ Redundancy payments.

These payments are made by the Redundancy Payments Offices. Employees can call the Redundancy Payments Helpline on 0845-1450004 or go to www.insolvency.gov.uk to download the leaflet *Redundancy and Insolvency – a Guide for Employees*. They need to fill in form RP1 which is in the back of that leaflet and send it to the Redundancy Payments Office which deals with the area they live in. The addresses for these are listed in the leaflet.

Chapter 17

Paper Money, Money Paper – Payslips and Deductions

In This Chapter

▶ Wading through wage slips

▶ Understanding tax and National Insurance wage deductions

▶ Being aware of other possible wage deductions

*W*hatever, however, and whenever you decide to pay your employees, a lot of calculations and paperwork are involved. Not only giving with one hand, you have to take back quite a bit with the other and hand it over to the taxman. People working for you on a freelance or self-employed basis usually send you an invoice at the end of the job or at intervals you've agreed and you pay them in full, leaving them to work out and hand over their own income tax and National Insurance payments to HM Revenue & Customs – the new name for the Inland Revenue, but you have a responsibility to collect tax and insurance from your own employees. On top of that you have to comply with the law on the National Minimum Wage (see Chapter 16), Statutory Sick Pay, maternity, paternity, and adoption pay, and holiday pay (see Chapter 18 for more on these deductions). Phew – is it any wonder that one of the first jobs many bosses farm out is the payroll?

Setting Everything Out on the Payslip

Employees have a legal right to a written pay statement – a *payslip* or *wage slip* – that itemises their pay and anything deducted from their pay. One of the main reasons for these written statements is that they notify employees of the deductions made from their pay. You have to give out these itemised statements each time (or just before) you pay your employees.

An employee's payslip must include:

- ✔ The *gross amount* of her wages (her salary before any deductions).

- ✔ The *net amount* she earns (what's left after you have made any deductions).

- ✔ Any amounts that you have deducted and why (some of these are fixed deductions made every pay-day and some are variable from pay period to pay period).

- ✔ The breakdown of different payment methods, if you pay your employees in this way (for example, what amounts are paid by cheque and what are paid in cash).

If you don't provide wage slips or don't include the correct details on them, your employees can complain to an Employment Tribunal (refer to Chapter 15 for more on Tribunals). The Tribunal can make you pay back any unnotified deductions you made in the 13-week period before the employee complained – even if you were entitled to make them.

Gross pay

Gross pay is the amount of pay your employee earns before you make any deductions. Gross pay comprises the basic wage and any other elements of pay due in the pay period, and may include elements such as:

- ✔ Bonuses

- ✔ Commission

- ✔ Holiday pay

- ✔ Statutory Sick Pay

- ✔ Maternity pay

- ✔ Overtime

The gross pay is the top line – earnings go downhill from there. Gross pay doesn't include items such as loans or advances in wages, expenses, or redundancy payments.

Deductions

Employees are entitled to know in advance what deductions you will be making from their gross pay and why.

Most deductions are regulated by the Employment Rights Act 1996 and are legal only when your employees' contracts clearly explain in what circumstances you will make such deductions, or when your employees give you written consent to make them. But some deductions are exempt from regulation by the Employment Rights Act (more details are given later in this chapter):

- ✔ Deductions for previous overpayment of wages.

- ✔ Deductions under statutory provisions such as tax and National Insurance.

- ✔ Deductions that you make by law and hand over to a third party, such as an attachment of earnings order.

- ✔ Deductions that you pay to a third party where the employee consents in writing, such as payments to a pension company.

- ✔ Deductions relating to strike action.

- ✔ Deductions to satisfy a ruling by a court or tribunal that an employee has to pay you a certain amount.

If you're intending to make any deductions not shown on this list, you need prior written consent from your employee (you must have the consent in writing before the event that gives rise to the deduction). If you get consent *after* you've deducted the money, that deduction is considered unlawful. That's because you have changed an employee's pay without her consent and were in breach of contract. In other words, the contract needs to include a provision (agreed to by the employee) that in the particular circumstances you can take money out of her wages.

If you're making exactly the same fixed deductions each pay period, you can give out *standing statements* notifying employees of these deductions in advance; standing statements may be valid for up to a year (so you'll have to issue them annually at the least). Any variable or additional deductions still have to appear on the monthly or weekly payslips, and any changes to the fixed deductions must be notified in writing or through an amended standing statement of fixed deductions.

Net pay

Net pay is what your employee's left with after the taxman and anyone else entitled to a cut has had their share; net pay amounts to gross pay minus any deductions. Net pay is the bottom line, and it's what your employee is left to play with to reward her for all her hard work!

Carrying out Your Duties as a Tax Collector

Small business owners often complain that life would be a lot simpler if – on top of running the business – they didn't have to act as unpaid collectors of taxes. But unfortunately, you do have to fulfil certain duties on behalf of HM Revenue & Customs. You must:

 ✔ Work out how much tax and national insurance your employees should be paying (along with any contributions you, as boss of the outfit, have to make to the Exchequer yourself)

 ✔ Collect these payments and get them to the right government department by the correct date.

Rather than doing this complicated task yourself and tackling the payroll on your own, you may wish to call in expert accountants. Not all employers can afford to do this, of course, and even if you can, it's still a good idea to read the following sections to understand what deductions you must make from your employees' payslips.

You must send the most recent amounts that you deduct from all your employees' pay to HM Revenue & Customs (formerly the Inland Revenue) by the 19th of each month. If you make your payments electronically you have until the 22nd of every month to pay up.

Deducting income tax

PAYE (or Pay As You Earn) is HM Revenue & Customs' system for collecting income tax from employees. As an employer, you're responsible for the administration of your employees' PAYE deductions.

All the help you need in calculating income tax is available from HM Revenue & Customs in the form of tables, forms, advice, and software. The Inland Revenue (now HM Revenue & Customs) used to have a reputation for being less than helpful, but that really isn't true any more. It runs helplines for just about every aspect of tax that you'll ever have to deal with. Two phone helplines are specifically for employers:

 ✔ 0845-6070143 for new employers.

 ✔ 0845-7143143 for established employers

> ✓ The HM Revenue and Customs Web site holds lots more information covering all aspects of tax in the UK: www.hmrc.gov.uk.

Employees normally have to pay income tax on just about every payment you give them:

- ✓ Wages

- ✓ Overtime and shift pay

- ✓ Tips

- ✓ Bonuses and commissions

- ✓ Statutory sick, maternity pay, paternity pay, and adoption pay

- ✓ Lump sums (such as redundancy payments) over and above any tax-free amount

- ✓ Some cash expense allowances

Not all of the money an employee earns is taxable. Certain sums must be earned before a person starts to pay tax; this amount is known as a *personal allowance*. The personal allowance for a person under 65 is currently £4,895, which means that the first £4,895 an employee earns in any tax year isn't taxable.

When an employee earns more than her tax-free amount the employer deducts tax from her pay at different rates. Table 17-1 shows the correct breakdown. And rather than paying an employee her full tax-free earnings in the first part of the tax year, you give her a proportion of these earnings in every wage packet throughout the tax year, adding up to her full tax-free earnings by the end of the year, but taxing her that little increment less throughout the year.

Table 17-1	Taxable Pay Breakdown
Taxable Pay	*Rate Taxed at*
The first £2,020	10%
£2,020 to £31,400	22%
Beyond £31,400	40%

Each employee's own circumstances dictate how much income tax she has to pay. HM Revenue and Customs (formerly the Inland Revenue) gives each of your employees a tax code each year showing how much tax-free earnings they're entitled to before you need to start deducting their tax contributions. When a new employee joins your staff her P45 shows you her current tax code.

Special PAYE situations

All sorts of reasons may occur allowing an employee to earn more than her personal allowance before starting to pay tax, or where she has to pay tax on some of the first £4,895 she earns. She may be entitled to some tax relief or have paid too much tax last year and so the figure will be higher. She may have paid too little tax last year and the figure will be lower. Any benefits that she gets on which she has to pay tax will affect that tax-free amount. Benefits in kind, such as company cars and medical insurance, are subject to tax – but only at the end of your tax year, rather than through the PAYE system. If you pay your employees with shares or vouchers, the Inland Revenue taxes these on their cash value under the PAYE system.

Help with childcare costs is an exception. If you give an employee childcare or childcare vouchers up to the value of £50 a week, this won't be taxed as long as:

✔ The childcare scheme is registered childcare or approved home childcare.

✔ The childcare scheme is available to all your employees.

If a new employee turns up without a P45 (which sometimes happens – usually because her previous employer hasn't handed over all the necessary paperwork), you won't immediately have the correct tax code for her. She needs to fill in a form P46, available from the HMRC Web site or your local office, which you must send off to HMRC (formerly the Inland Revenue); doing so eventually results in a new P45 and tax code being issued. In the meantime you have to deduct tax from any wages she gets using an emergency code, meaning that you may deduct more tax than necessary (but that can be refunded in future wage packets when you have received your employee's correct tax code).

Keeping PAYE records

Because PAYE is such a complicated system covering all sorts of individual situations, you should maintain your tax deduction records in good order. Using HMRC (Inland Revenue) forms is the easiest way to do this – you can get your local tax office to send them to you or download them from the HMRC Web site www. hmrc.gov.uk.

You need to keep the following for your own records:

✔ Records showing all wage and salary payments you've made in whatever form, including benefits in kind.

✔ Wage slips showing how you have calculated each employee's wages along with her tax deductions.

✔ P45s for each employee, showing her tax codes. (And when an employee leaves, you give her a P45 to pass on to her new employer.)

✔ P60s for each employee, showing the total amount of tax that you've deducted for the whole tax year.

At the end of the tax year, send HMRC (the Inland Revenue) the following:

✔ Details of each employee's pay and deductions.

✔ Details of all employee expenses and benefits.

✔ Details of National Insurance contributions (see 'Deducting National Insurance' for more details about this).

At the end of the tax year, you must also give each employee:

✔ Her P60.

✔ A copy of the information you've sent HM Revenue & Customs about her expenses and benefits.

Deducting National Insurance

National Insurance Contributions (NICs) fund future benefits for the contributor, such as state pensions and Job Seeker's Allowance. NICs fall into different classes, and the class of contributions paid affects the benefits the contributor's entitlements in future.

Most people who work have to pay NICs and as an employer you also have to pay NICs on most of your workers. HM Revenue and Customs collects National Insurance and again you get to play the role of unpaid collector. You don't have to pay NICs for people who are self-employed – they take care of their own NICs.

As with the PAYE scheme, it's up to you to calculate, deduct, and pay HM Revenue and Customs. Once you have registered as an employer with the HMRC you will get payment slips to fill in and return with your NICs.

NICs for employees

Different classes of NICs exist. Some classes are paid at a flat rate and some depend on earnings. Self-employed people pay their own contributions, so you don't have to deduct them from any money you pay out to people working for you on a self-employed basis. All other employees pay Class 1 contributions, and some employees may also pay Class 3 contributions. Here's how you know who pays what:

✔ **Employees pay Class 1 contributions on earnings over the** *Earnings Threshold* **(ET).** The ET usually changes at the beginning of each tax year. The 2005 rate was £94 a week. An employee pays 11 per cent of her gross earnings over the ET into National Insurance up to the *Upper Earnings Limit* (£630 per week in 2005). If she earns more than the Upper Earnings Limit, she just pays 1 per cent on any earnings above that rate.

✔ **People who haven't paid enough National Insurance in the past to qualify for certain benefits like a full state pension pay Class 3 contributions at a flat rate.** Usually that's because the person's been taking time out of work or she's been abroad. You usually pay Class 3 contributions direct to HM Revenue and Customs (the Inland Revenue).

NICs for employers

As well as organising the payment of your employees' NICs, and paying your own personal NICs, you must make two other National Insurance payments from your business:

✔ **Secondary Class 1 contributions.** You pay these at 12.8 per cent on all your employees' gross earnings over the Earning Threshold (refer to 'NICs for employees' for an explanation of that). Unlike your employees' own contributions, there's no Upper Earnings Limit on how much you pay.

✔ **Class 1A contributions.** You pay these on your employees' benefits in kind, such as the company car or medical insurance.

You have to pay Class 1 NICs to HM Revenue & Customs monthly and you calculate and pay the Class 1A contributions annually.

Keeping NIC records

All sorts of records need to be kept showing how you arrived at the calculations and what payments you have made. You need to keep the following records relating to NICs:

✔ Payroll records for all staff including payslips, deductions, salary details, and NICs deducted.

✔ Evidence of how you calculated the NICs.

✔ Records of NIC payment to the Inland Revenue.

✔ Copies of P60s given to employees each year showing NICs for the year.

✔ Copies of P11D forms for each employee showing the benefits in kind and the NICs due on them.

✔ Evidence of calculations and payments of any additional NICs over the year.

Reduced NICs

You may come across the occasional female employee who's paying Reduced NICs (sometimes known as the married woman's stamp). The government allowed these employees to choose to pay reduced contributions on the grounds that they were married and would be entitled to a full state pensions based on their husbands' National Insurance payments. Women paying reduced NICs pay 4.85 per cent on earnings between the Earnings Threshold and the Upper Earnings Limit and 1 per cent on anything over that. Women can no longer choose this option, so it's something of a rarity these days.

You need to keep these records for the current year and for at least the previous three tax years.

Counting Up Any Other Deductions

Your employees' wage deductions don't necessarily stop with tax and National Insurance. Depending on your employees' circumstances, you may need to deduct other amounts too.

Most students won't get through university without taking on a student loan and they have to pay this money back as soon as they are earning enough. HM Revenue and Customs (formerly The Inland Revenue) is responsible for collecting repayments on loans taken out after August 1998 meaning that you end up with the job of collecting them on HMRC's behalf. When you take on a new employee look on her P45 form for a box marked 'Continue Student Loans Deduction'. If there's a 'Y' for yes in that box you need to make deductions. Alternatively the Inland Revenue may send you a *Start Notice* (form SL1) relating to one of your employees; in this case you must start making deductions. Special student loan deduction tables are available to help you work out what to deduct and pay to HM Revenue & Customs.

Include details of student loan deductions on the employee's payslips; if she leaves you have to put details of the deductions on her P45 so that the next employer knows the score.

You can get help administering student loan repayments from HM Revenue and Customs' telephone helpline: 0845-7646646 or by looking at their Web site: www.hmrc.gov.uk.

Deducting pension contributions

If you have five or more employees, you must offer them the chance to belong to a pension scheme. This can be an occupational scheme, a group personal pension, or at the very least a stakeholder scheme. Chapter 20 has more detail about pensions.

If an employee is a member of a scheme you need her permission in writing to take her pension contributions out of her wages. It's your job to:

- ✔ Pass contributions to the pension scheme.

- ✔ Keep records of these payments.

- ✔ Pay the contributions by the date they're due or by the 19th of the following month.

Making child support payments

You can find yourself having to make deductions from an employee's pay to cover child support payments. The Child Support Agency sometimes has difficulties getting non-resident parents to pay towards their child's upbringing and has the right to ask the court to order that the employer takes the payments directly from an employee's wages. If that happens you are the one who will have to deduct the money and hand it over to the agency. This is known as a *Deductions from Earning Order*. The section on 'Handling Attachment of Earnings Orders' later in this chapter deals with these sorts of deductions.

Child support payments must be handed over to the Child Support Agency by the 19th of the month following the deduction from pay and it's an offence not to comply with one of these orders.

The Child Support Enquiry Line can provide assistance to you; the telephone number is 0845-7133133 and the Web site address is www. csa.gov.uk.

Giving to charity

Enabling staff to make regular charitable donations directly from their wages (known as a *payroll-giving scheme*) is an extra option you may want to provide. It's very little effort for many good causes; it makes it easier and more worthwhile for employees who want to give to charity; and it boosts your image as a caring, socially responsible employer. Employees don't pay tax on the amounts they give to charity and most of the paperwork is done by

Payroll-Giving Agencies approved by HM Revenue and Customs (the Inland Revenue). If you set up a contract with one of these agencies, you need to keep the following records:

- ✔ A copy of your contract with the payroll-giving agency.

- ✔ Forms filled in by your employees authorising you to take their contributions.

- ✔ Details of the deductions from pay.

- ✔ Receipts from the agency.

If you don't already have such a scheme in place, you can set one up. You may even qualify for a grant of up to £500 until March 2007! The HMRC (Inland Revenue) Charities Helpline can provide more advice; call them on 0845-3020203.

Dishing out union dues

Members of a union have to pay their regular union subscriptions, and if you have a recognised union in your workplace these subs will usually come directly out of pay – which you deduct and hand over to the union. You will need written consent from employees to make the deductions and should either show the deduction on each payslip or (as the deduction's likely to be a fixed deduction each month) give employees a standing statement of what the deductions will be for the next year.

Handling Attachment of Earnings Orders

You may sometimes have to take deductions from an employee's wages due to a court order. That is, a court may order that a certain amount of money must be taken directly from your employee's wages in order to pay someone she owes money to. This is called an *Attachment of Earnings Order* (or in some cases a *Deduction from Earnings Order*).

The order instructs you (the employer) to pay a certain sum of money at a regular interval – probably monthly – directly to the court office. You must take that sum of money directly from the employee's wages before you pay her. The main reasons a court will issue an attachment of earnings order are when someone:

- ✔ Owes child support.

- ✔ Owes maintenance to an ex-partner.

✔ Has a court judgment against them for debts of more than £50.

✔ Has to make payments under an *administration order* (an order for a single regular payment to cover a series of debts owed to various creditors).

✔ Has to pay fines having been convicted in a criminal court.

✔ Has to make contributions towards the repayment of legal aid.

 Under an Attachment of Earnings Order you have a legal obligation to make the deduction and send it on to the court. For the purposes of an order, 'earnings' means:

✔ Wages

✔ Bonuses

✔ Commission

✔ Overtime

✔ Pension payments

 These are called *attachable earnings*. But limits as to what can be deducted are in place – your employee can't be left with nothing to live on. The court has to assess what the employee needs to live on for her basic needs, and that amount is known as *protected earnings*. The court can't order deductions that will leave your employee with less than the protected earnings amount.

The courts can make more than one attachment of earnings order against an employee at any one time and these take priority in chronological order.

You're within your rights to charge your employee a small amount to cover any extra administration costs that you run up as a result of an Attachment of Earnings Order. You can deduct that amount from her wages too, but you have to give her notice in writing.

Be fair. If you can absorb the costs and forget about them it will be better for your working relationship. If you do charge her, don't charge more than your actual costs – such as postage and stationery. She can already be struggling to survive on what the court has left her to live on.

 If you're faced with an Attachment of Earnings Order you have no choice but to do the court's bidding or you'll be in the dock yourself. If you don't make the deductions and pass the money on to the court office, you can be convicted and fined.

Overpayments

If you have overpaid an employee you are usually legally entitled to have that money paid back to you. You can deduct it from future wages. In this situation, you don't have to have an employee's written consent to make the 'payback' deductions but you need her agreement in writing before you begin to make the deductions.

The employee may plead that she's already spent the money but that doesn't mean that she doesn't have to pay up. Take into consideration that she may have genuinely been unaware that she'd been overpaid – maybe through a clerical error. If the error has been made for a few months in a row it's possible she owes you quite a lot of money. It will be unreasonable to ask her to pay it back all in one lump sum. Be prepared to negotiate a deal whereby she pays back – or you deduct out of her wages – a certain manageable amount each pay-day. This is the kind of scenario where you'd certainly want her consent to the deal in writing.

The odd occasion may arise when an employee argues that (in good faith) as a result of the extra money she changed her financial standing and ran up bills that she wouldn't otherwise have run up. If you take her to court to get the money back or she takes you to an Employment Tribunal because she feels you were unlawfully deducting money from her wages to recover the overpayment and she can convince the court she spent the money in good faith, you won't get it back. The *good faith* element of this defence is crucial, implying that she didn't know and can't reasonably have known that she was being overpaid.

 Make sure that your pay system is very transparent so that your employees know what to expect in their pay packets and there's no chance of a member of staff getting extra pay without realising that it's a mistake.

Money to Make Up for Shortfalls

If you work in the retail industry the till may sometimes be short, or unexplained gaps in your stock may occur; if so, you can make deductions from wages to recover those. But you can only do so as long as this is covered in the employee's contract and:

- ✔ You tell the employee in writing what the total shortfall amounts to.

- ✔ You make a written demand for payment on the pay-day you're making the deduction from.

You have to make the deduction within 12 months of discovering that there was a shortfall and you can't take any more than one tenth of an employee's gross wages out of any wage packet (unless it's a final wage). Investigate fully and make sure the employee is the one responsible for the shortfall – otherwise the employee may make a claim against you for an unlawful deduction of wages. She may even feel that your actions had left her unable to go on working for you; that she had no choice but to quit and claim constructive unfair dismissal (see Chapter 4).

Chapter 18

Adding Up the Bill for Time Off

· ·

In This Chapter

▶ Handing out holiday pay

▶ Coughing up cash when employees are ill

▶ Calculating maternity, paternity, and adoption pay

▶ Getting some of the money back

· ·

*E*mployees do take time off work, whether they're on holiday, parental leave, or sometimes unwell. You have to pay for some of this time off out of your business profits and some of it you can recover from HM Revenue and Customs, the new department which combines the work of the Inland Revenue and Customs and Excise.

There's more information on holiday entitlements in Chapter 7; more on the rules about sick leave in Chapter 8; and more on time off for having a baby in Chapter 9. In this chapter, how to pay for it all is the issue.

Paying for Holidays

Most employers accept that there's a good business case for allowing members of staff to take time off to recharge their batteries and the law now says that employers must pay most people for a certain minimum amount of time off each year. A few employment exceptions still exist, as you can see in Chapter 7.

To keep matters clear for everyone, set out policies on how much annual leave your employees are entitled to, the dates your company's holiday year runs from and to, and your policy on public holidays.

Annual leave

Spell out the details of annual leave entitlement in your employees' contracts. The law entitles employees to at least four weeks' paid leave, but you may be more generous than that. You can count bank and public holidays as part of those four weeks, but again you may decide to give employees those days off on top. You can also increase the amount of annual leave depending on how long people work for you.

Whatever you decide, you can't give your employees less than the legal minimum. So if someone works 5 days a week he should get 20 days off. If he works 6 days a week he should get 24 days off, and if he works fewer days in a week he should get 4 times what he works on average (so someone who works a 3-day week should get 12 days' holiday).

The holiday year

For the sake of your payroll it's a good idea to make sure that all your staff have the same holiday year regardless of when they joined you. Otherwise calculating all their different entitlements and holiday pay will be a nightmare. Most bosses opt for a holiday year running from 1 January to 31 December, from 6 April to 5 April the following year, or a year that coincides with their accounting year.

If, for the sake of argument, your holiday year runs from 1 January to 31 December, someone who starts working for you on 1 January and stays with you for six months will only be entitled to half of his annual holiday entitlement by the time he leaves. If he works from 1 January through to the end of December he should have taken his full year's entitlement and be starting again from 1 January. If he joins you on 1 September and your holiday year runs from 1 January to 31 December, then by 31 December he will only be entitled to a quarter of a total year's holiday.

Public and bank holidays

There are eight bank and public holidays in England, Wales, and Scotland and ten in Northern Ireland. If you count them as part of your employees' total holiday entitlement you simply have to allow employees four weeks off a year and pay them for that time. They don't have to have those actual public holidays off. People assume that they are entitled to have those particular days off or to receive more than their normal pay if they work on those days, but that's only the case if that's what it says in their contracts.

Calculating Holiday Pay

If your employees work the same hours each week and get the same pay per hour, then when they take any holiday they simply get their usual week's wage, even though they're not at their desks. If they would normally get bonuses, shift payments, or guaranteed overtime payments, you should include these in their holiday pay. You basically pay them for 52 weeks a year but they only work for 48 of them.

If employees' hours and wages vary, as they do for *piece workers,* or output workers who are paid for each unit of work they do – for example each garment they stitch together – then on a week that they are on holiday, you should pay them an amount calculated by taking the average of the pay they took home in the previous 12 weeks. Again, that should include the extra wages like bonuses, commissions, and guaranteed overtime.

If you do give your employees more than the statutory four weeks' minimum holiday, the rate of pay for the days over and above the four weeks can be whatever you agree with your employees in their contract.

 When you're thinking about how much holiday pay to give, think about what your competitors are up to. If you offer less annual leave and lower rates of pay than those being paid in the rest of the market, you may not get or keep the best staff.

Paying in lieu of holiday

You have to make it possible for employees to take their holidays, but if they choose not to take them all by the end of the holiday year you aren't under any obligation to allow them to carry the untaken days forward or to pay extra for days lost. The only time you have to pay in lieu of employees taking holiday is when they leave and haven't taken the full proportion of annual leave they're entitled to.

Paying while sick on holiday

If an employee is off sick their future holiday entitlement continues to build up unless the illness becomes long-term (see Chapter 8). If they get sick when they're off on holiday, they may qualify for Statutory Sick Pay. They should notify you that they're sick in the same way as you expect them to notify you that they're sick on a work day (Chapter 8 gives more details). Because in most cases the employee won't be entitled to any payment for the first three days off sick, they may prefer to carry on taking their paid holiday.

Paying when changing jobs

It's possible that an employee leaves you in the middle of the holiday year but hasn't taken all of his holiday entitlement up to that date. If you can't let him take the remaining days off between handing in his notice and actually leaving, then you have to add those days' pay into his final pay packet.

If an employee has already taken more days off than he is entitled to at the time he leaves, you will be within your rights to deduct that money from his final pay, but only if this is stated in the employee's contract.

Rolling up holiday pay

There is another way of paying holiday pay. Some employers give employees their basic pay plus an amount for holiday pay each week. They then expect employees to save up the holiday pay element throughout the year and use that to pay for their weeks off.

If you do roll up holiday pay you have to set out the details of the holiday pay in employees' contracts and it has to be a genuine additional amount on top of basic pay. The details need to be stated on the employee's wage slip.

Rolling up holiday pay in this way is illegal in Scotland because of the outcome of a court dispute over the issue, but not in the rest of the UK.

Paying While Off Sick

The most common reason for having to pay someone while they're not at work is because they're sick. Chapter 8 gives you the details of procedures to follow for a sick employee. Apart from the first few days of any period of sickness, employees can usually expect that you will pay them.

The minimum amount of pay an ill employee is entitled to is set down by law, and is known as Statutory Sick Pay (SSP). In many cases employers pay well over the SSP amounts and sometimes even give full pay for at least the first few weeks of a period of illness.

Statutory Sick Pay

In smaller firms most employees depend on Statutory Sick Pay to tide them over an illness. But employees aren't all entitled to SSP; the following employees can't get it:

- Employees who haven't yet done any work for you under their contract of employment.
- Employees who are sick for less than four days in a row.
- People working for you on a freelance or self-employed basis.
- Employees who are under 16 or over 65 on the first day of their sickness.
- Employees who earn less than the Lower Earnings Limit for Nation Insurance (£82).
- Employees who have claimed incapacity benefit or severe disablement allowance from the state within the last eight weeks.
- Employees who are pregnant and go off sick during the maternity pay period (Statutory Maternity Pay starts immediately instead; see the section 'Paying mum' for more details).
- Employees who are off sick during a stoppage at work due to a trade dispute – on strike – unless they can prove that at no time did they have a direct interest in that dispute.
- Employees who are in police custody on the first day they're sick.
- Employees who have already had 28 weeks of SSP from you in any one period of incapacity for work or in any two periods of illness separated by eight weeks or less in a period of three years.
- Employees who are outside the European Economic Area.
- Employees who have already had 28 weeks of SSP from a previous employer and, having moved to your firm go off sick again within eight weeks or less.

To qualify for SSP employees must:

- Have four or more consecutive days off sick on which they would normally work (including weekends, non-work days, and holidays). These are the *qualifying days*.
- Notify you of their absence as soon as possible and in accordance with your company's rules (but see chapter 8 Assessing Illness: 'Calling in sick' for rules about what you can't demand from employees).

✔ Supply you with evidence that they are too sick to work – such as a self-certificate for the first seven days and a doctor's sick note for the eighth day onwards.

Unless you've allowed for it in their contracts your employees won't be entitled to any pay at all for the first three days they're off sick. The first three days are the *waiting days* and a period of sickness of four days or more is known as a *Period of Incapacity for Work* (or PIW), during which you pay SSP if the employee qualifies from the information shown in the bulleted lists.

You may be able to claim back some of the SSP you pay out to your employees through the income tax and National Insurance Contributions you pay to HM Revenue and Customs (formerly the Inland Revenue). If your total SSP payments in a month are more than 13 per cent of the total Class 1 National Insurance liability (see chapter 17) for your whole company for that same tax month, you can get the difference back. You do the calculations yourself and deduct the amount you are reclaiming from the amount you are due to pay over to HMRC. You can get help with this from HMRC. There is a lot of information for employers on its Web site www.hmrc.gov.uk including a section called 'What to do if your employee is sick'; you can pick up relevant leaflets from your local HMRC office or call the HMRC Employer's Helpline on 0845-7143143.

If an employee goes off work sick for four days or more, comes back to work, and goes off sick again within eight weeks for another four days or more, SSP will start immediately on the second occasion – without a second period of three waiting days.

SSP is paid for up to a maximum of 28 weeks. To qualify employees have to have been earning more than the Lower Earnings Limit for National Insurance Contributions over the eight weeks before the illness (£82 a week). SSP is £68.20 per week.

If an employee has used up his entitlement to the maximum 28 weeks SSP and you don't have any contractual agreement to pay him for longer, he will have to apply through the benefits system via his local Benefit Agency office or Job Centre Plus for Sick Benefit from the State. The same applies if he's not eligible for SSP in the first place.

If you don't pay SSP when one of your employees qualifies for it he can complain to an HM Revenue and Customs (formerly Inland Revenue) adjudication officer, leading to a decision as to whether or not you must pay. Chapter 8 has more details. However, you can decide not to pay SSP if you believe that the employee isn't really ill or he doesn't notify you in accordance with the rules you operate on notification of sickness.

You have to keep records for at least three years of any SSP you pay and of the dates of any periods of sickness lasting at least four days in a row.

Contractual sick pay

If your employees' contracts state that they get better sick pay than the SSP rates, you have to stick to those contractual amounts or be in breach of the contract. Some employers pay their employees their full salary for up to six months of sick leave and then half their normal pay for another six months. Some have contractual agreements where people can be off sick long term and still get some pay from the company. In most cases these contracts have been negotiated between the employer and a recognised union. You can't claim back any amounts you pay over and above Statutory Sick Pay.

Paying Parents

Employees who are about to become parents, whether because they're pregnant, soon to be a father or adopting a child, will be entitled to leave and will usually be entitled to be paid for some or all of that leave. HM Revenue and Customs produces leaflets that explain all the procedures for paying Statutory Maternity, Paternity and Adoption Pay. Visit the Web site at www.hmrc.gov.uk, call the employers' helpline on 0845-7143143, contact the HMRC office that deals with your business accounts or call into the local office to pick up leaflets.

Paying mum

Chapter 9 explains when a woman is entitled to maternity leave. All your pregnant employees are entitled to 26 weeks of ordinary maternity leave regardless of how long they've been employed by you, and they may be entitled to a period of additional maternity leave too. Your pregnant employee may be entitled to Statutory Maternity Pay (the minimum amount set out in law). To qualify for Statutory Maternity Pay (SMP) a pregnant employee:

- ✔ Has to have worked for you continuously for at least 26 weeks by the Qualifying Week (the fifteenth week before the expected week of the birth).

- ✔ Has to earn more than the Lower Earnings Limit for National Insurance Contributions (which is £82 a week).

✔ Must still be pregnant or have given birth at the beginning of the eleventh week before the expected week of childbirth.

✔ Has to give you proper notification (see Chapter 9).

✔ Must provide you with medical evidence (a MAT B1 form) of the expected week of the birth.

Statutory Maternity Pay lasts for 26 weeks. If an employee chooses to stay off longer than the ordinary maternity leave period of 26 weeks, Statutory Maternity Pay doesn't cover the additional maternity leave. You may of course have made more generous provisions for paying for maternity leave in your employees' contracts. The government is planning to change the rules about Statutory Maternity Pay to give mothers the right to be paid for more of their maternity leave and to transfer some of the leave and pay to the father. The best way to keep up to date is to check on the HMRC Web site each time an employee informs you that she's pregnant.

For the first six weeks of Statutory Maternity Pay, an employee's entitled to nine-tenths of her average earnings (averaged for the last eight weeks up to and including the Qualifying Week). Shift allowances, overtime payments, bonuses, and commission are included. For the other 20 weeks, she's entitled to either the £106 set by the Government or 90 per cent of her average earnings – whichever is the lower amount.

An employee doesn't have to intend to come back to work in order to get SMP. You have to keep on paying SMP for the full 26 weeks even if she leaves your employment after she qualifies for the money. Payment of SMP can't begin until the Sunday after the employee leaves work to start her maternity leave (see Chapter 9), and can start at any time from the start of the eleventh week before the expected week of childbirth. But if she decides to work right up until the baby is born, the maternity pay starts from the Sunday following the birth. If your employee decides to come back to work before the end of the 26 weeks of SMP, her SMP stops. From the point of view of income tax and National Insurance, SMP is regarded as earnings.

If you don't pay SMP when an employee is entitled to it she can apply to HM Revenue and Customs for a formal decision. If HM Revenue & Customs decides that you should be paying SMP and you still don't pay up within the time allowed, you can be fined up to £1,000.

Getting help with SMP

The good news is that employers do get some help from the government to pay SMP bills. You can usually get a refund of 92 per cent of the SMP for any employee by taking money back through the National Insurance Contributions system (see Chapter 17). If you're a small employer whose total National Insurance Contributions are under £45,000 a year, you can recover the full amount of SMP paid out plus 4.5 per cent compensation. As with Statutory Sick Pay you calculate how much you should be entitled to reclaim and deduct that from the amount of Income Tax and National Insurance you are due to pay over to HM Revenue and Customs each month.

If your finances are a bit tight and you can't afford to pay an employee's SMP, you may be able to claim funding in advance from HM Revenue and Customs. Contact the HMRC office that deals with your Income tax and National Insurance accounts.

Contractual maternity payments

After the 26 weeks of Statutory Maternity Pay are finished, nothing in law accounts for payments for any further maternity leave. But some employers do give their employees better terms for both maternity leave and pay. If you have written better terms into your contracts and don't deliver you can be sued for breach of contract.

Paying dad

New dads are entitled to two weeks' paid leave to help care for their child and the mother. To be eligible the employee must have responsibility for the child's upbringing, be the father of the baby or the mother's husband or partner, and have worked for you continuously for 26 weeks as at the fifteenth week before the baby is due. He is entitled to take either one week or two consecutive weeks off, but can't take the time off in odd days here and there. He'll be entitled to Statutory Paternity Pay (SPP) for the time off if he earns more than the Lower Earnings Limit for National Insurance (£82 a week). SPP is £106 a week or 90 per cent of his average weekly wage if that's a lower amount.

As with SMP, if you have to pay fathers' paternity pay you'll be able to recover most of it through National Insurance payments in the same way. See the section on 'Paying Mum' above for more details.

Adopting

Most employees who adopt children are entitled to adoption leave for up to 52 weeks and to Statutory Adoption Pay (SAP) for 26 weeks. It's very similar to Statutory Maternity Pay. To qualify, your employee has to have worked for you continuously for at least 26 weeks by the date she is notified that she has been matched with a child for adoption. Chapter 9 includes more details on your employees' rights regarding adoption.

Individuals who adopt, or one partner of a couple who adopt jointly, can qualify for adoption leave and SAP. The other partner of an adopting couple may be eligible for paternity leave and pay. Step-parents adopting their partner's children don't qualify for adoption leave or SAP.

SAP is the same amount as SPP: £106 a week for up to 26 weeks or 90 per cent of average weekly earnings if that's a lower amount. Adopters who earn less than the Lower Earnings Limit for National Insurance Contributions (£82 a week) don't qualify.

If you do have to pay out for SAP you can claim it back in the same way as SMP and SPP. See the section on 'Paying Mum' for more details.

Parental leave

Parents have a right to take time off to look after children or to make arrangements for their welfare. Chapter 9 explains how this works. But although each parent can take up to thirteen weeks off work in the first five years of the child's life, it is unpaid leave and you're under no obligation to pay for that time off unless you've written better terms into your employees' contract.

Paying Part-Timers

The rules are the same for part-timers as full-timers. If an employee works a three-day week and you've given him the statutory holiday entitlement of four weeks, he's entitled to four times three days off in the year. If he works different hours each week he is entitled to four times the average number of hours he works.

Part-time employees are entitled to Statutory Sick, maternity, paternity, and adoption pay too, in the same way as full-time employees. The same rules apply.

Unpaid Leave

Sometimes no matter how generous you are with holiday allowances, an employee needs a bit more time off to get over a domestic crisis or just to sort his life out. If he has no paid leave left he may ask you to agree to unpaid leave. If you agree you don't pay him for the time he takes off so there are no Income Tax, National Insurance, or other usual deductions to be made. Because he isn't leaving and you aren't dismissing him all his employment rights under the terms and conditions of his contract continue (see Chapter 3) unless you both agree otherwise. So for instance he'll still be building up holiday entitlement, have the same rights to private health care if you make that available to your employees, and the same right to a redundancy payment if you have to make him redundant in future.

 Whether or not you can grant his wish depends on what effect his absence will have on your business – but if you can afford to let him take the time away you may be rewarded with a more productive and loyal employee when he comes back.

Laying off Staff and Guarantee Payments

Sometimes there's temporarily no work for your employees and rather than having to make them redundant, you just need to lay them off for a few days. You can do this if your employees' contracts of employment state that you can. But you will have to pay most of them some money. Unless they haven't worked for you for at least a month they're entitled to guarantee pay. It's not a lot – a maximum of five days' payments in any period of three months – at a maximum of £18.40 each day. If they normally earn less in a day you can pay them less. You can find more in Chapters 6 and 16 on guarantee payments, who doesn't qualify, and your situation if your employees' contracts don't allow for you to lay employees off.

Chapter 19

Figuring Out Final Payments

. . . .

In This Chapter

▶ Adding up final payments and deductions for departing employees

▶ Working out payments in lieu of notice, for unused holidays, and pensions payments

▶ Calculating redundancy payments

. . . .

*W*hen an employee leaves your firm, for whatever reason, you'll have to work out what should be in their final pay packet. A few people move on each year from most businesses, so this is something you may find you get a lot of practice at!

Some employees choose to leave to go to another job, and others leave to retire. You may have to let others go because you have to reduce your workforce or because you have reason to sack some-one. Whatever the situation, handle it as well as you possibly can, because people do talk afterwards and your reputation as an employer can be affected.

If someone resigns, don't take it personally! She may have picked up skills and experience with you and want to move on to learn new skills and take on new responsibilities. Or she may simply want an easier life with fewer responsibilities. And no matter how tempting, don't jump up and down with glee because you can't wait to get rid of her. Organise a leaving party and a present so that everyone feels good about the event. Use your employee's exit to take another look at your workforce and see if you need to make changes in its structure.

Give the person who's leaving the opportunity to have a final inter-view with you. You may learn something valuable from what she has to say about the way you run the company.

If you have to sack an employee, make sure you are doing so for a fair reason and that you follow all the correct dismissal and dis-pute resolution procedures – refer to Chapters 4 and 15 for more advice. If you have to make people redundant, don't select them unfairly for redundancy or discriminate against anyone, and remember that those left will feel vulnerable and need to be kept informed (see Chapter 5 for more on this).

Above all – get the final wages right! The last thing you want is a dispute over money that ends up at an Employment Tribunal and drags on well after the employee has left.

Working Out What's Owed When Staff Leave You

An employee's last wage packet should have all the money in it that your employee is entitled to up to the date she leaves. This includes:

- ✔ Wages up to the employee's final day.

- ✔ Any bonuses, commission, shift pay, overtime, or share of tips.

- ✔ Any money in lieu of notice.

- ✔ Any holiday pay the employee's entitled to for days that she was entitled to take off but wasn't able to.

- ✔ Any redundancy payments.

- ✔ Any sick, maternity, paternity, or adoption pay due.

- ✔ Any guarantee payments which are due for a period when the employee has been laid off (see Chapters 6 and 16 for more details).

See the section 'Paying Redundancy Money' for more details about redundancy pay. Chapter 16 gives more details about wages, and Chapter 18 provides information on holiday pay, sick pay, and payments for new parents.

After you know exactly how much you owe in the employee's final pay packet, any income tax and National Insurance has to be deducted along with any other deductions that you normally make (such as student loan repayments, Attachment of Earnings Orders, or union dues). The final pay packet is the last time you can make those deductions, so you need to make sure that you let everyone know that your employee is no longer working for you and that you will be making no more of those deductions – see Chapter 17 for more information. The people you need to inform include HMRC and other organisations who need to know about changes to salary deductions – student loan companies, for instance.

The employee may owe you some money too, such as an outstanding loan, advances, overpayments of wages, or money for shortfalls in the till or stock (these are all covered in Chapter 17). You're usually entitled to take any overpayments and shortfalls out of the employee's final pay packet, and will probably be entitled to take any advances of wages and remaining loan repayments too – if that's the agreement you drew up when you gave your member of staff the money. If you didn't make an agreement that anything still to be paid on a loan can come out of final wages but that the employee will repay it at a certain amount over a particular period of time, then that agreement still stands. Such agreements are separate to employment contracts and have their own terms and conditions.

An employee is entitled to a final wage slip detailing all the payments and deductions you've made, and a P45 showing how much tax and National Insurance you have deducted for the year to date. There's more on P45s in Chapter 17.

Paying Redundancy Money

Regardless of your financial situation, most employees you make redundant are entitled to a redundancy payment as compensation for losing their jobs and to tide them over until they get back into work.

A departing employee may already have a new job to go to before she leaves or she may find a new job straight away, but she's still entitled to her redundancy payment.

Knowing who's entitled to redundancy payments

The law entitles most people who've been employed by you for two years or more to a *statutory redundancy payment* (the minimum amount that the law says you have to pay an employee when you make them redundant – there's more in the section 'Payments the law says you must give'). To qualify, an employee has to have been employed by you for two years continuously and to have been dismissed by you because of redundancy. Chapter 5 explains more about redundancy, continuous employment and dismissal.

Employees aren't entitled to a redundancy payment if they:

- ✔ Have their fixed-term contract renewed.
- ✔ Have their contract renewed with a break of less than four weeks.
- ✔ Accept an alternative job offer from you.
- ✔ Resign before the redundancy notices were issued.
- ✔ Unreasonably turn down a suitable alternative job offer from you.

If you employed a member of staff before she was 18, that time won't count when working out what her redundancy payment should be.

An employee aged 65 or more when she's made redundant doesn't qualify for a redundancy payment as the law stands at the moment but the government may give over-65s the same rights to redundancy payments as their younger colleagues when the new age discrimination legislation comes in, in 2006. There's more on this proposed legislation in Chapters 13 and 20.

If you've given your employees redundancy notices but don't pay redundancy money, they can apply to an Employment Tribunal to decide whether you owe them money and how much. Anyone who doesn't claim within six months of leaving loses her entitlement.

Payments the law says you must give

No flat rate covers all statutory redundancy payments. The amount you have to pay each employee depends on how long she's worked for you, how old she is, and how much she earns. The best way to work out the exact entitlement is to use Table 19-1.

A *week's pay* means the employee's gross wage for the week in which you hand out the redundancy notices. If your employees get a fixed amount each week, use that in the calculation; if their pay varies from week to week, take the average over the previous 12 weeks. A limit to what constitutes a week's wages is in place for redundancy calculations; you calculate the payment using your employees' normal week's wages up to a maximum of £280 a week and anything they earn over £280 doesn't count. The calculation is made starting at the date of redundancy and working backwards to take into account the years of service that give the greatest entitlement. The table below shows you how many weeks money you have to pay out depending on age and total number of years worked.

Table 19-1					Calculating Redundancy Pay from Years of Service													
Service (years)	2	3	4	5	6	7	8	9	10	11	12	13	14	15	16	17	18	19	20
Age (years)																		
20	1																		
21	1	1½	1½	1½	1½														
22	1	1½	2	2	2	2													
23	1½	2	2½	3	3	3	3												
24	2	2½	3	3½	4	4	4	4											
25	2	3	3½	4	4½	5	5	5	5										
26	2	3	4	4½	5	5½	6	6	6	6									
27	2	3	4	5	5½	6	6½	7	7	7	7								
28	2	3	4	5	6	6½	7	7½	8	8	8	8							
29	2	3	4	5	6	7	7½	8	8½	9	9	9	9						
30	2	3	4	5	6	7	8	8½	9	9½	10	10	10	10					
31	2	3	4	5	6	7	8	9	9½	10	10½	11	11	11	11				
32	2	3	4	5	6	7	8	9	10	10½	11	11½	12	12	12	12			
33	2	3	4	5	6	7	8	9	10	11	11½	12	12½	13	13	13	13		
34	2	3	4	5	6	7	8	9	10	11	12	12½	13	13½	14	14	14	14	

(continued)

Table 19-1 (continued)

Service (years)	2	3	4	5	6	7	8	9	10	11	12	13	14	15	16	17	18	19	20
Age (years)																			
35	2	3	4	5	6	7	8	9	10	11	12	13	13½	14	14½	15	15	15	15
36	2	3	4	5	6	7	8	9	10	11	12	13	14	14½	15	15½	16	16	16
37	2	3	4	5	6	7	8	9	10	11	12	13	14	15	15½	16	16½	17	17
38	2	3	4	5	6	7	8	9	10	11	12	13	14	15	16	16½	17	17½	18
39	2	3	4	5	6	7	8	9	10	11	12	13	14	15	16	17	17½	18	18½
40	2	3	4	5	6	7	8	9	10	11	12	13	14	15	16	17	18	18½	19
41	2	3	4	5	6	7	8	9	10	11	12	13	14	15	16	17	18	19	19½
42	2½	3½	4½	5½	6½	7½	8½	9½	10½	11½	12½	13½	14½	15½	16½	17½	18½	19½	20½
43	3	4	5	6	7	8	9	10	11	12	13	14	15	16	17	18	19	20	21
44	3	4½	5½	6½	7½	8½	9½	10½	11½	12½	13½	14½	15½	16½	17½	18½	19½	20½	21½
45	3	4½	6	7	8	9	10	11	12	13	14	15	16	17	18	19	20	21	22
46	3	4½	6	7½	8½	9½	10½	11½	12½	13½	14½	15½	16½	17½	18½	19½	20½	21½	22½
47	3	4½	6	7½	9	10	11	12	13	14	15	16	17	18	19	20	21	22	23
48	3	4½	6	7½	9	10½	11½	12½	13½	14½	15½	16½	17½	18½	19½	20½	21½	22½	23½
48	3	4½	6	7½	9	10½	11½	12½	13½	14½	15½	16½	17½	18½	19½	20½	21½	22½	23½
49	3	4½	6	7½	9	10½	12	13	14	15	16	17	18	19	20	21	22	23	24

Service (years)	2	3	4	5	6	7	8	9	10	11	12	13	14	15	16	17	18	19	20
Age (years)																			
50	3	4½	6	7½	9	10½	12	13½	14½	15½	16½	17½	18½	19½	20½	21½	22½	23½	24½
51	3	4½	6	7½	9	10½	12	13½	15	16	17	18	19	20	21	22	23	24	25
52	3	4½	6	7½	9	10½	12	13½	15	16½	17½	18½	19½	20½	21½	22½	23½	24½	25½
53	3	4½	6	7½	9	10½	12	13½	15	16½	18	19	20	21	22	23	24	25	26
54	3	4½	6	7½	9	10½	12	13½	15	16½	18	19½	20½	21½	22½	23½	24½	25½	26½
55	3	4½	6	7½	9	10½	12	13½	15	16½	18	19½	21	22	23	24	25	26	27
56	3	4½	6	7½	9	10½	12	13½	15	16½	18	19½	21	22½	23½	24½	25½	26½	27½
57	3	4½	6	7½	9	10½	12	13½	15	16½	18	19½	21	22½	24	25	26	27	28
58	3	4½	6	7½	9	10½	12	13½	15	16½	18	19½	21	22½	24	25½	26½	27½	28½
59	3	4½	6	7½	9	10½	12	13½	15	16½	18	19½	21	22½	24	25½	27	28	29
60	3	4½	6	7½	9	10½	12	13½	15	16½	18	19½	21	22½	24	25½	27	28½	29½
61	3	4½	6	7½	9	10½	12	13½	15	16½	18	19½	21	22½	24	25½	27	28½	30
62	3	4½	6	7½	9	10½	12	13½	15	16½	18	19½	21	22½	24	25½	27	28½	30
63	3	4½	6	7½	9	10½	12	13½	15	16½	18	19½	21	22½	24	25½	27	28½	30
64	3	4½	6	7½	9	10½	12	13½	15	16½	18	19½	21	22½	24	25½	27	28½	30

The maximum number of weeks' pay the law says you have to pay is 30. That would be due to a member of staff aged 61 to 64, employed continuously by you for 20 years at the time you were making her redundant (20 years at one-and-a-half week's pay per year = 30 weeks). A 64-year-old who had been with you for 40 years from the age of 24 still wouldn't be entitled to any more money beyond the maximum 30 weeks' pay.

Under current law once an employee is 64 the amount of money she's entitled to reduces by one twelfth for every month she is over 64 – so by the time she reaches 65 her redundancy payment will be nil. But that could change when the government brings in new age discrimination legislation in 2006. There are more details in Chapters 13 and 20.

Paying what the contract says

As with any payment where the law lays down a minimum, you can pay more if you choose to. Although some firms do make enhanced payments, most small employers don't exceed the letter of the law. But if you have in the past made people redundant with enhanced redundancy payments and nothing in your current employees' contracts states otherwise, your staff may interpret those enhanced payments as 'custom and practice' that have become part of their contracts (see Chapter 3 for more on custom and practice). So you need to make clear in employees' contracts what your terms will be if you have to make people redundant.

On the other hand, some employers try to wriggle out of making redundancy payments by making employees contract themselves out of their rights to payments. You can't force employees to waive their rights to redundancy payments. Such contracting-out agreements are void unless the employee

✔ was on a fixed-term contract of two years or more made before the Fixed Term (Prevention of Less Favourable Treatment) Regulations 2002 came into force.

✔ agreed in writing, before she started work, to waive her rights to redundancy payments at the end of the contract.

Taxing redundancy payments

No-one pays tax or National Insurance contributions on statutory redundancy payments. But if you're paying out enhanced redundancy payments there may be tax to consider. The payments are tax free up to £30,000. If the redundancy plus any other amounts that have to be paid to someone who's leaving come to more than £30,000, income tax has to be paid on the amount over £30,000.

Lay-offs and short-time working

Some situations allow an employee to claim a redundancy payment without being dismissed. The Redundancy Payments Scheme prevents dodgy bosses from deliberately laying off a worker or putting her on *short-time work* (where an employee has less than half a normal weeks work and pay during any week in which she has a contract of employment with you) instead of dismissing her when little work is available, avoiding having to give a redundancy payment.

An employee who's worked for you continuously for two years, whose pay is directly linked to the number of hours she works or her output, may be entitled to a redundancy payment even though you don't dismiss her. An employee can resign and claim a redundancy payment within four weeks of the last day of lay-off or short-time working if she has:

✔ Been laid off or put on short time for at least four consecutive weeks.

✔ Been laid off or put on short time for six weeks or more in a total of thirteen weeks.

If an employee in this situation claims a redundancy payment, you can give her notice in writing within seven days that you fully expect to give her full-time working for at least thirteen weeks, starting within the next four weeks. If she doesn't accept that offer she can resign – giving you the correct period of notice – and ask a tribunal to settle the argument.

Understanding pension implications

If an employee is entitled to an occupational pension, that can reduce or even wipe out her redundancy payment. Any pension starting within 90 weeks of an employee being made redundant can be taken into consideration. Under the Redundancy Payments Pensions Regulations 1965 employers can offset pensions or lump sums which are paid immediately on redundancy or within a short time after – up to 90 weeks – against the statutory redundancy payment so that the payment is reduced or even wiped out altogether. Employers don't have to do this, but if you decide to you have to tell the employee in writing what you intend to do, show the amount the employee would have been entitled to, and how the reduction in the redundancy payment has been calculated. The calculation is quite complicated so you should take advice. The Department of Trade and Industry Web site has the details at www.dti.gov.uk or talk to your local Business Link office. You'll find details in the phone book or call 0845-6009006.

Getting on the wrong side of the law

If you aren't careful, you can commit various offences when it comes to redundancy payments, and the consequences can be fairly severe. Here are a few key offences to be aware of:

- ✔ If you don't make redundancy payments when you should, an employee can make a claim against you at an Employment Tribunal or can claim from the National Insurance Fund.

- ✔ If you fail to hand over any information the National Insurance Fund adjudication officer asks for to help decide whether a payment should be made.

- ✔ If you don't give an employee written details of the calculation of her redundancy payment they can bring a claim to an Employment Tribunal.

- ✔ If you are making multiple redundancies (20 or more), you must notify the Secretary of State – through the Department of Trade and Industry – by letter, or fill in form HR1. You can download this from the DTI Web site www.dti.gov.uk or get it from your local Job Centre Plus or through the Redundancy Payments Helpline. If you don't notify the Secretary of State you can be fined up to £5,000.

Money Instead of Notice

Whether an employee's leaving you voluntarily, you have sacked her, or made her redundant, the question of notice periods must raise its head. Normally an employee works until the end of her notice period, but sometimes you may want to let her go immediately or before the end of the notice period. For example, if you are letting go someone who has access to sensitive materials and for any reason think they may do something irresponsible with those materials, you probably don't want the person coming into work during the notice period, even if she's been a trustworthy employee to this point.

Likewise, sometimes the employee is giving you notice of a change of jobs, but is really hoping you'll offer the money instead of asking her to come in the next couple of weeks because she'd rather have the time off before starting her next job. However, if your employee wants to leave before the end of the notice period by her own choice, she's not entitled to money in lieu. For example, if you really need her expertise to make sure she has time to pass along what she knows to the next person to fill her slot, you don't have to let her go early.

If you do let an employee go before the end of her notice period, you have to pay her for those weeks even though she's no longer working for you. Otherwise she can bring a case against you for the money on the grounds of wrongful dismissal (refer to Chapter 4 for more details). If your employee wants to leave before the end of the notice period by her own choice, she's not entitled to money in lieu.

When it comes to paying money in lieu of notice, there's no limit on what constitutes a week's wages (unlike the caps placed on redundancy payments). You will have to pay the employee's normal week's wages or, if the pay and hours vary, a week's wages are calculated as the average of the last 12 weeks immediately preceding the first day of the notice period.

 If you've given your employee notice and she gets sick during that notice period, she is still entitled to be paid her notice weeks at her normal weekly wage. If you have given her more notice in her contract than the statutory amount, the extra weeks can be paid at the Statutory Sick Pay rates (see Chapter 18 for more on sick pay).

Retiring Staff

You have to work out final payments for a member of staff when she's retiring. That may be at whatever the normal retirement age is for your company or at 65 if you haven't set one. Some people want to retire earlier but, on the whole, the same applies as in any other situation when staff leave you. You need to work out what exactly you owe her and anything she owes you, make the necessary deductions, and then pay her what's left. Retirement and pensions are covered more in Chapter 20.

Paying Up If You're Going Bust

If you've totted up final payments but can't pay them, you're likely to be at the point of having to wind up your business or go into liquidation. In this situation, your employees are creditors of your business and as such are entitled to what's owed to them if there's enough money in the pot. They are *preferred creditors* and should get their money after your *secured creditors*, who have security such as a mortgage. You need to keep employees informed of what's going on and make sure they know that if you can't pay, the state, through the National Insurance Fund, will pick up at least some of the bills.

It can be a long process. If you are formally insolvent and an insolvency practitioner or official receiver has been appointed to deal with your business affairs your employees can contact the Redundancy Payments helpline on 08451450004 for help to make a claim. If you simply stop trading and aren't formally insolvent but can't pay what you owe them, your employees have to claim through an Employment Tribunal and if you still can't pay they can then apply to the fund. They may not get all the pay or notice pay they're entitled to – a week's wage is calculated up to a maximum of $280 – but they will be paid the amount of statutory redundancy payment they're entitled to. Chapter 16 has more information on this situation.

If your business is about to go 'pop', you need to try to keep all employees on your side, especially your finance and payroll people, while you're going through the process.

Chapter 20

Making Provisions for Life after Work

*I*n an ironic twist of the business world, to attract and keep the best employees in your business, you may need to look at what you offer them when they are ready to stop working – namely, your pension or retirement plan. There *is* life after work . . . and a whole generation of retirees out there on golf courses and foreign beaches can prove it. But many employees work on beyond the *state pension age* of 60 for women born on or before 6th April 1955 (by 2020 it will be 65 for women) or 65 for men. Nothing in the law stops people working as long as they like or are able to, as long as their employer is willing to keep them on or they can find another job. As well as the people who've had to keep working because they don't have sufficient pensions to retire on, for some people the prospect of not working is a nightmare, whether they have money or not. They may leave their careers and move into less pressurised, less lucrative jobs, but they want to carry on working to keep themselves busy.

You need to plan ahead to make sure that your staff have as easy a transition into retirement as possible and are as well taken care of financially as you'd like to be yourself – so this chapter also helps you think through the pensions options to offer staff. If you don't, you may find that you aren't getting the best staff because they're going to employers who offer better working conditions and pensions.

In 2006 new age discrimination legislation comes in, stopping employers using age as a reason for getting rid of employees.

Retiring Your Workforce

If you have set a retirement age for your employees it should be in their contract. Most employers set a retirement age that's the same for most of their industry. If you haven't set one it will be whatever has become custom and practice in your workplace or industry, and if no history of retirement exists then it will usually be 65 (see 'Taking account of custom and practice' in Chapter 3 for more about custom and practice).

If the contract states a clear retirement age, once employees reach that age you don't have to do anything other than make sure that they get all their final payments and give them a nice send-off. If you don't specify an age in the contract then you have to give the correct notice period – see Chapter 4 for more details.

You have to make plans to replace an employee who's retiring and who's handing over his work to a new person. Think about whether or not the outgoing and the incoming employees need to work together for a while to smooth the transition. You might also want to include your retiring employee in the recruitment process. After all, he's been doing the job and probably knows more about it than you do.

Exit interviews with departing employees can be very useful to both parties. An *exit interview* gives the employee the opportunity to have his say about how the place is run and anything he's not been happy about during his employment. You're losing an employee with a lot of knowledge of your business and with the best will in the world not everything he knows can be written down, put in files or databases, and left behind. An exit interview gives you the chance to gain useful insights, from your soon-to-be-departing employee, into the running of your business. And the fact that you listen will enhance your reputation no end. There is an example of an Exit Questionnaire you can adapt to use at exit interviews in Chapter 22.

Easing employees into retirement

Many people are very excited about retiring. They have plans or are motivated to find new ways to fill their time. How often do you

Retiring (but maybe not so shy)

Big companies can afford to send their people on retirement courses that spell out all the details of pensions, benefits, financial planning, work opportunities, or voluntary work and so on. One retiring friend even had advice on exercise for the over-60s. You probably can't afford to do all that, but you can let an employee have time off to make appointments with a pensions adviser or the local Citizen's Advice Bureau if he's worried about living on less money. He can talk to various organisations locally about any voluntary work available if he's worried about having too much time on his hands and becoming isolated at home. And maybe you can encourage him to use your work computers to look for courses or classes he'd like to do. The Pre-Retirement Association and the University of the Third Age are just a couple of organisations to contact. The Pre-retirement Association can be contacted on 01483-301177 or at www.pra.uk.com and the University of The Third Age is on 0208-4666139 or at www.u3a.org.uk.

hear retired people say 'I have no idea how I ever found time to work'? But retirement can look like a big black void to others. The gloom hanging over them can affect their work for a long time before they leave and can rub off on everybody else, especially if you have a small staff. Think about what you can do to help lift the gloom.

Talk to staff well before retirement about how they feel about it and what concerns they have and try, together, to come up with ways of making it easier. Sometimes information is all that's needed. Sometimes it's something practical such as having a computer at home when you've been used to having one at work. You may even have an old one you don't need or stretch to one for a leaving present.

You can pay for your employees to take advice on pensions as an employee benefit. It's not a taxable benefit as long as the advice or information is offered to all employees and costs you less than £150 per employee per year. Your local Business Link can give you more information and you'll find their details in the phone book or on the Web site www.businesslink.org.uk.

If a member of staff looks forward to retirement he'll be a valuable member of staff right up until the last day and remain loyal to you after he's left. And the remaining staff are likely to recognise that you're a good employer and do their best to earn their own comfortable retirements. You know it makes sense!

Offering early retirement

An employee who doesn't want to carry on working up to retire-ment age always has the option simply to hand in his notice and leave. But if you want an employee to go early you'll have to:

- ✔ Have a reason to dismiss him

- ✔ Make him redundant if you genuinely have to cut jobs

- ✔ Offer employees who retire early an incentive package

The last is an option open to employers who have occupational pension schemes (explained in the section 'Offering an occupa-tional pension', later in this chapter). Depending on the particular scheme there may be enough money in the pot to allow you to offer an employee a retirement package that encourages him to go before his normal retirement age.

As in any situation where someone leaves of their own volition, you give them the pay due to them and their P45. There may be no pension payments involved unless they are old enough to start taking their occupational pension if there is one in place.

Managing older employees

Current employment trends see employees working on to a greater age than used to be the case. Some employers have dropped retire-ment ages completely and encourage employees to stay on. And as with any employees you have a duty of care for their welfare, mean-ing that bosses have to pay more attention to the health and safety of older workers. For example, older workers may need more help to make sure that their workstations are ergonomically set up. They may have more problems with viewing computer screens. Simple things like more *screen breaks* (working away from the computer), more opportunities to walk around, and bigger text size on computer screens don't need to cost much but can make a big difference. Refer to Chapters 10, 11, and 12 for more information on health and safety.

You need to talk to all employees about any problems they're having around the workplace and that's probably even more true as they get older. The best way of doing this is to incorporate frequent, brief informal chats into the general running of the workplace so that employees feel you care without being intrusive. If problems do crop up deal with them quickly and involve your employees in coming up with solutions. They've probably all got older relatives and may have some useful ideas.

Encourage your older and younger staff to work together – they can all learn from each other. Some older staff think that just because they've always done something in one particular way that's the only way to do it. They can learn new tricks from younger dogs, who in turn will benefit from older employees' experience and knowledge.

Many people don't want to retire or would like to retire gradually rather than being in work one day and out of it the next. If your employee has been good at his job it's worth thinking about whether or not he'd still be useful to have around in another capacity. Perhaps he can work fewer hours and reduce his hours over a period of time to ease him into retirement. Maybe he can continue working for you as a consultant on a self-employed basis after he leaves. You're not only looking after his welfare but making sure that you don't lose all his knowledge and expertise at once.

If you want to keep an employee, and he wants to stay on there's nothing to stop you keeping him on the payroll past the normal retirement age for your company – or 65 if there isn't one. If they are taking their occupational pension payments, however, your occupational pension scheme may stipulate that people have to retire at a certain age. Past 65 they won't have the right to claim unfair dismissal or redundancy payments.

Avoiding discrimination

Employers are becoming increasingly dependent on older workers as demographics shift and the pool of younger people becomes smaller. But some employers feel that older people are more trouble around the workplace and because they've worked their way up are probably more expensive than younger replacements would be. So the temptation exists to get rid of older employees if the opportunity arises or not to hire them in the first place.

Older workers have the same basic rights as younger workers – until they reach retirement age at 65 and then they have none. For example, 65-year-old (and older) employees have no right to claim compensation for unfair dismissal or redundancy payments. The government may give employees those rights when the age discrimination legislation comes in, in 2006 but as the law stands at the moment nothing stops you deciding that if you have to make someone redundant you'll choose the older one for no other reason than that he's older. But Beware. Employers have used redundancy as an excuse to dump people in their 50s for years, but new laws come into force in 2006 to stop this discrimination.

A Department of Work and Pensions Code of Practice that tries to address these issues of age discrimination does exist (flick back to Chapter 13), but hasn't proved terrifically successful. Until the new laws come in, employees can use the code of practice to support their claims of age discrimination against employers. As the 2006 age discrimination legislation approaches, tribunals are likely to expect employers to be changing their attitudes.

Pensioning Off Your Employees

Pension planning is important. Even young people see pension provision as an increasingly important part of the whole employment and pay package that prospective employers offer. More paranoia exists now about pensions than there has been for decades. People are worried about changing jobs in case their new employer's pension scheme is worth less than their existing one. Where people used to say 'I've just got a couple of years until I get my pension – much as I hate my job I'm going to stay put', they're now saying the same with six or eight years to go. So you need to understand the pension system.

Pensions broadly break down into four categories:

✔ **State pensions.** The basic state pension, the state second pension and SERPS. State pensions are available to all workers who've paid the right National Insurance Contributions.

✔ **Occupational pensions.** Including final salary, money purchase, and group personal pensions; occupational pensions are organised privately by employers.

✔ **Stakeholder pensions.** Like occupational pensions, stakeholder pensions are private pensions, but are available to self-employed workers too and people who aren't working but can afford them.

✔ **Personal pensions.** These are private plans that people arrange for themselves.

If you employ five or more workers you have to offer an occupational scheme, or a stakeholder scheme, or pay contributions worth at least 3 per cent of your employees' wages into your employees' private schemes.

An employee may already have his own (non-employment-related) personal pension plan when he joins you and not want to join whatever scheme you offer for some reason. That may not be the most sensible decision and you should advise him to talk to a financial adviser: If employees don't have access to an occupational scheme and don't save into a personal pension or a stakeholder scheme, they're dependent on the state pension.

You should encourage your employees to apply for *combined pension forecasts* from the Pension Service – allowing them to see forecasts of their state, private, and occupational pension provisions together. If they have that information they can plan better for their retirement. The Pension Service Web site is at www.thepensionservice. gov.uk or on 0845-6060265.

Depending on the State

A *state pension* is the sum of money paid to all retired workers by the government; everyone who works saves for their future by paying National Insurance Contributions (NICs), which contribute to their final pension. As an employer, you're responsible for collecting these NICs (see Chapter 17 for more about this).

Several types of state pension exist, and which one retired workers qualify for depends on their circumstances. As an employer you need to be familiar with the state scheme and encourage your employees to find out how much they can expect when they retire. They'll be entitled to some or all of the elements explained in this section and they can ask for a pension forecast from the Pension Service so that they know how much to expect from the state on retirement. Call the Pensions Service on 0845-3000168 for a State Pension forecast or visit the Web site (details above).

The state of state pensions

People are often very shocked when they find out how little they can expect from their state pension. Newspaper headlines for years were full of stories of well-off pensioners indulging their every whim and the importance of their spending power to the economy. As a result, an expectation arose among employees approaching retirement age that all pensioners can expect to be well off.

The reality is that unless they can afford to save money into an occupational pension provided by an employer, or into a private pension that they arrange themselves, retired workers are unlikely to be able to live the high-life as pensioners. In 1975 the full state pension was worth around 22 per cent of the average wage. Now it's worth about 16 per cent . . . and falling.

Basic state pension

The *basic state pension* is for people who've reached state pension age. At the time of writing, that's 60 for women and 65 for men. From 2010 women will have to retire later and by 2020 the state pension age will be 65 for both sexes.

The amount paid by the basic state pension depends on the number of years an employee has paid National Insurance Contributions – NICs – during his working life. *Working life* is 49 years for men and 44 for women, starting at the age of 16. If an employee has paid enough NICs during his working life, he gets the full amount (for example, £79.60 per week in April 2005).

Employees who haven't paid enough can add voluntary Class 3 contributions to make up the difference. They pay these direct to HM Revenue and Customs (formerly the Inland Revenue). If that's not an option the amount the employee gets will be reduced. If he hasn't worked he can claim on his spouse's contributions and will get £47.65 (that applies for both men and women). If the two members of a couple have both paid enough NICs they will both be entitled to a full pension.

People who have been out of work looking after children and getting child benefit are protected and have to pay fewer years' NICs to qualify for a full basic pension. Additional amounts are available for adult and child dependants. If you or your employees want to know more, go to the Pension Service Web site (www.thepension service.gov.uk) for a full explanation.

State second pension

The *state second pension*, sometimes known as an *additional state pension*, is for low and moderate earners. Employees earning up to £26,600 can get the state second pension on top of the basic state pension. It replaced SERPS (see the next section) in April 2002 and the government claims that the state second pension gives people earning up to £26,600 a better second pension than SERPS did.

Employees can leave, or *contract out* of, the additional state pension as long as they join a personal scheme, your employer's contracted-out occupational scheme, or a stakeholder scheme (all explained in the following sections). If they do choose to opt out and pay into your occupational scheme instead, you and they will both pay smaller NICs. If they contract out with a stakeholder or personal pension the NICs aren't reduced, but once a year HM Revenue & Customs rebates some NICs directly into their scheme.

SERPS – State Earnings Related Pension Scheme

The *State Earnings Related Pension Scheme* (SERPS) was the second state pension until April 2002, although employees who qualified for SERPS still accumulate a pension through the scheme. It started in 1978 and anyone who earned more than the lower earnings limit for National Insurance Contributions (see Chapter 17) built up an entitlement to a SERPS. The amount contributed to SERPS increased the more you earned.

Working out SERPS is complicated and employees can fill in form BR19 (available from the local Benefits Agency or Job Centre Plus) and send it to the Pension Service or visit the Web site at www.thepensionservice.gov.uk or call 0845-3000168 for a forecast of how much they'll get on retirement.

Graduated pensions

Anyone who worked between 1961 and 1975 may be entitled to a graduated pension. Lots of people coming up to retirement age in the early twenty-first century fall into that category. They would have to have paid Graduated National Insurance Contributions to qualify and the amounts paid out are very small. A state pension forecast from the Pensions Service will tell employees about any graduated pension they are entitled to and it will be paid to them with their state pension payments.

Offering an occupational pension

The government offers tax relief on contributions paid into personal, stakeholder, or employer's pension schemes. *Occupational pensions* are run by private financial companies rather than the government, and allow workers and employers (if they choose to – many typically pay around 3 per cent of an employee's earnings) to contribute to their own pension scheme.

Two types of occupational pension schemes are available:

- ✔ **Final salary schemes.** Salary-related schemes promise to pay an employee a pension of a certain percentage of his final salary or an average over his total employment.

  You pay contributions for each of your employees who join the scheme and your employees pay contributions at a certain percentage of their salary. As their salary goes up so the contributions increase and what's in the pot when they retire is dependent on their earnings and how long they've been a member. All the money paid into the fund is invested by the fund managers and if the investments do well everybody wins. If the investments do badly your contributions have to increase.

You take all the risk with a scheme of this sort, so fewer employers are setting them up and some who are already operating them are closing them to new members because they say they're too expensive to run.

In some cases firms have gone bust and there hasn't been enough money in the pot to pay out the pension obligations.

✔ **Money purchase schemes.** These operate in a similar way to final salary schemes – up to a point. Each member pays contributions into the scheme and builds up his own pot. The size of the pot will depend on how much employers and employees contribute and how the pension fund has been invested. When an employee retires his money is used to purchase an annuity. An *annuity* is an investment product sold by a range of insurance companies, and pays out regular payments to the employee after retirement until he dies.

✔ No guarantees are made about how much an employee will get after he retires because this depends on how the money in the annuity is invested and how well it does. Another problem for the employee when he retires is that he has a pension fund but he has to use it to buy an annuity – and a big choice of annuities exists. Getting it right is a gamble.

✔ More employers are opting to set up money purchase schemes and some are using them to replace final salary schemes.

The Pensions Regulator regulates pension schemes as the name suggests. That's the place to start for advice and information on your role as an employer. The Web site is at www.thepensions regulator.gov.uk or you can call 0870-6063636. The Pensions Service and your local Business Link can also help. Details for both are given earlier in this chapter. The Office of the Pensions Advisory Service has a wealth of general information on the whole range of pension schemes. The Web site is at www.opas.org.uk or you can call 0845-6012923.

You can't force employees to join an occupational pension scheme just because you offer it, but by not joining they miss out on the contributions you may choose to make to the scheme on their behalf. Most schemes will also provide for employees who have to retire early on the grounds of ill health and have a life insurance element so that their dependants get a lump sum if they die while they're a scheme member.

If you don't offer an occupational pension scheme or offer to make contributions worth at least 3 per cent of your employees' wages into their personal schemes, you may have to provide access to a stakeholder scheme (see 'Offering a stakeholder pension', later in this chapter).

If you do decide to go ahead with an occupational pension, you have to follow all the rules and regulations in place to protect the members, your employees. HM Revenue and Customs (Inland Revenue) approved occupational pension schemes give tax relief on contributions, allow members to take part of their eventual benefits as a tax-free lump sum, and allow members to contract out of the state second pension in return for a reduction in, or a rebate of, National Insurance Contributions (see 'State second pension', earlier in this chapter).

You don't have to set up and run an employer's or occupational scheme, but if you don't you may miss out on all the best recruits. Check out what your competition is offering and what the situation is throughout your industry. You may think you can't afford to run a pension scheme, but maybe you can't afford not to.

Running an occupational pension scheme

If you're thinking of running an occupational pension scheme you'll need a *pension provider* – one of the companies that sells and designs pension schemes – to set up and operate the scheme on a day-to-day basis, investing the money and administering it with the trustees who make the decisions. The scheme has to be registered with the Pensions Regulator (see above) and the pension provider usually does that.

Your scheme must have a qualified scheme auditor and, if it's a salary-related scheme, a qualified scheme actuary. Trustees have to be appointed to run the scheme and they have to be trained. The scheme has to be run in the interests of the people who will benefit from it, not in the interest of your business, and its assets and money have to be kept separate from those of your business.

Fulfilling your duties

Your role is to give employees access to the scheme and information about it, and to make contributions to their pensions. Employees should have:

- ✔ A booklet explaining the scheme
- ✔ An annual benefits statement showing how their pension is doing

✔ The trustees' report and accounts

✔ Information about their options if they leave the scheme

You have to get your employees' agreement when they join the scheme that you can take their contributions out of their wages. You have to send those contributions and your own contributions if you make any to the pension provider by the 19th of each month and you can be fined if you don't. You need a system for making deductions, paying them, and keeping records. Chapter 17 gives advice on money matters.

Appointing trustees

You have to appoint *trustees* to hold and make decisions about your scheme's assets for the people who will eventually receive pensions from it. Trustees have to act separately from you for the benefit of the scheme members, and their powers are set out in the trust deed – the legal document detailing their duties and responsibilities – and the scheme's rules.

The Pensions Act 2004 (which took effect from April 2005) requires trustees to be trained so they know exactly what they're taking on and what they have to do.

The Trust Deed sets out how new trustees are to be appointed. Members of the scheme have the right to elect or appoint at least half the trustees, and normally other trustees are appointed by you or by the existing trustees. One third of trustees should normally be Member Nominated Trustees (but the rules are very complicated and changing in 2006). You can't remove trustees yourself; only the other trustees, the regulatory authority – The Pensions Regulator – and a court have the power to do so. As long as they are over 18 trustees can be:

✔ A scheme member

✔ An employee

✔ A professional trustee or trustee company

✔ You, the employer

✔ A business associated with the scheme

Becoming a trustee of your own scheme creates the potential for a conflict of interests: You have to act in the best interests of the members not your own business.

Trustees have a legal duty to:

✔ Register a scheme, pay the annual levy, and take decisions for example about investments

✔ Take and keep records of meetings, decisions, and transactions

✔ Keep financial and member records

✔ Keep scheme assets separate from business assets

✔ Appoint professional advisers

✔ Get auditor's statements and actuarial certificates

✔ Approve and file the annual report

✔ Take investment decisions and appoint advisers

✔ Provide information for members, beneficiaries, and prospective members

✔ Sort out disputes for example where members complain about the scheme

Being a trustee isn't easy, and you should give employees time off to carry out their duties as trustees. They can be personally and jointly liable for scheme losses and be fined by OPRA if they don't comply with legislation. Your trustees do a very important job, so they need to be chosen carefully.

Making employer contributions

You don't have to make contributions to occupational pensions for your employees. Some employers pay all the contributions and don't expect their employees to make any from their salaries; on the other hand, sometimes the contributions the employer makes aren't big enough to provide a decent pension. Some employers have been cutting their contributions to salary-related schemes because they're no longer willing to carry so much of the risk.

Another option is to make contributions to your employees' private pensions. If you contribute at least 3 per cent to private pensions, you won't need to provide employees with access to a stakeholder or occupational scheme.

Overseeing workers' contributions

Some employers run schemes where employees don't have to make any contributions, but such generosity is rare. Usually employees join a scheme where the percentage of salary they're expected to contribute is already set.

Employees don't have to join any scheme you offer. They can make their own arrangements or decide they can't afford to pay into a pension at all. So far it's not compulsory.

If you do provide a salary-related scheme, you also have to give employees the opportunity to build up extra savings through *Additional Voluntary Contributions* (AVCs) which do what they say on the tin and allow employees to make extra contributions to enhance their pensions. You might choose to have the same company provide your AVC scheme that operates your occupational scheme or choose a different one.

Making contributions to group personal pensions

One other type of occupational pension you can consider offering is the group personal pension, a variation on personal (non-employment-related) pensions. *Group personal pensions* are arranged by individual employees, each having their own individual plan. However as the employer, you choose the plan for your employees. These pensions are money purchase schemes (see 'Money purchase schemes', earlier in this chapter) but are cheaper in terms of charges than the other occupational schemes due to group discounts.

Changing jobs

If an employee has been with you for less than two years and leaves, he's entitled to a refund of the pension contributions he's made into an occupational scheme, minus tax. If he's contributed to it for at least two years he can leave the money in your scheme where it remains invested and grows (with luck) and provides him with a preserved pension when he reaches the retirement age set down by that scheme. Alternatively, he may be able to transfer the value of what he has built up so far into his new employer's scheme. He may want to do that so he doesn't have to keep track of more than one pension, or it may be that the new scheme seems a better prospect. You should advise him to get financial advice.

The employee will carry on making NICs towards his state pension through his new employer.

Offering a stakeholder pension

Stakeholder pensions are a way for your employees to save for their retirement, but they can also be used by people who aren't employed. These low-cost schemes are intended for people who don't have access to an occupational or personal pension. They must have low charges, flexibility, and security. Minimum contributions should be £20 or less.

You have to provide your employees with access to a stakeholder pension if you have five or more employees and:

> ✔ You don't offer an occupational pension.
>
> ✔ You don't pay an amount equal to at least 3 per cent of your employees' wages into all private pensions for all your employees who are 18 or over.

Stakeholder pensions are chosen from a range offered by financial services companies. Take a look at several of the schemes, all of which must be registered with the Pensions Regulator (contact details earlier in this chapter), get all the information so that you can compare them, discuss the options with your employees, and together choose which one they should access. Giving employees *access* to a stakeholder pension scheme means:

> ✔ Giving them all the details of the scheme and the stakeholder provider
>
> ✔ Consulting them about deducting their payments directly from their wages
>
> ✔ Collecting their contributions and sending them to the stakeholder provider by the deadlines if that's what they want
>
> ✔ Keeping records of all the payments you make

You don't have to make employer contributions to the stakeholder pension if you choose not to.

Carrying on working and pensions

Nothing stops people going on working as long as they like, provided they can find the work. Occupational pension schemes may allow them to start taking their pension at 60 – and perhaps they can take the pension and find another job as well. Depending on the type of scheme, workers may be able to defer taking their pension until they do decide to retire, or take money out in stages to provide some income to top up earnings and take the remainder at 75.

Unfortunately you can't keep someone on your payroll and allow them to receive their occupational pension at the same time, but that may change in 2006 when the age discrimination legislation comes in, as the government looks for ways to encourage people to work longer.

Employees can receive the state pension and carry on working, or delay receiving it until they've retired fully. If they do carry on working after state pension age, they won't need to make any more NICs. Workers can defer taking the state pension as long as they like, and if an employee carries on working and wants to have a bigger state pension later he'll earn an extra state pension worth around 7.5 per cent of pay for every year he defers.

All pension payments are taxable.

Spouses, unmarried partners, and same-sex partners

State pensions and additional state pensions have regulated amounts that can be passed on to spouses, widows, and widowers, but similar payments from occupational pensions are determined entirely by the trustees.

You can write into the provisions of the scheme that unmarried partners and same-sex partners should be treated in the same way as spouses. These days when more people do live together without marrying or in same-sex partnerships, that's something that you should consider and discuss with your employees and trustees.

Part VI
The Part of Tens

"This might be construed as ageism."

In this part . . .

*E*very *For Dummies* book has its Part of Tens. This one has ten ways to avoid problems at work and ten documents I think make employing other people a bit easier.

Chapter 21

Ten Ways to Avoid Problems at Work

In This Chapter

▶ Knowing your obligations and responsibilities

▶ Keeping the lines of communication open

▶ Knowing when to ask for help

*W*hen it comes to employing people, you have to stick to the law but the law is the minimum that you must do. You can do much more to make the workplace somewhere that your employees want to be. The law is also littered with the word *reasonable*. You have to take *reasonable* care and do what's *reasonably* practicable. If you do have problems at work and end up in a court or an Employment Tribunal, the people hearing the case will want to know that you did all that a *reasonable* employer would do. In deciding what a *reasonable* employer would do the judges and tribunal members are making sure that you didn't cut corners with your employees' welfare and that you erred on the side of caution when it came to putting the law into practice. The better an employer you are, the fewer problems you will have at work. You don't have to spend a lot of money to become an employer people want to work for. It's more a matter of good practice and remembering that old adage – do unto your employees as you would be done by yourself!

Recruiting with Care

Employers sometimes make the mistake of thinking that because they have a vacancy they have to fill it at all costs. Filling it with the wrong person can be a big mistake. Sometimes leaving the vacancy unfilled until the right person comes along is the better option. Recruiting is about more than merely finding someone to do the job.

You have a duty to provide a safe working environment for your employees and that includes recruiting competent colleagues who work safely and take care of fellow workers. That can be someone who knows how to use the machinery properly and doesn't put colleagues at risk; or someone who pulls her weight and doesn't leave other people to do extra work because she's shirking, which can create a stressful environment. Check out potential employees' references and qualifications. Make sure their training is up to date or be prepared to put them through the latest training before they start work.

You have to recruit without discriminating against any of the applicants on the grounds of race, sex, sexual orientation, religion or other beliefs, or membership of or refusal to join a union (see Chapter 13). The age discrimination legislation due in October 2006 will make it illegal to discriminate on the grounds of age too. However, you are entitled to think about the best mix for your team. If you have too many men on your workforce, for example, because that's how it's always been, you can justify taking positive action to recruit women on the grounds that you are trying to achieve a balance.

Communicating Clearly

In many cases problems arise because of poor communication. Communication isn't just about you telling employees what you want them to know. It's also about listening to them and making them feel a part of the whole operation. Employees need to know what your ethos for your business is and they can't be expected to know or understand that if you don't discuss it with them. If people get used to an air of openness, where communicating is the norm, you can spot problems early and deal with them before they can cause any real damage.

Some big firms can afford to give employees share options or a share of the annual profit as a way of motivating them and making them feel they have a stake in the venture. Those aren't usually options for small firms where making enough to pay everyone, including yourself, is hard enough. But good communication can go a long way to playing a similar role.

The more employees know about how their workplace operates and the more they're involved in decisions about how it's run, the more they feel some ownership of it. That sense of ownership helps people feel empowered and motivated. They are more likely to take responsibility and to perform better. Be consistent in how you communicate with them. Don't just talk to them when things are going well and keep them in the dark over problems or when things aren't so hot. Having regular staff meetings and inviting employees to put issues on the agenda is a good way of developing valuable communication. You can learn a lot from the people you work with and good communication breeds trust.

Good communication is most essential when change is in the air. People get very insecure if they feel that there's something going on that you are keeping from them and their imagination can come up with much worse scenarios than the reality. If that happens, people start looking for new jobs. In a competitive marketplace, where many small business bosses worry about skills shortages, you can't afford to lose good people. Apart from having the costs of recruiting all over again, you may well have to pay for training. After one employee leaves there's often a period of unrest when more follow and productivity can suffer until everything beds down again.

You also need to create clear lines of communication within the workplace community so that all those who need to know about specific aspects of the business know who they must pass information on to and get information from. Without clear channels, people make mistakes and accidents happen. Make it clear that you won't allow personality clashes and differences of opinion to block up those lines of communication.

The more open everyone is around the workplace about anything to do with work, the better the atmosphere will be. Any vacuum of silence you create will simply be filled with gossip, speculation, and discontent.

Spelling Out Staff Responsibilities

Your employees need to understand what their responsibilities are to you, to the firm, to your customers and clients, to themselves, and to each other. Good Written Statement of Employment Particulars (see Chapter 3) with job descriptions, set out each specific position's responsibilities. But everyone shares the added responsibilities of working with and around other people. A staff handbook is a very useful tool for setting out all of those responsibilities, such as working safely so that employees don't put colleagues in danger, reporting accidents, or keeping certain information about your business confidential. You don't have to put everything in writing – but it's much better for everyone, including you, if you do. Make sure that people not only understand what their responsibilities are but why they have them and what the consequences are of not taking them seriously.

If you decide you want certain employees to take on more responsibility in their jobs, don't just impose the additional work on them. Simply expecting more of people without getting them to buy into the idea can breed resentment. Discuss your proposals with the employees concerned and get their agreement. You may think people are ready to take on more, but they may feel that they aren't or that any more responsibility will make them stressed. People often assume that having more responsibility merely means having to work harder for more hours. They may relish the challenge but not be prepared to give up any more time with their families. Think about ways to give people more responsibility without too much extra workload and don't forget to reward them. If people turn down the opportunity, don't take it out on them. Try together to work out ways to develop people's potential over time until they are ready to accept the extra responsibility.

Following Disciplinary Procedures

Your disciplinary procedures (see Chapter 15) have to be in writing and available to all your employees. Employees need to know exactly where they stand and the process they go through if they do something that you decide, following investigation, is a disciplinary matter. Make it clear what will trigger disciplinary proceedings, what will count as gross misconduct, and what will lead to dismissal. Forewarned is forearmed. If you do decide that you have to discipline someone, stick to the procedures. If you sack someone without following all the correct procedures you will risk being taken to an Employment Tribunal for automatic unfair dismissal. Tribunals can order you to pay the employee increased compensation.

Don't view your disciplinary procedure simply as a process for getting rid of someone. It's much more valuable if you use it to try to come up with a solution and a way of being able to retain someone. The more opportunities your procedure gives you for sitting down with an employee and discussing the problem and why it arose in the first place, the more likely it is that you'll be able to resolve issues without unpleasantness and the more you'll learn about what works and what doesn't in your workplace.

Don't dismiss anyone in anger, on the spot, even if you think she's been guilty of gross misconduct. Always investigate the situation fully before you decide what action to take. Unless someone has been guilty of gross misconduct, don't sack her for a first offence. Give the alleged offender the benefit of the doubt and help her to avoid making the same mistake in future.

At the same time, though, don't ignore problems – deal with them quickly and fairly. You never gain anything from dragging things out beyond the period of time it takes to follow the correct procedures. The same goes for dealing with complaints from your employees. Make sure they know how to complain and that you take them seriously.

Avoiding Any Kind of Discrimination

Allowing any kind of discrimination in the workplace can land you in big trouble. There's no limit on the amount of money that a tribunal can award to an employee who has been discriminated against and she can take a case against you even if it wasn't you but another of your employees who was guilty of discrimination such as harassment. You have to lead by example and make it clear that you simply won't tolerate discrimination from anyone in any shape or form.

It pays to have a policy on discrimination so that everyone knows how you will deal with it (see Chapter 13). Make sure you spell out that harassment and victimisation come under the same category. Quite often the discrimination shows up in the form of bullying. This can be hard to spot as victims are often scared that if they complain you won't believe them and the situation will just get worse. You have to create a culture where bullying simply isn't acceptable, so that people know you will take any suggestion of it seriously and will take action.

Taking Good Care of Staff

If you take good care of your employees they will take good care of your customers and clients. Your good reputation is very important in a competitive market – not only because your customers want to deal with a firm with a good reputation, but because people are more likely to want to work for you. Your employees are your ambassadors and your reputation protectors or breakers. If you take care of them they'll spread the good news; if you don't they'll spread the bad news even further.

Taking care of them means looking after their health and safety, as in Chapters 10, 11, and 12, and making sure that you don't break any of the employment laws. But it also means going that bit further so that if, say, three employers in the area are trying to hire similar people, with the same kinds of qualifications, you're the one people choose to work for. Paying the going rate is important, but money isn't always the top priority for a prospective employee. She may be more concerned about having flexible working patterns in case she needs time off to be with her young children or her elderly mother.

Taking care of employees also means keeping their workloads at a manageable level and making sure they know that they can talk to you as soon as they see a hint of a problem and that you will do whatever has to be done to deal with a situation. It's also about inspiring them with good leadership so that they're motivated; giving rewards for good performance; involving them in the running of the company and in decision-making; being open to new ideas about how to do the work; communicating well with them; and allowing for some fun from time to time so that stress levels are kept well under control.

Just because something has always been done in one particular way doesn't mean a better way of doing it doesn't exist.

Paying Everything You Owe

All employees need to know what your policy is on pay: how much they earn an hour, how and when you pay them, bonuses, overtime, commission, how and what you pay them for holidays and bank holidays, what the situation is if they go off sick, and when they can take time of without pay. Leave nothing to chance! And if you say you are going to pay people on the tenth of each month then don't delay until the twelfth. Two days can be long enough to mess up people's finances; the bank may refuse to pay out standing orders and direct debits or may bounce cheques. If you do have cash-flow problems, make sure that you talk to employees about the situation and come to an arrangement with them, rather than just leaving them without any money and being in breach of your contract.

Make sure that all the deductions you make from employees' pay are lawful (see Chapter 17). Tax and National Insurance are straightforward, but if you make other deductions without their agreement you are in breach of contract. Right at the beginning when you take someone on and draw up their Written Statement of Employment Particulars, get their agreement that if necessary you can make deductions to cover things like damage to your business property or to take back any extra money you have paid them by mistake. Even though you do have their agreement in writing, if the need ever arises to make those deductions, investigate fully and be sure that you really are entitled to take the money and give them fair warning that it's going to happen.

When people leave your employment, make sure you pay them all the outstanding amounts you owe them (see Chapter 19). Just because they're no longer working for you doesn't mean that you can short-change them. They are more likely to take a claim against you after they've left precisely because they no long have to work with you.

Consulting Correctly

If you're planning to change something around your workplace that will affect your employees, consult them about it. You can just go ahead and make changes and then inform them as and when they need to know, but that causes resentment and creates trouble. Some changes you want to make may in effect change employees' contracts and you can't do that without their agreement. If there is a recognised union in your workplace (see Chapter 8) you have to consult with the union representatives too.

You may feel that you're having to make decisions by committee if you have to consult employees at every turn, but if they understand why you need to make changes and feel they have a real opportunity to voice and iron out their concerns, they're much more likely to accept what you want to do. They may even have better ideas to contribute about how to carry out the changes you want to make. If they aren't consulted and you simply spring changes on them, they may feel like pawns in your game and that you are manipulating them, become demotivated, and get less work done. While consultation may seem like a pain in the neck, it makes good business sense.

Using Mediation

If problems do arise despite all your best endeavours and you can see yourself heading for a tribunal, get help. The Advisory, Conciliation and Arbitration Service (ACAS) does all the things its title suggests. It can arbitrate by hearing both sides of the argument and coming to a legally binding decision about how the dispute should be resolved. It can help you to come to an agreed settlement with the employee – conciliation. Or it can help with a mediator who can suggest ways of reaching a voluntary agreement. The contact details for ACAS are given in the next section 'Taking Good Advice'. Often when you're locked into a row with an employee you may feel that the only way out is to sack her. But don't forget that you can only sack an employee if you have a fair reason and you have to go about it in a fair way, so occasions can arise where sacking isn't an option (see Chapter 4). Stepping back from the situation and letting a third party listen to both of you can help you to see things much more objectively. Sometimes you don't really need the services of a professional mediator, just someone who can help you both to get your points of view across without shouting and come up with a few suggestions you haven't thought of. A visit to your local Business Link office to talk to an adviser may be enough to reach a solution acceptable to both parties. The contact details for Business Link are also given in the section 'Taking Good Advice'.

Taking Good Advice

Running a small business can leave you feeling very isolated. You probably don't have a management team to turn to for advice and support. Your solicitor and accountant are both useful, but you should choose people who are used to dealing with small businesses. Some very good big law and accountancy firms deal very well with large businesses but don't really understand the peculiarities of running a small operation. Don't forget your bank manager either – many banks provide business account holders with all sorts of useful publications and services. But other organisations can also help and you should never be too proud to admit that you can do with a helping hand:

✔ **ACAS** has an advisory role. Contact the helpline on 0845-7474747 or check out the website www.acas.org.uk if you are in any doubt about some aspect of the law and about what action to take.

✔ **The Federation of Small Businesses** lobbies government on behalf of small business owners on the whole range of business issues and runs a legal advice service for its members. For an annual subscription you have instant access to all the legal advice you can possibly need about running a business, including employment law. Contact the FSB on 01253-336000 or visit www.fsb.org.uk.

✔ **Business Link** is a government-funded business advice office with branches all around the country. You can find the details of your nearest branch in the phone directory and the organisation has a very good Web site, www.businesslink.gov.uk.

To enjoy some camaraderie with fellow small business owners and perhaps even share problem-solving innovations with people in similar sectors, try joining local business organisations such as the British Chambers of Commerce (phone 0207-6545800; www.chambersonline.co.uk) or nationwide business associations like the Association of Convenience Stores (phone 01252-515001; www.thelocalshop.com), to name but one of thousands. Just talking to other people working in similar areas or sectors can give you ideas for dealing with potentially difficult work situations. Other useful organisations which aim to reflect employers views to government, and to influence laws and policies affecting businesses are the Forum of Private Business – 01565-634467 www.fpb.co.uk and The Institute of Directors – 0207-8391233 www.iod.co.uk.

Chapter 22

Ten Sample Documents

In This Chapter

▶ Documents that will help you draw up your employment contracts

▶ Documents that you can adapt for your own use

▶ Documents that will help you draw up policies for your business

*I*n this chapter there are ten sample documents which will help you to see some of the information in the previous chapters in action. You can just read them to give you a better understanding of how disciplinary, grievance, sickness or redundancy policies might be put together. You can adapt them for your own use. The example of an application form, for instance, or the holiday request form will give you some ideas as to how your own might look. They all come from the Federation of Small Businesses (FSB) which provides its members with a wealth of information on all aspects of running a business including employment law. There are more details of the FSB in Chapter 21.

SPECIMEN APPLICATION FOR EMPLOYMENT

This form has been designed to tell us all we need to know about you at this stage. Please complete the form in black ink and block capitals.

Personal Information

Surname:	
Forenames:	
Title (Mr, Mrs, Miss, etc):	
Previous names (if any):	
Date of birth:	
Address for communications:	
Daytime telephone number:	
Are you subject to immigration control?	YES / NO
Are you free to take up employment in the UK?	YES / NO
Dates you are not available for interview	

Education

From GCSE or equivalent to degree level in chronological order

From	To	Establishment	Qualifications gained

Postgraduate education or study or any other professional qualifications

From	To	Establishment	Qualifications gained

Figure 22-1: Specimen application for employment form.

<u>Work experience</u>

Please give details of your last three jobs. Any relevant posts held before then may also be mentioned. Please begin with your present or most recent position and then work chronologically backwards.

From	To	Name and address of employer	Description of duties and responsibilities and reason for leaving

<u>Other Information</u>

Do you have any other relevant qualifications or skills (e.g. knowledge of a foreign language, a full driving licence, computer literacy, etc.)?

Please give details of any time not accounted for elsewhere in this application form.

Have you made a previous application to the Company? If so, when was this and what was the outcome?

Please give details of your main extra-curricular activities and interests.

Please use this space to say why you are interested in the post for which you have applied and mention anything else which supports your application.

If you are successful, when could you take up your post?

If you are disabled or suffer from an acute or chronic ill-health problem, please give details of any special arrangements you would require to attend interview.

Referees

Please give details of two referees. Neither should be a relative or contemporary.

First referee	Second referee

Declaration

I declare that the information I have given on this form is, to the best of my knowledge and belief, true and complete. I understand that if it is subsequently discovered that any statement is false or misleading, or that I have withheld relevant information, my application may be disqualified or, if I have already been appointed, I may be dismissed.

Signed: ....

Date: ....

SPECIMEN CONTRACT OF EMPLOYMENT

Between *(name of Company)* Limited and *(name of employee)* meeting the requirements of section 1 of the Employment Rights Act 1996 (as amended).

This Agreement is made between *(name of Company)* Limited ('the Company') and you. It supersedes any earlier written or oral arrangement between you and the Company.

The headings in this Agreement are for convenience only and shall not affect its interpretation.

1   JOB TITLE AND PLACE OF WORK

1.1   The Company will employ you as a *(job title)*. You will be required to undertake (such duties and responsibilities as may be determined by the Company from time to time.) *(or)* (the following duties and responsibilities: *(list of duties)*.) The Company reserves the right to vary your duties and responsibilities at any time and from time to time according to the needs of the Company's business.

1.2   Your normal place of work will be *(address)*. If necessary, you will work at and, if requested, change your normal place of work to any other branch office which the Company has already set up or may set up within a 10 mile radius of your normal place of work.

1.3   The Company's business premises are no smoking premises and any other premises that it may establish in the future will also be no smoking premises. *(Details of smoking areas provided, if any.)*

2   START OF EMPLOYMENT

2.1   Your employment with the Company started on *(date)*. (No period of employment with a previous employer counts towards your period of continuous employment.) *(or)* *(where the business was acquired as a going concern under the TUPE Regulations or the old employer was an associated employer:* Your period of employment with *(name of old employer)* which began on *(date)* counts as part of your continuous period of employment with the Company.)

3   PROBATIONARY PERIOD

3.1   The first *(number)* months of your employment will be a probationary period during which time your performance and conduct will be monitored and appraised. At the end of that period, your employment will be reviewed and may be terminated if you are found for any reason whatsoever to be incapable of carrying out, or otherwise unsuitable for, your job. Alternatively, the Company may extend your probationary period by up to three months.

4   NOTICE

4.1   Your employment is not for a fixed term and there is no anticipated duration for your employment but it may be terminated by notice. During any probationary period, your employment may be ended either by you giving the Company or by the Company giving you one week's written notice.

4.2   After the successful completion of any probationary period, your employment may be ended by you giving the Company (one month's) written notice. The Company will give you (one month's) written notice and after 4 years service a further one week's notice for each additional complete year of service up to a maximum of 12 weeks' notice.

Figure 22-2: Specimen contract of employment.

Your contract of employment is terminable by written notice as follows:

<u>Notice by the Company</u>

Length of continuous service	Minimum period of Notice
Less than one month	one day
One month to two years	one week
Two years to 12 years	one week for each continuous year of employment
12 or more years	12 weeks

<u>Notice to the Company</u>

Length of continuous service	Minimum period of Notice
Less than one month	One day
One month onwards	One week

4.3   The Company will not be obliged to provide you with work at any time after notice of termination shall have been given by either party and the Company may, in its absolute discretion, pay your salary entitlement in lieu of all or any part of the unexpired period of notice (subject to deduction at source of income tax and applicable national insurance contributions).

4.4   If you leave without giving the proper period of notice or leave during your notice period without permission, the Company shall be entitled as a result of your agreement to the terms of this contract to deduct a day's pay for each day not worked during the notice period, provided always that the Company will not deduct a sum in excess of the actual loss suffered by it as a result of your leaving without notice and any sum so deducted will be in full and final settlement of the Company's claim for your breach of contract. This deduction may be made from any final payment of salary which the Company may be due to make to you. The amount to be deducted is a genuine attempt by the Company to assess its loss as a result of your leaving without notice. It is not intended to act as a penalty upon termination.

5   **HOURS OF WORK AND OVERTIME**

5.1   The Company's normal hours of work are from *(time)* until *(time)* on *(day)* to *(day)* with *(duration)* break for lunch. These hours will be your normal hours of work unless otherwise agreed between you and the Company. You may be required to work such additional hours as are reasonably necessary for the proper performance of your duties. (No extra payment will be made for any additional hours worked, unless expressly authorised by your line manager.) *(or)* (Any overtime worked by you at the request of the Company will be paid at (the rate of £*(amount)* per hour) *(or)* *(number)* times your normal hourly rate).)

6   **SALARY**

6.1   Your salary will be £*(insert details)* per *(hour/day/week/annum)* payable in equal *(monthly/weekly)* instalments in arrears on or before the last working day of each *(month/week)* for the *(month/week)* up to and including that day. Payment will be made (by direct credit transfer to a bank or building society account nominated by you) *(or)* (by cheque made payable to you). Your salary will be reviewed annually in *(month)*.

6.2   In addition to your remuneration, you will be reimbursed all reasonable expenses, properly, wholly and exclusively incurred by you and authorised by your line manager in the discharge of your duties under this contract upon production of receipts or other evidence for them as the Company may reasonably require.

7   **REVIEW OF PERFORMANCE**

7.1   A performance review will be carried out in relation to you at least once in each year. The timing of that review will vary depending upon your job and, in any event, is in the discretion of the Company. Details of any review procedures relating to you will be given to you and you are required to comply with them at the time of any review of you in order to assist in making the process worthwhile.

7.2   Your performance will also be reviewed, independently of the annual review process, during and at the end of the probationary period.

8   **HOLIDAY**

8.1   The Company's holiday year is from *(date)* to *(date)*. (In addition to paid holiday on all statutory and other public holidays,) you will be entitled to *(number)* days' holiday in each holiday year throughout which you are employed by the Company *(or)* (which includes statutory and other public holidays (and any period during which the Company closes down for Christmas and the New Year)). You will accrue holiday at the rate of *(number)* days per calendar month from your first day of employment with the Company.

8.2   The Company will operate a system that you must follow for obtaining prior approval for holiday plans. Details of that system and of any changes to it from time to time will be made known to you. The Company will try to co-operate with your holiday plans wherever possible subject to the requirements of the Company. However, you must not book holidays until your request has been formally authorised in writing by your line manager.

8.3   You must use all of your holiday entitlement by the last day of each holiday year and, unless there are exceptional circumstances, you may not carry your holiday entitlement forward into the next holiday year. Holiday entitlement not used by the correct date will usually be lost and under no circumstances will payment be made for holiday entitlement that is lost through not being exercised by the correct date.

8.4   No more than two weeks' holiday may be taken at any one time without the prior written agreement of your line manager. *(Amount)* notice must be given by you of the proposed date of commencement of any holiday.

8.5   In your first and last year of employment, your holiday entitlement will be that proportion of your annual holiday entitlement equivalent to the proportion of the holiday year in question during which you have been employed (to the nearest half-day and assuming that holiday entitlement accrues at an even rate from day to day).

8.6   Subject to clause 8.1, on termination of your employment, holiday pay will be given for earned and unused days of holiday entitlement in that year. If, on termination, you have taken more holiday than you have earned in that year, the Company shall be entitled as a result of your agreement to the terms of this contract to deduct the value of the unearned holiday from any final payment of salary made to you. Holiday pay will be at a rate derived from annual salary accruing at *(number)* days per month.

8.7   Should you be incapacitated for work during any period of pre-booked holiday (whether in whole or in part) the Company may in its absolute discretion reimburse the period of holiday entitlement lost due to incapacity. You have no contractual right to reimbursement and before considering whether reimbursement is appropriate in the circumstances, you must deliver to the Company a relevant medical certificate covering the period of incapacity.

9   **COMPASSIONATE LEAVE AND TIME OFF FOR FAMILY EMERGENCIES**

9.1   The Company will consider all requests for compassionate leave and time off to deal with family emergencies. If you need to take compassionate leave or time off to deal with a family emergency, you should raise the matter with your line manager and that person will consider your request. There is no contractual entitlement to remuneration for absences relating to compassionate leave or time off to deal with family emergencies. Any payment will be made at the absolute discretion of the Company.

10   **SICK PAY**

10.1   You are entitled to Statutory Sick Pay ('SSP') during periods of sickness absence. Any payment over and above SSP will be made at the absolute discretion of the Company.

11   REPORTING SICKNESS ABSENCE

11.1   On the first day of any sickness absence you must ensure that your line manager is informed by telephone of your sickness at the earliest possible opportunity. You should also give details of the nature of your illness and the day on which you expect to return to work. You must inform the Company as soon as possible of any change in the date of your anticipated return to work.

11.2   Sickness absence of up to and including seven consecutive days must be fully supported by a self-certificate and thereafter by one or more doctor's certificates provided to the Company at intervals of no more than seven days during the period of sickness absence.

11.3   You must inform your line manager on the first day of your return to work after a period of sickness absence and complete a self-certificate form if applicable. Self-certification forms are available from *(name)*.

12   MEDICAL EXAMINATIONS

12.1   The Company may require you to undergo a medical examination by a medical practitioner nominated by it at any stage of your employment. The cost of any such examination or examinations will be met by the Company and you will co-operate in the disclosure of all results and reports to the Company. The Company will only request such an examination where reasonable to do so.

13   PENSION

13.1   (The Company does not operate or participate in any pension scheme applicable to your employment and no contracting-out certificate is in force in respect of this employment.) *(or)* (In accordance with Government legislation, the Company has in place a Stakeholder Pension Scheme and after three months' service you will be invited to make your own contributions to that scheme should you so wish. No contracting-out certificate is in force in respect of this employment.) *(or)* (The Company provides you with a pension (and life assurance) scheme which you may join on becoming eligible to do so. Details of the scheme, including the conditions of eligibility and the rates of contributions and of benefits, are available from *(name)*. If you become a member of the scheme, you will be contracted (in/out) of the State Scheme. The Company reserves the right to withdraw or amend any of the rules or benefits of the scheme at any time.)

14   RETIREMENT AGE

14.1   The Company's normal retirement age is *(age)* years. When you reach the normal retirement age, your employment will come to an end without breach or fault on either side.

15   COLLECTIVE AGREEMENTS AND PERIODS OUT OF THE U.K.

15.1   There are no collective agreements that directly affect the terms of your employment.

15.2   You will not be expected to work outside the United Kingdom for one month or more.

16   DISCIPLINARY RULES

16.1   The Company's disciplinary rules and procedures that apply to your employment are set out in Appendix 1 to this contract.

17   GRIEVANCE PROCEDURE

17.1   The Company's grievance procedures that apply to your employment are set out in Appendix 2 to this contract.

18   EQUAL OPPORTUNITIES

18.1   It is the Company's policy to provide employment, compensation, training, promotions and other conditions of employment without regard to race, colour, ethnic origin, nationality, national origin, religion or belief, sex, sexual orientation, marital status and/or disability unrelated to an individual's ability to perform essential job functions. It is also the Company's policy to conform to all employment standards required by law.

19   LAY-OFFS

19.1   The Company reserves the right to lay you off or put you on short-time working where the needs of the Company's business make this necessary. You will be paid statutory guarantee payments during a period of any lay-off or short-time working.

20   RESTRICTIONS

20.1   During your normal hours of work you may not, without the prior written consent of the Company, devote any time to any business other than the business of the Company or to any public or charitable duty or endeavour.

20.2   During the period of your employment you will not, without the prior written consent of the Company, undertake any work or other activity which may prejudicially affect your ability properly and efficiently to discharge your duties and responsibilities. The decision as to whether or not an activity would have a prejudicial effect shall be in the absolute discretion of the Company.

20.3   You will not at any time either during your employment or afterwards, to the detriment or prejudice of the Company or the Company's customers, use or divulge to any person, firm or company, except in the proper course of your duties during your employment by the Company, any confidential information identifying or relating to the Company, details of which are not in the public domain, or such confidential information or trade secrets relating to the business of any customer of the Company which have come to your knowledge during your employment.

21   DELIVERY UP OF DOCUMENTS

21.1   Upon the termination of your employment under this contract for whatsoever cause, you shall forthwith deliver up to the Company all keys and any swipe cards, credit cards, computer hardware or software, books, documents, account records and any other papers which may be in your possession, custody or control and which are the property of the Company or which otherwise relate in any way to the business or affairs of the Company and no copies of the same or any part thereof shall be retained by you. You shall then (if required by the Company) make a declaration that the whole of the provisions of this Clause have been complied with.

22   DEBTS AND OVERPAYMENTS

22.1   If, on the termination of your employment, you owe the Company money as a result of any loan, overpayment, default on your part or any other reason whatsoever, the Company shall be entitled as a result of your agreement to the terms of this contract to deduct the amount of your indebtedness to it from any final payment of salary which it may be due to make to you.

I hereby confirm that I have read, understood and accept the above contract of employment. I undertake to observe the terms and conditions of employment contained therein.

....
(Name of employee)

....
For and on behalf of the Company

Date: ....

Date: ....

This contract of employment was prepared by the **Employment Unit** of **Abbey Legal Protection Limited's Legal Services Centre**. It is intended only as a guide and is not to be regarded as a definitive contract. Neither is it to be regarded as a substitute for consultation with one of our Legal Advisors, since every case will ultimately turn on its own particular facts and circumstances. Should you require legal advice please contact the **Legal Services Centre** on **0870 513 3307**.

APPENDIX 1 - DISCIPLINARY PROCEDURE

Whilst the Company does not wish to impose unreasonable rules of conduct on its employees, certain standards of behaviour are necessary to maintain good employment relations and discipline in the interest of all employees. The Company prefers that discipline be voluntary and self-imposed and in the great majority of cases this is how it works. However, from time to time, it may be necessary for the Company to take action towards individuals whose level of behaviour or performance is unacceptable.

This disciplinary procedure is in two parts. Section A generally applies to those employees who have less than one year's continuous employment with the Company, although the Company reserves the right to apply Section B instead to any such employee. Section B applies to those employees who have one or more years' continuous employment with the Company.

This disciplinary procedure is <u>entirely non-contractual</u> and does not form part of an employee's contract of employment.

Section A

Before taking a decision to dismiss an employee on the grounds of misconduct or poor performance, the Company will, as a general rule and subject to any permitted statutory exceptions, comply with the following procedure:

Stage 1: Notification of allegations

The Company will notify the employee in writing of the allegations against him or her and will invite the employee to a disciplinary meeting to discuss the matter. The Company will also notify the employee of the basis for the complaint of alleged misconduct or poor performance.

Stage 2: Disciplinary meeting

Having given the employee a reasonable opportunity to consider his or her response to the allegations, a disciplinary meeting will then take place at which the employee will be given the chance to state his or her case. The employee may be accompanied, if requested, by a trade union official or a fellow employee of his or her choice. The employee must take all reasonable steps to attend that meeting. Following the meeting, the employee will be informed of the Company's decision in writing and notified of his or her right to appeal against it.

Stage 3: Appeals

If the employee wishes to appeal against the Company's decision, he or she can do so to a Director of the Company within five working days of the decision. Appeals should be made in writing and state the grounds for appeal. The employee will be invited to attend an appeal meeting chaired by a senior manager or a Director. At the appeal meeting, the employee will again be given the chance to state his or her case and will have the right to be accompanied by a trade union official or a fellow employee of his or her choice. Following the appeal meeting, the employee will be informed of the appeal decision in writing. The Company's decision on an appeal will be final.

The Company reserves the right not to follow this Section A procedure in relation to the imposition of a period of suspension with pay on, or the issuing of a disciplinary warning to, any employee who has less than one year's continuous employment with the Company.

Section B

Minor faults will be dealt with informally through counselling and training. However, in cases where informal discussion with the employee does not lead to an improvement in conduct or performance or where the matter is considered to be too serious to be classed as minor, for example, unauthorised absences, persistent poor timekeeping, sub-standard work performance, etc the following disciplinary procedure will be used. At all stages of the procedure, an investigation will be carried out.

The Company will notify the employee in writing of the allegations against him or her and will invite the employee to a disciplinary hearing to discuss the matter. The Company will also notify the employee of the basis for the complaint of alleged misconduct or poor performance. Having given the employee a reasonable opportunity to consider his or her response to the allegations, a formal disciplinary hearing will then take place, conducted by a manager, at which the employee will be given the chance to state his or her case, accompanied if requested by a trade union official or a fellow employee of his or her choice. The employee must take all reasonable steps to attend that meeting. Following the meeting, the employee will be informed in writing of the Company's decision in accordance with the stages set out below and notified of his or her right to appeal against that decision. It should be noted that an employee's behaviour is not looked at in isolation but each incident of misconduct is regarded cumulatively with any previous occurrences.

Stage 1: Written warning

The employee will be given a formal WRITTEN WARNING. He or she will be advised of the reason for the warning, how they need to improve their conduct or performance, the timescale over which the improvement is to be achieved, that the warning is the first stage of the formal disciplinary procedure and the likely consequences if the terms of the warning are not complied with. The written warning will be recorded but nullified after six months, subject to satisfactory conduct and performance.

Stage 2: Final written warning

Failure to improve performance in response to the procedure so far, a repeat of misconduct for which a warning has previously been issued, or a first instance of serious misconduct or serious poor performance, will result in a FINAL WRITTEN WARNING being issued. This will give details of, and grounds for, the complaint, how he or she needs to improve their conduct or performance, the timescale over which the improvement is to be achieved and warn that dismissal will probably result if the terms of the warning are not complied with. This final written warning will be recorded but nullified after twelve months, subject to satisfactory conduct and performance.

Stage 3: Dismissal

Failure to meet the requirements set out in the final written warning will normally lead to DISMISSAL with appropriate notice. A decision of this kind will only be made after the fullest possible investigation. Dismissal can be authorised only by a senior manager or a Director. The employee will be informed of the reasons for dismissal, the appropriate period of notice, the date on which his or her employment will terminate and how the employee can appeal against the dismissal decision.

Gross misconduct

Offences under this heading are so serious that an employee who commits them will normally be summarily dismissed. In such cases, the Company reserves the right to dismiss without notice of termination or payment in lieu of notice. Examples of gross misconduct include:

- Any breakage of the law, such as theft and unauthorised possession of Company property, fraud, deliberate falsification of records or any other form of dishonesty.
- Wilfully causing harm or injury to another employee, physical violence, bullying or grossly offensive behaviour.
- Deliberately causing damage to the Company's property.
- Causing loss, damage or injury through serious carelessness.
- Wilful refusal to obey a reasonable management instruction.
- Incapacity at work through an excess of alcohol or drugs.
- A serious breach of health and safety rules.
- Harassing or victimising another employee on the grounds of race, colour, ethnic origin, nationality, national origin, religion or belief, sex, sexual orientation, marital status, age and/or disability.

The above is intended as a guide and is not an exhaustive list.

Suspension

In the event of serious or gross misconduct, an employee may be suspended on full basic pay while a full investigation is carried out. Such suspension is a neutral act, which does not imply guilt or blame, and will be for as short a period as possible.

Appeals

An employee may appeal against any disciplinary decision, including dismissal, to a Director of the Company within five working days of the decision. Appeals should be made in writing and state the grounds for appeal. The employee will be invited to attend an appeal hearing chaired by a senior manager or a Director. At the appeal hearing, the employee will again be given the chance to state his or her case and will have the right to be accompanied by a trade union official or a fellow employee of his or her choice. Following the appeal hearing, the employee will be informed of the appeal decision, and the reasons for it, in writing.

The Company's decision on an appeal will be final.

<u>**APPENDIX 2 - GRIEVANCE PROCEDURE**</u>

<u>**Object**</u>

The object of the procedure is to provide an employee who considers that he or she has a grievance with an opportunity to have it examined quickly and effectively, and where a grievance is deemed to exist, to have it resolved, if possible, at the earliest practicable opportunity. Most grievances can be settled informally with line managers and employees should aim to settle their grievances in this way if possible.

<u>**Procedure**</u>

If a grievance cannot be settled informally with the relevant line manager, the employee should raise it formally. This procedure has been drawn up to establish the appropriate steps to be followed when pursuing and dealing with a formal grievance.

Stage 1

In the event of the employee having a formal grievance relating to his or her employment he or she should, in the first instance, put their complaint in writing and address it to their line manager. Where the grievance is against the line manager, the complaint should be addressed to an alternative manager. A manager (who may not be the manager to whom the grievance was addressed) will then invite the employee to a grievance meeting to discuss the grievance and the employee has the right to be accompanied at this meeting by a trade union official or a fellow employee of their choice. The employee must take all reasonable steps to attend that meeting.

Following the meeting, the Company will endeavour to respond to the grievance as soon as possible and, in any case, within five working days of the grievance meeting. If it is not possible to respond within this time period, the employee will be given an explanation for the delay and be told when a response can be expected. The employee will be informed in writing of the Company's decision on the grievance and notified of their right to appeal against that decision if they are not satisfied with it.

Stage 2

In the event that the employee feels his or her grievance has not been satisfactorily resolved, the employee may then appeal in writing to a more senior manager or to a Director of the Company within five working days of the grievance decision.

On receipt of such a request, a more senior manager or a Director (who again may not be the person to whom the appeal was addressed) shall make arrangements to hear the grievance at an appeal meeting and at this meeting the employee may again, if they wish, be accompanied by a trade union official or a fellow employee of their choice. The employee must take all reasonable steps to attend that meeting.

Following the meeting, the senior manager or Director will endeavour to respond to the grievance as soon as possible and, in any case, within five working days of the appeal hearing. If it is not possible to respond within this time period, the employee will be given an explanation for the delay and be told when a response can be expected. The employee will be informed in writing of the Company's decision on their grievance appeal.

This is the final stage of the grievance procedure and the Company's decision shall be final.

<u>**Former employees**</u>

Grievances may also be raised by ex-employees after employment has ended. In this case, the grievance procedure set out above will continue to apply, unless both parties agree in writing that a modified form of grievance procedure will apply instead.

SPECIMEN DISCIPLINARY PROCEDURE

Whilst the Company does not wish to impose unreasonable rules of conduct on its employees, certain standards of behaviour are necessary to maintain good employment relations and discipline in the interest of all employees. The Company prefers that discipline be voluntary and self-imposed and in the great majority of cases this is how it works. However, from time to time, it may be necessary for the Company to take action towards individuals whose level of behaviour or performance is unacceptable.

This disciplinary procedure is in two parts. Section A generally applies to those employees who have less than one year's continuous employment with the Company, although the Company reserves the right to apply Section B instead to any such employee. Section B applies to those employees who have one or more years' continuous employment with the Company.

This disciplinary procedure is <u>entirely non-contractual</u> and does not form part of an employee's contract of employment.

Section A

Before taking a decision to dismiss an employee on the grounds of misconduct or poor performance, the Company will, as a general rule and subject to any permitted statutory exceptions, comply with the following procedure:

Stage 1: Notification of allegations

The Company will notify the employee in writing of the allegations against him or her and will invite the employee to a disciplinary meeting to discuss the matter. The Company will also notify the employee of the basis for the complaint of alleged misconduct or poor performance.

Stage 2: Disciplinary meeting

Having given the employee a reasonable opportunity to consider his or her response to the allegations, a disciplinary meeting will then take place at which the employee will be given the chance to state his or her case. The employee may be accompanied, if requested, by a trade union official or a fellow employee of his or her choice. The employee must take all reasonable steps to attend that meeting. Following the meeting, the employee will be informed of the Company's decision in writing and notified of his or her right to appeal against it.

Stage 3: Appeals

If the employee wishes to appeal against the Company's decision, he or she can do so to a Director of the Company within five working days of the decision. Appeals should be made in writing and state the grounds for appeal. The employee will be invited to attend an appeal meeting chaired by a senior manager or a Director. At the appeal meeting, the employee will again be given the chance to state his or her case and will have the right to be accompanied by a trade union official or a fellow employee of his or her choice. Following the appeal meeting, the employee will be informed of the appeal decision in writing. The Company's decision on an appeal will be final.
The Company reserves the right not to follow this Section A procedure in relation to the imposition of a period of suspension with pay on, or the issuing of a disciplinary warning to, any employee who has less than one year's continuous employment with the Company.

Section B

Minor faults will be dealt with informally through counselling and training. However, in cases where informal discussion with the employee does not lead to an improvement in conduct or performance or where the matter is considered to be too serious to be classed as minor, for example, unauthorised absences, persistent poor timekeeping, sub-standard work performance, etc the following disciplinary procedure will be used. At all stages of the procedure, an investigation will be carried out.

The Company will notify the employee in writing of the allegations against him or her and will invite the employee to a disciplinary hearing to discuss the matter. The Company will also notify the employee of the basis for the complaint of alleged misconduct or poor performance. Having given the employee a reasonable opportunity to consider his or her response to the allegations, a formal disciplinary hearing will then take place, conducted by a manager, at which the employee will be given the chance to state his or her case, accompanied if requested by a trade union official or a fellow employee of his or her choice. The employee must take all reasonable steps to attend that meeting. Following the meeting, the employee will be informed in writing of the Company's decision in accordance with the stages set out below and notified of his or her right to appeal against that decision. It should be noted that an employee's behaviour is not looked at in isolation but each incident of misconduct is regarded cumulatively with any previous occurrences.

Figure 22-3: Specimen disciplinary procedure.

Stage 1: Written warning

The employee will be given a formal WRITTEN WARNING. He or she will be advised of the reason for the warning, how they need to improve their conduct or performance, the timescale over which the improvement is to be achieved, that the warning is the first stage of the formal disciplinary procedure and the likely consequences if the terms of the warning are not complied with. The written warning will be recorded but nullified after six months, subject to satisfactory conduct and performance.

Stage 2: Final written warning

Failure to improve performance in response to the procedure so far, a repeat of misconduct for which a warning has previously been issued, or a first instance of serious misconduct or serious poor performance, will result in a FINAL WRITTEN WARNING being issued. This will give details of, and grounds for, the complaint, how he or she needs to improve their conduct or performance, the timescale over which the improvement is to be achieved and warn that dismissal will probably result if the terms of the warning are not complied with. This final written warning will be recorded but nullified after twelve months, subject to satisfactory conduct and performance.

Stage 3: Dismissal

Failure to meet the requirements set out in the final written warning will normally lead to DISMISSAL with appropriate notice. A decision of this kind will only be made after the fullest possible investigation. Dismissal can be authorised only by a senior manager or a Director. The employee will be informed of the reasons for dismissal, the appropriate period of notice, the date on which his or her employment will terminate and how the employee can appeal against the dismissal decision.

Gross misconduct

Offences under this heading are so serious that an employee who commits them will normally be summarily dismissed. In such cases, the Company reserves the right to dismiss without notice of termination or payment in lieu of notice. Examples of gross misconduct include:

- Any breakage of the law, such as theft and unauthorised possession of Company property, fraud, deliberate falsification of records or any other form of dishonesty.
- Wilfully causing harm or injury to another employee, physical violence, bullying or grossly offensive behaviour.
- Deliberately causing damage to the Company's property.
- Causing loss, damage or injury through serious carelessness.
- Wilful refusal to obey a reasonable management instruction.
- Incapacity at work through an excess of alcohol or drugs.
- A serious breach of health and safety rules.
- Harassing or victimising another employee on the grounds of race, colour, ethnic origin, nationality, national origin, religion or belief, sex, sexual orientation, marital status, age and/or disability.

The above is intended as a guide and is not an exhaustive list.

Suspension

In the event of serious or gross misconduct, an employee may be suspended on full basic pay while a full investigation is carried out. Such suspension is a neutral act, which does not imply guilt or blame, and will be for as short a period as possible.

Appeals

An employee may appeal against any disciplinary decision, including dismissal, to a Director of the Company within five working days of the decision. Appeals should be made in writing and state the grounds for appeal. The employee will be invited to attend an appeal hearing chaired by a senior manager or a Director. At the appeal hearing, the employee will again be given the chance to state his or her case and will have the right to be accompanied by a trade union official or a fellow employee of his or her choice. Following the appeal hearing, the employee will be informed of the appeal decision, and the reasons for it, in writing.

The Company's decision on an appeal will be final.

This procedure was prepared by the **Employment Unit** of **Abbey Legal Protection Limited's Legal Services Centre**. It is intended only as a guide and is not to be regarded as a definitive procedure. Neither is it to be regarded as a substitute for consultation with one of our Legal Advisors, since every case will ultimately turn on its own particular facts and circumstances. Should you require legal advice please contact the **Legal Services Centre** on **0870 513 3307**.

SPECIMEN EMPLOYEE CONFIDENTIALITY AGREEMENT

THIS AGREEMENT is dated *(date)*

And is made between:

(Name of Company) Limited whose registered office is at *(registered office details)* ('the Company'); and

(Name of employee) of *(address of employee)* ('the Employee')

It is hereby agreed as follows:

Definitions

1.   In this Agreement, unless the context otherwise requires, 'Confidential Information' means all information in respect of the business of the Company, including, but not limited to, any ideas, business methods, prices, finance, marketing, research, development, manpower plans, processes, market opportunities, intentions, design rights, product information, customer lists or details, trade secrets, computer systems and software, know-how or listings imparted by the Company, and other matters connected with the products or services manufactured, marketed, provided or obtained by the Company, and information concerning the Company's relationships with actual or potential clients or customers and the needs and requirements of such clients' or customers' operations.

Obligation of confidentiality

2.   The Employee agrees to treat as confidential all information supplied by or on behalf of the Company in connection with the Company's business and all other confidential aspects of the business as defined in 'Confidential Information' above.

Exclusions

3.   This obligation of confidentiality does not apply to:

- any information received from a third party who was legally free at the time of disclosure to disclose it; or
- any information already in the public domain.

Duties of Employee

4.   The Employee shall not, without the prior written consent of the Company, permit any of the Confidential Information:

- to be disclosed, except to those of the Company's employees who may need to have such information; or
- to be copied or reproduced; or
- to be commercially exploited in any way; or
- to pass outside the control of the Employee.

5.   The Employee will keep a record of Confidential Information received and of the people holding that information and will make that available to the Company on request.

Figure 22-4: Specimen employee confidentiality agreement.

6.   The Employee will return to the Company all documents containing
      Confidential Information and all copies of those documents on demand which
      are in their possession or under their control, and for this purpose the term
      'documents' includes computer discs and all other materials capable of
      storing data and information.

SIGNED:

....
Director
For and on behalf of the Company

SIGNED:

....
(Name of employee)

This agreement was prepared by the **Employment Unit** of **Abbey Legal Protection
Limited's Legal Services Centre**. It is intended only as a guide and is not to be
regarded as a definitive agreement. Neither is to be regarded as a substitute for
consultation with one of our Legal Advisors, since every case will ultimately turn on
its own particular facts and circumstances. Should you require legal advice please
contact the **Legal Services Centre** on **0870 513 3307**.

SPECIMEN EXIT QUESTIONNAIRE

It is both regrettable and potentially expensive when an employee decides to leave the Company. It is therefore essential that we find out the reason why, if we are going to avoid losing good people in the future. Once an individual decides to leave, they are likely to give a frank and honest input which is invaluable to the Company in identifying why people leave and giving ideas which can be implemented to change the Company for the better. We would therefore ask you to complete the following questionnaire and return it promptly to *(name)*.

With your permission, selected information gained from this completed questionnaire will be discussed with the management of the Company. The aim of this is to ensure that any problem issues can be discussed and resolved before you leave. It also means that if we discover you are leaving as a direct result of perceived problems of which we were previously unaware, the Company can try to resolve these to the mutual satisfaction of all parties before you leave. A copy of this questionnaire will be placed on your personnel file.

Your name and department:	
What did you like most about your job and why?	
What did you like least about your job and why?	
Do you think your job duties and responsibilities were clearly defined and how did you feel about your workload?	
What made you decide to leave the Company?	
Is there anything the Company could have done to make you stay?	
Would you recommend the Company as an employer to others?	
Have you generally been happy during your time with the Company?	
What do you think you have gained from your time with the Company?	
Were you given sufficient opportunities for training and development? If not, what more did you need?	
Did you feel that your health and safety at work was provided for?	
What do you think is good about the Company?	
What do you think the Company could improve on, both generally and in terms of your current job?	

Figure 22-5: Specimen exit questionnaire.

How do you feel about the pay and benefits package provided by the Company?	
What was your working relationship like your line manager? In particular: • Did he/she explain the job properly? • Did he/she show fair treatment? • Do you feel he/she provided you with encouragement and help when needed? • Did he/she give praise for work well done? • Did he/she listen to your suggestions? • Were you made to feel that your contribution was valuable?	
How would you describe the level of morale in your department?	
Please add any other comments you wish to make e.g. you may wish to comment on your place of work, the people you work with or the job that you do.	
Do you have any objection to this questionnaire being discussed with your line manager?	YES / NO

Signed by employee:

……………………………….

Date: …………………………..

Thank you for your comments.

SPECIMEN FLEXIBLE WORKING POLICY

It is the Company's view that the promotion of flexible working arrangements increases staff motivation, reduces employee stress, improves employee performance and productivity and encourages staff retention.

Employees who are parents of young or disabled children have a statutory right both to request a change to the terms and conditions of their employment in order that they can have flexible working arrangements to look after their children and to have that request considered seriously by the Company. This right to request flexible working can be exercised at any time up until two weeks before the child's sixth birthday (or 18th birthday if the child is disabled). In order to make a request under the statutory right, an employee must have worked for the Company for a continuous period of six months at the date the application is made.

For the avoidance of doubt, employees must meet each of the following eligibility criteria in order to qualify for the statutory right to request flexible working:

- They have responsibility for the upbringing of either a child under six or a disabled child under 18.
- They are either the mother, father, adopter, guardian or foster parent of the child or they are married to or the partner of the child's mother, father, adopter, guardian or foster parent.
- They are making the request to help care for the child.
- They make the request no later than two weeks before the child's sixth birthday or 18th birthday where the child is disabled.
- They have worked continuously as an employee of the Company for the previous 26 weeks.
- They have not made a request to work flexibly under the statutory right during the past 12 months.

The Company implements the right to request flexible working set out in legislation. [In addition, it is the Company's policy to try and be flexible on working patterns for all employees, not just those who have a statutory right to submit such requests, although priority will always be given to those employees who do have the statutory right to request flexible working in order that the Company can comply with its legal obligations.]

Employees can apply to vary the number of hours they work, the times they work or their place of work (between their home and the Company's place of business).

The following procedure will apply to flexible working requests:

- The employee should first make their request in writing to the Company setting out the flexible working arrangement they seek in order to care for a child. A Flexible Working Application Form can be obtained from *(name)*.

- Within 28 days of receipt of this application, the Company will set up a meeting with the employee to discuss the changes the employee has proposed, the effect of the proposed changes and any possible alternative work patterns that might suit both parties. The employee has a right to be accompanied at this meeting by a work colleague or trade union official.

- The Company will properly consider the request and will make a practical business assessment on whether, and if so how, the flexible working request could be accommodated.

- The Company will notify its decision to the employee within 14 days of the meeting. If the Company accepts the employee's request, it will write to the employee, establishing a start date and providing a written note of the contract of employment variation. If the application is refused, the Company will explain the grounds for refusal in writing and confirm the internal appeal procedure.

- Where a request is agreed to, it constitutes a permanent change to the employee's terms and conditions of employment. This means that the new working arrangement will not lapse merely because the child reaches the age of six and neither has the employee a right to revert to their previous pattern of working at a future date.

- The employee can appeal against a refusal within 14 days of receipt of the Company's rejection letter. The Company will then set up a meeting with the employee to discuss the appeal within 14 days after receiving the employee's appeal letter. After that meeting has been held, the Company will write to the employee within 14 days to notify the employee of the outcome of the appeal.

Figure 22-6: Specimen flexible working policy.

The Company will only refuse an application on one of eight grounds. They are:

1. The burden of additional costs.
2. Detrimental effect on ability to meet customer demand.
3. Inability to reorganise work among existing staff.
4. Inability to recruit additional staff.
5. Detrimental impact on quality.
6. Detrimental impact on performance.
7. Insufficiency of work during the period when the employee proposes to work.
8. Planned structural changes.

Each request for flexible working will be dealt with individually, taking into account the likely effects the changes will have on the Company, the work of the department in which the employee making the request is employed and the employee's colleagues. This means that if the Company agrees to one employee's request, this does not set a precedent or create a right for another employee to be granted the same or a similar change to their work pattern.

This policy was prepared by the **Employment Unit** of **Abbey Legal Protection Limited's Legal Services Centre**. It is intended only as a guide and is not to be regarded as a definitive policy. Neither is to be regarded as a substitute for consultation with one of our Legal Advisors, since every case will ultimately turn on its own particular facts and circumstances. Should you require legal advice please contact the **Legal Services Centre** on **0870 513 3307**.

SPECIMEN GRIEVANCE PROCEDURE

Object

The object of the procedure is to provide an employee who considers that he or she has a grievance with an opportunity to have it examined quickly and effectively, and where a grievance is deemed to exist, to have it resolved, if possible, at the earliest practicable opportunity. Most grievances can be settled informally with line managers and employees should aim to settle their grievances in this way if possible.

Procedure

If a grievance cannot be settled informally with the relevant line manager, the employee should raise it formally. This procedure has been drawn up to establish the appropriate steps to be followed when pursuing and dealing with a formal grievance.

Stage 1

In the event of the employee having a formal grievance relating to his or her employment he or she should, in the first instance, put their complaint in writing and address it to their line manager. Where the grievance is against the line manager, the complaint should be addressed to an alternative manager. A manager (who may not be the manager to whom the grievance was addressed) will then invite the employee to a grievance meeting to discuss the grievance and the employee has the right to be accompanied at this meeting by a trade union official or a fellow employee of their choice. The employee must take all reasonable steps to attend that meeting.

Following the meeting, the Company will endeavour to respond to the grievance as soon as possible and, in any case, within five working days of the grievance meeting. If it is not possible to respond within this time period, the employee will be given an explanation for the delay and be told when a response can be expected. The employee will be informed in writing of the Company's decision on the grievance and notified of their right to appeal against that decision if they are not satisfied with it.

Stage 2

In the event that the employee feels his or her grievance has not been satisfactorily resolved, the employee may then appeal in writing to a more senior manager or to a Director of the Company within five working days of the grievance decision.

On receipt of such a request, a more senior manager or a Director (who again may not be the person to whom the appeal was addressed) shall make arrangements to hear the grievance at an appeal meeting and at this meeting the employee may again, if they wish, be accompanied by a trade union official or a fellow employee of their choice. The employee must take all reasonable steps to attend that meeting.

Following the meeting, the senior manager or Director will endeavour to respond to the grievance as soon as possible and, in any case, within five working days of the appeal hearing. If it is not possible to respond within this time period, the employee will be given an explanation for the delay and be told when a response can be expected. The employee will be informed in writing of the Company's decision on their grievance appeal.

This is the final stage of the grievance procedure and the Company's decision shall be final.

Former employees

Grievances may also be raised by ex-employees after employment has ended. In this case, the grievance procedure set out above will continue to apply, unless both parties agree in writing that a modified form of grievance procedure will apply instead.

This procedure was prepared by the **Employment Unit** of **Abbey Legal Protection Limited's Legal Services Centre**. It is intended only as a guide and is not to be regarded as a definitive procedure. Neither is it to be regarded as a substitute for consultation with one of our Legal Advisors, since every case will ultimately turn on its own particular facts and circumstances. Should you require legal advice please contact the **Legal Services Centre** on **0870 513 3307**.

Figure 22-7: Specimen grievance procedure.

SPECIMEN HOLIDAY REQUEST FORM

This form is to record requests for holiday leave and is to be completed by the employee and countersigned by their line manager. It must be completed for all requests for holiday leave of _ day or more.

Full name of employee:	
First date of proposed holiday absence:	
Last date of proposed holiday absence:	
Total number of working days of proposed absence:	
Balance of annual leave entitlement remaining if this request is authorised:	
Please give any information you would like your line manager to take into account in relation to this request:	

I declare the above information to be correct. I understand that my request for holiday is not authorised until this form has been countersigned by my line manager.

I accept that any leave that I purport to take without the prior authorisation of my line manager will be viewed by the Company as unauthorised absence, which is a gross misconduct offence and could result in my summary dismissal.

Signed by employee: Signed by line manager:

....

Date: ....   Date: ....

Figure 22-8: Specimen holiday request form.

SPECIMEN SICKNESS & ABSENCE POLICY

Should you be unable to attend work due to illness or injury, you must comply with the following Company sickness absence policy:

1. On the first morning of your sickness absence, you must contact the Company and speak to your line manager at the earliest possible opportunity and as close to your normal start time as possible. In any event, this must be no later than two hours after your normal start time. You should give details of the nature of your illness. If you are unable to speak to your line manager personally, you should speak to *(names)*. If the illness is of a minor nature, you should indicate when you believe you will be fit to return to work. You must inform your line manager as soon as possible of any change in the date of your anticipated return to work.

2. For an absence of seven consecutive calendar days or less, you are required to telephone your line manager on a daily basis in accordance with the reporting procedure set out above. You must also complete a self-certification form immediately on your return to work. Self-certification forms are available from *(name)*. On completion, the form should be forwarded to *(name)*. You are reminded that it is a serious disciplinary offence to knowingly provide false information on a self-certification form.

3. Should the absence be for a period in excess of seven calendar days, you are required as an absolute minimum to contact your line manager on a weekly basis in order to provide an update on your illness or injury. A doctor's certificate must also be obtained. A new doctor's certificate must be submitted each week. The doctor's certificate must be forwarded to *(name)* as quickly as possible and in any event no later than the end of the calendar week in respect of which the certificate applies. Each subsequent doctor's certificate must be forwarded in the same manner.

4. You should have certificates (either self-certification forms or doctor's certificates) to cover the entire period of your sickness absence.

5. For long-term absence, your line manager may request to visit you at home.

6. For all periods of sickness absence, your line manager may require you to attend a 'back to work' interview on your return to work to discuss the reasons for your absence and, in particular, whether it was work-related.

7. For long-term sickness absence or frequent periods of sickness absence, the Company may request further information from your GP or consultant or alternatively request that you visit a doctor selected by the Company to undergo a medical examination. The cost of any such examination will be met by the Company and you are required to co-operate in the disclosure of all results and reports to the Company. The Company will only request such an examination where reasonable to do so.

8. The Company reserves the right to withhold sick pay in circumstances where the certification procedure described above has not been followed or it has reason to doubt the validity of the sickness absence claim and may request you to undertake a medical examination by a doctor selected by it.

9. On being fit to return to work, you must contact your line manager and let them know as far in advance as possible of the proposed date of your return.

Persistent short-term sickness absence is, in the absence of any underlying medical condition or other reasonable excuse, a disciplinary matter and will be dealt with in accordance with the Company's disciplinary procedure.

This policy was prepared by the **Employment Unit** of **Abbey Legal Protection Limited's Legal Services Centre**. It is intended only as a guide and is not to be regarded as a definitive policy. Neither is it to be regarded as a substitute for consultation with one of our Legal Advisors, since every case will ultimately turn on its own particular facts and circumstances. Should you require legal advice please contact the **Legal Services Centre** on **0870 513 3307**.

Figure 22-9: Specimen sickness and absence policy.

SP6 (September 2004)

SPECIMEN REDUNDANCY POLICY

Should circumstances arise where redundancy is seen to be a possibility, the first steps the Company will take will be to:

- Reduce overtime to a workable minimum
- Restrict recruitment
- Investigate measures such as short-time working and/or lay-offs as a means of avoiding redundancies
- Investigate whether there are any opportunities for redeployment to other departments within the Company
- Explore other methods by which desired cost cuts can be achieved
- Explore whether there are any other options available in order to avoid the redundancy situation.

If redundancies cannot be avoided, consideration will then be given by the Company to asking for volunteers for redundancy.

If the selection of employees for compulsory redundancy becomes necessary, having ascertained the relevant pool for selection, the Company will then apply one or more of the following as objective selection criteria:

- Length of service with the Company
- Relevant knowledge and skills
- Relevant qualifications
- Job performance
- Achievement of targets
- Geographical location
- The ability to transfer to a new location and/or a different job
- The ability to take on additional job responsibilities
- Disciplinary record for misconduct/poor performance
- Attendance record (excluding absences relating to maternity leave, pregnancy-related illnesses and disabilities within the meaning of the Disability Discrimination Act 1995)
- Timekeeping record
- *(Any other applicable criteria)*

The chosen selection criteria will be capable of objective substantiation and verification.

In deciding which criteria will apply for a particular redundancy programme, the overriding consideration will always be the future needs of the Company's business. This means that a particular criterion may carry more weight than another criterion, even though both criteria may be applied.

There will be full consultation with employees throughout the redundancy selection process. Employees will be encouraged to be fully involved in the consultation procedure. It is important for the Company to take full account of employees' views and suggestions before final decisions on redundancies are made.

This policy was prepared by the **Employment Unit** of **Abbey Legal Services**. It is intended only as a guide and is not to be regarded as a definitive policy. Neither is it to be regarded as a substitute for consultation with one of our Legal Advisors, since every case will ultimately turn on its own particular facts and circumstances. Should you require legal advice please contact **Abbey Legal Services** on **020 8730 6000**.

Figure 22-10: Specimen redundancy policy.

Index

• *I* •

FOR DUMMIES®

The easy way to get more done and have more fun

UK editions

PROPERTY

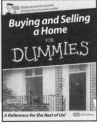

Understand the system and get the price you're after

Buying and Selling a Home

FOR DUMMIES

A Reference for the Rest of Us!

0-7645-7027-7

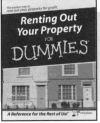

The easiest way to rent out your property for profit

Renting Out Your Property

FOR DUMMIES

A Reference for the Rest of Us!

0-7645-7016-1

Affordable options to get you feet on the ladder

Buying a Home on a Budget

FOR DUMMIES

A Reference for the Rest of Us!

0-7645-7035-8

PERSONAL FINANCE

A plain language guide to multiplying your money

Investing

FOR DUMMIES

A Reference for the Rest of Us!

0-7645-7023-4

Pile on the pounds with this insider's guide to reducing your tax bill

Paying Less Tax 2005/2006

FOR DUMMIES

A Reference for the Rest of Us!

0-7645-7053-6

The easy way to make your pounds go further

Sorting Out Your Finances

FOR DUMMIES

A Reference for the Rest of Us!

0-7645-7039-0

BUSINESS

Understand business basics and be your own boss

Starting a Business

FOR DUMMIES

A Reference for the Rest of Us!

0-7645-7018-8

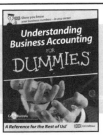

Show you know your business numbers — in any sense

Understanding Business Accounting

FOR DUMMIES

A Reference for the Rest of Us!

0-7645-7025-0

An insider's guide to successfully planning your business

Business Plans

FOR DUMMIES

A Reference for the Rest of Us!

0-7645-7026-9

Other UK editions now available:

British History For Dummies
(0-7645-7021-8)

Cleaning and Stain
Removal For Dummies
(0-7645-7029-3)

CVs For Dummies
(0-7645-7017-X)

Diabetes For Dummies
(0-7645-7019-6)

Divorce For Dummies
(0-7645-7030-7)

Formula One Racing
For Dummies
(0-7645-7015-3)

Neuro-Linguistic
Programming For Dummies
(0-7645-7028-5)

Pregnancy For Dummies
(0-7645-7042-0)

Rugby Union For Dummies
(0-7645-7020-X)

Wills, Probate and Inheritance
Tax For Dummies
(0-7645-7055-2)

FOR DUMMIES®

The easy way to get more done and have more fun

LANGUAGES

0-7645-5194-9   0-7645-5193-0   0-7645-5196-5

Also available:

French Phrases For Dummies
(0-7645-7202-4)

German For Dummies
(0-7645-5195-7)

Italian Phrases For Dummies
(0-7645-7203-2)

Japanese For Dummies
(0-7645-5429-8)

Latin For Dummies
(0-7645-5431-X)

Spanish Phrases For Dummies
(0-7645-7204-0)

Hebrew For Dummies
(0-7645-5489-1)

MUSIC AND FILM

0-7645-5106-X   0-7645-2476-3   0-7645-5105-1

Also available:

Bass Guitar For Dummies
(0-7645-2487-9)

Blues For Dummies
(0-7645-5080-2)

Classical Music For Dummies
(0-7645-5009-8)

Drums For Dummies
(0-7645-5357-7)

Jazz For Dummies
(0-7645-5081-0)

Opera For Dummies
(0-7645-5010-1)

Rock Guitar For Dummies
(0-7645-5356-9)

Screenwriting For Dummies
(0-7645-5486-7)

Songwriting For Dummies
(0-7645-5404-2)

Singing For Dummies
(0-7645-2475-5)

HEALTH, SPORTS & FITNESS

  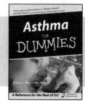

0-7645-5167-1   0-7645-5146-9   0-7645-4233-8

Also available:

Controlling Cholesterol
For Dummies
(0-7645-5440-9)

Dieting For Dummies
(0-7645-4149-8)

High Blood Pressure
For Dummies
(0-7645-5424-7)

Martial Arts For Dummies
(0-7645-5358-5)

Menopause For Dummies
(0-7645-5458-1)

Nutrition For Dummies
(0-7645-4082-3)

Power Yoga For Dummies
(0-7645-5342-9)

Thyroid For Dummies
(0-7645-5385-2)

Weight Training For Dummies
(0-7645-5168-X)

Yoga For Dummies
(0-7645-5117-5)

Shell Cottage as it was in 1955 with visitors admiring part of an unusual garden at 'Harvey Dene', Smite Hill, which took the owner, Sidney Dowdeswell, and his wife Elsie, over 50 years to complete. Miniature statues, a castle, concrete arches, fountains and mosaic work in shells, porcelain and glass were all to be found among the flower beds. Friends and relatives who had holidayed in this country or abroad provided the shells, and the coloured glass and porcelain came from a variety of sources such as broken china, beer bottles, etc. People from all over the world visited the garden and it was featured in many guide books and overseas magazines. Mr Dowdeswell worked as inspiration struck him, creating no regular pattern but adding, at his whim, goldfish, flowers, penguins, peacocks, butterflies or fishermen. Many visitors commented that 'it must be a full-time job', but it was not. Mr Dowdeswell worked all his life in a factory at Worcester and claimed to have cycled 40,000 miles on his way to and from work. His garden was his hobby. There was no charge for admission – only a charity box. Mr Dowdeswell died in 1977 at the age of 93 and his wife, unfortunately, was unable to continue his work. The house was sold and the garden sadly broken up in 1980.

The early seventeenth-century dovecote at Lower Smite farm.

The late sixteenth-century timber-framed former Hindlip Rectory, 1979.